HOUSEHOLD FINANCIAL MANAGEMENT

Tony Larson, CFP®

ISBN-13: 978-15-1519766717
ISBN-10: 1519766718

Final PDF prepared by Rose Bradshaw at So Fast Printing, Kerrville, TX.

COVER DESIGN: Create Space

To C,

whose questions as a new widow led me to write this, and

to everyone who's looking here for answers, and

to Louise, and John and Sienna, and Douglas and Michele,

to whom I was always, in my mind, trying to explain things.

Disclaimer

No one should rely upon anything in this book in making any significant decisions relating to any of the subjects discussed. I am certainly not an expert on any of them and everything I have written about undergoes frequent change. I'm just sharing what I know at a particular point in time about a particular subject in the belief that I may know more about it than most of my readers do and, by sharing what I know, can help them get up to speed and so be able to manage their affairs more ably and confidently going forward. But when a reader has a question or problem whose answer or solution could have real ramifications, he or she needs to consult an expert. Depending on the nature of the question or problem, that's an attorney, a broker, a professional tax preparer, an insurance agent, or a Social Security specialist.

Acknowledgments

I wish here to thank all of the people who helped with editing and vetting this book and encouraging me to stick with it when I wearied of the thing. Chief among my encouragers has been my wife, Louise. She is my angel.

Another encourager has been my friend Ben Doerries. I never had a conversation with Ben in which we discussed my book that I didn't come away re-energized and ready to get back to work. He helped me more than he knows.

I am grateful to our lifelong friend Judy Ware, our son Douglas, and our daughter-in-law Sienna for reading the book through and pointing out the many instances where I had left a word out, misused a word, needed a comma (or didn't need one), or failed to hyphenate two words that needed connecting.

Rose Hall, a local Kerrville writer, also did me the very great favor of reading the book through and telling me what she thought about it insofar as its usefulness to someone who had been recently widowed and might need help understanding the financial issues he or she would now have to contend with. She worried—and rightly so, I know— that someone still grieving over the loss of a spouse would struggle with the book, which isn't always an easy read, and suggested I encourage anyone in that situation to enlist the help of a close friend or relative to help them with it. I certainly would encourage that.

Rhonda Wiley-Jones, another Kerrville writer, also read the book, but from a much broader perspective, and gave me her thoughts and suggestions. I am indebted to Rhonda for my title and for straightening me out on em-dashes, the use of italics and a host of other things I was doing wrong. I hope that on going back to correct my mistakes I got all of the really egregious ones.

I am indebted to my attorney, Stuart Lohmeyer, for vetting the chapter on Estate Planning; my friend and former colleague at A.G. Edwards, Bill Matthews, and my financial counselor at Fisher Investments, John Eussen, for vetting the chapters on Saving for Retirement and Investing; Casey Mikeska, a local CPA with Massey Itschner & Company of Kerrville, John Mallory and Ruth Ann Ohler, Enrolled Agents at H&R Block in Kerrville, and Roger McRoberts and Nita Brown with Kerrville's AARP's Tax-Aide program for vetting the chapter on Income Taxes; and my friend and insurance lady, Linda Arreola, of Garrett Insurance, also of Kerrville, for vetting the chapters dealing with Insurance. Any errors that remain I take responsibility for. There are some I'm sure.

I am also deeply indebted to Rose Bradshaw of So Fast Printing. Rose assembled all my files into one PDF for uploading into Create Space. Actually, she did this for me not once but countless times owing to the fact that every time she'd give me a printout to review, I'd find something I'd done wrong that needed to be corrected. I am very grateful to Rose for her help and for her great patience.

Finally, it would be unpardonable if I did not express my gratitude to my brother-in-law Mike DeArmond for the help he has given me throughout with all the *Word 2007* and *Excel* issues and questions I've had. Without his help, I'm sure that early on I would have chucked my PC into the pond and said to hell with writing a book.

Table of Contents

PREFACE

I got the idea for this book while trying to help an elderly lady in our church organize her affairs after losing her husband who had handled all the household office chores up until his death. He had paid the bills, kept the checkbook, done their tax return, managed their investments and so on, never bothering her to get involved in any way. Which, I'm sure, had suited her just fine…right up until the day he had a heart attack and died. Suddenly confronted with having to do all these things herself, she felt overwhelmed by the seeming enormity of what she didn't know. And by the realization that there were things she didn't know that she didn't know.

My first thought, then, was to write a book for new widows,[1] but as I got into it I began to ponder several things. The first was that, when it came to managing their affairs, my friend's husband, a guy I respected as being extremely capable, clearly hadn't understood what he was doing much of the time. The other was the response I got from nearly everyone with whom I discussed my project. The common refrain was, "Oh man, I need a book like that too," or "They ought to teach this stuff in the schools." After

---

[1] And widowers, too, because in many households today, and possibly most, it's the wife who handles all the office-type work.

mulling all this over for awhile, I decided it wasn't just new widows who needed help; it was apparently everybody. Everybody, then, is who I've ended up writing for.[2]

But not everybody is going to find the book a good read. It's not a book you're going to want to curl up in bed with and read for the sheer pleasure of it. By its nature, most of the material is dry and only interesting when you feel the need to understand it because you've got a question or a problem. There's also a lot of material packed into each chapter. One friend, a former financial advisor, remarked after vetting Chapters 5 and 6 that it was like studying for the Series 7. That's the licensing exam to sell securities. She was exaggerating, but I took her point. It's almost too much information. None of it, however, should be over your head. Just take your time. If you need help understanding something, don't be ashamed to pick other people's brains. You may not think so, but chances are you have just as good a head on your shoulders as your attorney, your broker, the person who does your taxes, and your insurance guy or gal.

My professional background includes a thirty-year career with Chiquita Brands International, nearly all of it as a division controller and group CFO/CAO[3], and a five year stint with A. G. Edwards & Sons as a financial consultant. In the short interlude between the end of my first career and the beginning of the second, I briefly experimented with selling real estate and doing taxes. Though I long ago let my securities and insurance licenses go, I continue to keep up my certification as a Certified Financial Planner.

I have divided the book into four parts. The first part, *The Basics*, deals with the five jobs you've got to worry with more or less day-in and day-out, namely: planning your day, dealing with mail, paying bills, recordkeeping, and budgeting. It tells you how I manage these tasks.

The second part, *Financial Planning 101*, deals with all the other things that you, as the person ultimately responsible for how well your affairs are managed, need to be aware of and to understand, in at least a general way, in order not to be helpless in the

---

[2] That said, some of the chapters are written primarily for a particular audience. Chapter 4, which I believe is the first thing I wrote, was written with new widows and soon-to-be widows in mind; Chapter 5 for young people who can make compound interest work for them; and Chapters 13 and 14 for seniors.
[3] Chief Financial Officer/Chief Administrative Officer

hands of the professionals on whom you must rely for products and services. I'm referring here to estate planning (which is all about passing your property on to the people you want to get it after your death), doing your taxes, saving for retirement, managing your investments, and protecting yourself against various forms of risk through insurance.

The third part, *Social Security & Medicare*, covers those two programs, which for many seniors are their financial and healthcare mainstays.

The last part deals with a few topics that it occurred to me, after I had thought I was done, might be helpful to discuss. I call it *Loose Ends*.

The reader should understand that to a lesser or greater degree nearly everything I've written about here is in constant flux. Every few years the financial services industry comes out with an innovative new product or service, Congress tinkers with the tax code, or somebody develops new software that makes some task a bit easier. This has caused me, as the author of this small book, some annoyance, but it shouldn't concern you. These are minor details.[4] The standard deduction may have changed this year, it may change again next year or the year after, but how to understand Form 1040 and all its supporting schedules, which is the important thing, didn't and won't any time soon. Of that I'm fairly confident. I feel the same confidence about the essentials of everything else I've tried to get across here.

Finally, before closing, I feel the need to explain that while it is fashionable these days to avoid using "he," "his" or "him" when the pronoun doesn't refer unambiguously to a member of the male sex, I find the more fastidious "he or she," "his or her" and "him or her" irksome after a point. About halfway through the book, having had enough of this, I went back and wherever I wasn't clearly referring to a lady removed most of the "or she's" and "or her's." The few that remain I deemed necessary.

[4] You can stay current with these by going to the internet.

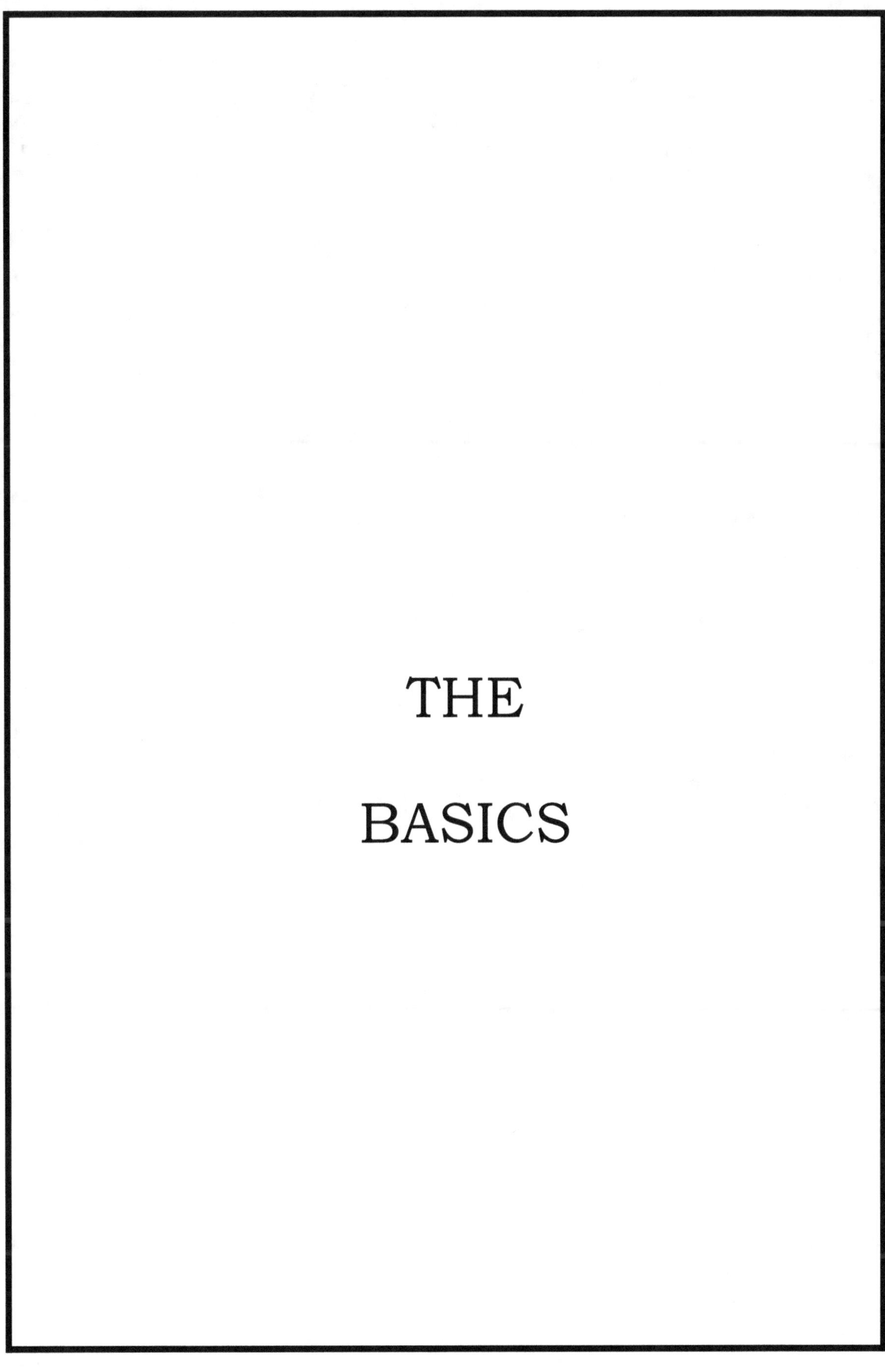

THE

BASICS

ONE

Planning Your Day, Dealing with Mail & Paying Bills

My three topics here—planning your day, dealing with mail and paying bills—make strange bedfellows, but I'm taking them up together because there's not enough to say about any one of them to warrant a separate chapter. What there is to say, however, can make your life easier and possibly spare you some grief.

****

I have nothing against day planners, organizers, appointment books, tickler files, and all the rest, but for whatever reason they've never worked for me. Plus some are expensive. What *has* worked for me are simple *to-do lists,* which I do on scratch paper, and those big desk calendar pads with a sheet for each month that office supply stores like OfficeMax sell for about $7.

A to-do list, if you're unfamiliar with the term, is merely a list of things you need to do during the day. Or soon. If that's a loopy definition, I'm sorry but I know no better way to explain it. Here's what a to-do list might look like:

- Call MN & Tom
- Write check to Keith
- Send condolence to Amy
- Get gas
- Take Pete to dr. @ 1:30

I make, update, and/or revise a list of to-do's almost daily. I do this soon after having my morning coffee and may add to my list during the day as and when other things occur to me or come up. It's never a work of art. When I've accomplished an item, I cross it off.

Some people after making their list go back and prioritize the things on it as a way of disciplining themselves to tackle the important ones first. I see the logic in this practice but don't bother with it myself. I don't need numbers to tell me what's first, second, third, and so on in importance; I just know. And sometimes if my list is long, I may do a few unimportant, quickly-done things first, just because I find the act of crossing them off energizing.

Keeping a to-do list is a habit I was urged to acquire by one of my first bosses many years ago. He may have done this after I had dropped the ball on something. It's likely, although I don't remember. In any event, I took the advice to heart and know it has served me well since. Whatever other faults I may have, allowing myself to be distracted from what I need to be doing and forgetting things aren't among them. In my old job, that would have been fatal.

The particular desk calendar pad that I'm referring to measures roughly 17.25"×22" and has twelve (12) sheets, one for each month. It looks something like Figure 1.1 on the next page.

You can't see them in my illustration, but there are six horizontal lines running through each day on which to note whatever you've got scheduled that day (e.g., "12:00: lunch w/ Jim @ Rio Ranch," "3:00 appt w/ Dr. Poindexter"). As things come up that you wish to be reminded of—appointments, deadlines, invitations, meetings etc.—you write them down. It's all there in plain view and instantly understandable. Plus it's always in the same place when you want to refer to it, which should be at least once a day, preferably first thing in the morning when you're making your to-do list.

Figure 1.1 ~ Desk Calendar

February, 2016						
Sunday	Monday	Tuesday	Wednesday	Thursday	Friday	Saturday
31	1	2	3	4	5	6
7	8	9	10	11	12	13
14	15	16	17	18	19	20
21	22	23	24	25	26	27
28	1	2	3	4	5	6

If you don't already have some aids or tools or practices you're using to plan your day, and maybe as a result are prone to forget things and not be as productive as you need to be, try making a daily to-do list and using a desk calendar like the one I've just described. You'll see immediate results.

****

With mail, the cardinal rule for avoiding trouble is to open it every day. If you don't, if you let it pile up, when eventually you do get around to opening it, I promise you that hidden somewhere in that muddle will be some little horror that's going to ruin your day—a reminder of a meeting held two days ago that you needed to attend, a bill that's now past due, a bank overdraft notice, an invitation to something from someone important to which you were to RSVP by yesterday… The list of possible unpleasant surprises is endless.

The other bad thing about a pile of unopened mail is that it's a rebuke. It says that you're not managing very well. Who needs that?

Where you do your mail is obviously a matter of personal preference. The logical choice might be a kitchen or dining room table where you've got plenty of room to sort it according to whatever criteria you find useful. I sort my mail according to what I'm going to do with it when I'm finished. Because we don't ordinarily get that much mail, most days I end up with just two or three little stacks, but occasionally I'll have as many as five:

- ***Periodicals & catalogs*** ~ This includes newspapers, newsletters, magazines, and catalogs—stuff we can look at later. Often these will just stay right where I tossed them until sometime later that day or evening when one of us—my wife or I—picks something up to go off and read. The newspapers generally get put into recycling a day or two later. Neither of us minds a bit of clutter. It helps make a house a home.
- ***Personal correspondence*** ~ This means letters, cards, and photos from friends and family, of which, owing to the telephone and internet, we nowadays receive very little, except around Christmas. On the rare occasions that we do, needless to say, we stop everything to read it. Where it ultimately ends up is anyone's guess.
- ***Junk mail*** ~ This covers a multitude of stuff that we didn't ask for, including: credit card offers; solicitations of money from charities, political parties, etc.; promotional materials from everybody under the sun; privacy notices and other communications from banks and brokerage firms aimed at covering their fannies; etc. The first thing I do when I'm finished opening my mail is to gather this stuff up and put it in recycling. I've learned over the years not to give any of it a second thought.
- ***Action items*** ~ This is the occasional paperwork that comes in on which some action needs to be taken—bills and account statements; *proxy statements; court notices of class action lawsuit settlements*; magazine and newspaper subscription renewal notices; requests for information from the Internal Revenue Service, etc. Unless there's something there that urgently needs attending to, I deposit anything of this nature in the middle of our desk to be dealt with the next morning when we're fresh and a little smarter.[1] *I never,*

[1] We usually get our mail in the mid to late afternoon.

ever, in the interest of being neat, stick action items in a desk drawer. That's a formula for disaster.

- ***Statements, etc.*** ~ This refers to bank statements, brokerage statements, trade confirmations, credit card statements, automatic deduction notices for insurance premiums, utility bills and the like paid by bank draft or charged to our credit card, and so on. I look at these and, after I'm done with our mail, immediately file them for future reference. It takes me only a couple of minutes. In Chapter Two ~ Recordkeeping and Records Retention, I will explain where and for how long I keep documents.

Most of the kinds of correspondence that I've mentioned here will be familiar to you. Two possible exceptions are *proxies* and *court notices of class action lawsuits*, which I know baffle lots of people, particularly people encountering them for the first time. Although I put them into the category of "action items," they aren't things you *have* to take action on. Here's the deal:

A *proxy* is an authorization you give someone to vote your shares at a meeting you won't be attending called to pass on some measure(s) requiring shareholder approval. If you own stocks or mutual funds, you'll get these from time to time. A proxy statement lays out what the resolutions are and provides a place for you to indicate whether you're for or against them. I would encourage anyone who has the time and inclination to be a good shareholder and thus to read, complete, and return the proxies he or she receives. The postage is paid by the company.

If you own stocks, you'll also occasionally receive a slightly sinister-looking package from some U.S. District Court having to do with the *settlement of a class action lawsuit*. It will include paperwork for you to complete and return if you want to share in the monies awarded to the plaintiffs. It may or may not be worth your while to take action on these. I personally tend to treat them as junk mail for the simple reason that our stake in such matters is invariably miniscule. Anything we might recover from a class action settlement would hardly ever compensate us for the time, effort and aggravation required to do the paperwork. That may not be true in your case. Consult your financial advisor. And if your stake in a settlement is significant and you need help with the specifics of when you bought a security, what you paid for it, when you sold it, and what you received, ask your financial advisor for help. He or she will have a financial assistant who can track down this information for you.

Before leaving mail, there are two other things I want to say, one having to with solicitations of money and the other with identity theft.

I think we all feel a little conflicted about what to do with the myriad solicitations for money that we receive. How can we not support cancer research, the March of Dimes, disabled veterans, public broadcasting, shelters for abused women, our alma mater, and all the political causes we believe in? It's not easy. All I can say is: be as generous as you can, but realize that there are more worthy causes out there than you have money to support. Sooner or later you must decide what, if anything, you can afford to give away and whom you want most to support so you can stop agonizing over everyone else's request.

Concerning identity theft, be careful how you get rid of junk mail. Or for that matter, any mail. I tear my name off anything that is going into the trash or recycling if there is even the remotest possibility of someone being able to do something mischievous with it. As the old saying goes, an ounce of prevention is worth a pound of cure.

****

There are basically five ways to pay your bills:

- By ***check*** ~ The old, time-honored way of paying bills is, of course, to pay them by check. That said, next to paying with cash, it's my least favorite. The risk you run with paying bills by check is forgetting to get your check off in time to arrive by the payment due date. Paying bills by check also entails an outlay for a first-class stamp.
- ***Online*** ~ Many banks now offer an online bill paying facility, which I find handy. I like being able when I get a bill to go ahead while I'm thinking about it to arrange to have it paid, so that I don't have to deal with it later and run the risk of being delinquent. You indicate when the payment is due, and the bank sees to it that it gets to the payee on time. Guaranteed. That can be just about any date in the future that's at least a week away. The first time you pay

somebody online using this facility you'll have to provide the bank with the payee's name, telephone number and address. Unless that changes, you won't have to do it again. The system remembers it. The next time you pay that vendor or utility or whoever, you just tell the system how much to pay and when, and it will do the rest. It will also save you a stamp.

- With ***cash*** ~ My barber expects to be paid in cash, and I will occasionally use it to purchase something like a soda at a convenience store, but I never pay bills or buy groceries, gas and the like with cash because it would make tracking my spending difficult. (More about that in Chapter 3.)
- By ***ACH debit*** ~ ACH stands for Automatic Clearing House, which is an electronic network for processing credit and debit financial transactions between account holders at banks operating within the Federal Reserve System. If your payroll check or your Social Security check is direct-deposited into your checking account each month, it's being done through the ACH network. You may have forgotten, but before your employer or the Social Security Administration could begin doing this, they needed your consent, plus a voided check showing the name on your account, your bank's routing number[2] and your account number. If you have a mortgage, chances are that your monthly payment is being handled through the ACH as well; only in this case, of course, your account is being debited, not credited. But just as with the direct-deposits, you would have had to authorize this payment arrangement and provided your lender with a voided check. Payment by ACH is not always an option, but when it is, it can simplify your life and keep you out of trouble. All of our insurance premiums are paid by ACH debit, saving us the time and expense of mailing in our payments and, more importantly, assuring that our policies do not lapse because we forgot that a premium payment was due. I think, really, that paying insurance premiums through the ACH is the only prudent way to go. Loan payments, as well. Many public utilities, like the power company, gas company, phone company, and water

[2] Your bank's routing number is the nine-digit series of numbers at the bottom, left-hand side of your checks. Your account number is to the right of the routing number. The number to the right of your account number is the check number.

company, will also happily let you pay your bills this way, provided you give them the paperwork they need. You just need to be sure, if you set something up to be paid by ACH debit, that there is money in your checking account to honor the charge when it comes through each month. The company can tell you when that will be.

- By ***credit card*** ~ You can also arrange with many service providers to collect what you owe every month by charging it directly to your credit card. Some utilities seem to prefer doing this to debiting your checking account. I'm more than happy to go the credit card route because a) the charge doesn't hit our checking account immediately and b) we earn "cash rewards" on our purchases, which can accumulate over time to be worth something.[3] We use credit cards to pay for a host of services and subscriptions—garbage collection, telephone, DSL, cable TV, Netflix, and the Wall Street Journal. We also use them to pay for groceries, gas, and much else. Needless to say, with the lion's share of our monthly expenses being paid by credit card, our balance at the end of the billing cycle is pretty hefty. To avoid any possibility of being late with our payment, which might tarnish our credit and add interest and a penalty to what we owe, we have arranged for our balance to be settled every month by ACH debit on the day it is due.

If you presently are paying your insurance premiums and utility bills and the like by check and would like to pay them instead by ACH debit or credit card, talk to the companies involved. They'll make it real easy for you. Once you've got everything set up, I think you'll be glad you did. Just remember that if you set something up to be paid by ACH debit there must be sufficient funds in your account to cover the charge. (To be doubly sure that there are, I log into our accounts every three or four days to check our balances.[4])

---

[3] We earn one (1) cash rewards point for every dollar we spend, and once we have a certain number of points, we can redeem them for cash rebates on things we buy or to apply to the purchase of airline tickets. Just last month, we redeemed 50,000 points for $500 off airline tickets.

[4] I have more to say about ACH debits and credits in Chapter 15 under the heading of *Reconciling Bank Accounts*.

A further comment or two on credit cards: A lot of older folks really distrust credit cards and for good reason. The main problem with credit cards is that by extending credit they enable you to purchase stuff without having the money in the bank to pay for it. Thus, they encourage impulse-buying and living beyond your means. They're the reason so many people, especially young people, are in debt up to their eyeballs with no hope of getting out short of declaring bankruptcy. But that is not all. Credit cards and credit card numbers can also fall into the wrong hands and be misused. It happens all the time. And lastly, the interest rates charged on credit card balances can be usurious. My bank charges 9.9% to 25.9%, depending on the cardholder's credit.

All that notwithstanding, I'm in favor of people having at least one card, because they're a great convenience. Plus, it is also pretty hard to secure an airline or hotel reservation without one. Just be sure if you have a card to observe a few rules: First, pay your balance off each month to avoid the finance charges. Second, do not leave the card lying around where it could fall into the wrong hands. When a clerk asks to see it or a waiter goes off with it, be sure you get it back. Third, when you're ready to discard your old credit card statements, be sure that you destroy them, so that no one can get your number.

TWO

Recordkeeping & Records Retention

There is always much confusion about what records and documents to keep, where to keep them, and how long to keep them. I've heard of people who just threw anything they weren't sure about into a big box against the eventuality that they might need it someday. If the need materialized, they'd go rummaging through their box or boxes until they found whatever it was.

Actually, for most people, including me, the uncertainty is less about what to keep and where to keep it than it is about *how long to keep it*. You know, of course, that some documents you need to keep pretty much forever—things like your birth certificate, Social Security card and college diploma—because someone, someday, like a prospective employer, may want to see them; but other records, like your tax returns or a release of lien, you may be very uncertain about. The reason for this uncertainty is that there are no laws that say how long you have to keep them. You keep these kinds of records and documents not to comply with the law; you keep them against the possibility of needing them at some point to prove something. When, thanks to the statute of limitations or whatever, it becomes all but inconceivable to think of a situation in which you might need a particular record or document, either to defend yourself against the claim of some third-party or to assert some claim of your own, you may safely assume that you can get rid of that piece of paper. In my opinion, that's pretty much the premise on which records retention guidelines should be based.

Much of the discussion here will focus on tax records. That's because I think most people's chief concern when it comes to recordkeeping is being able to produce whatever the IRS might want to see if it came calling because something on their tax return raised a red flag.[1] Fortunately, most of what I have to say here is pretty straightforward.

It's some of the non-tax related documents that are problematic in terms of what you should keep and for how long. I'll cover these too. Those that I suspect may cause some people a bit of angst I'll try to explain, which hopefully will help, and I'll tell you what I do. And in those instances where what I do is different from what other guidance suggests, I'll disclose that. You can then do what you want.

As to what I keep, where I keep it, how I label things and so on, my "system," if I may call it that, is entirely my own. That's not to suggest that there's anything very special about it; it's just to say that it's *not* a compilation of all the best ideas out there gleaned from extensive reading on the subject. That I know of, there are no brilliant ideas out there. Most of this stuff, except for how long you should keep records, is fairly intuitive, and of course we all use the same kinds of office equipment and supplies. It's just a question, really, of putting it all together. If you're struggling with how to do that, I think this will help. It's simple and low-maintenance.

****

Before we get started here, I want to warn you: This will be very tedious reading if you attempt to do it all in one sitting. My suggestion is to break the chapter up into bite-size pieces, reading the section on Income Taxes one day, Property Records another, and so on. And don't get discouraged if something doesn't make perfect sense on the first

---

[1] Your return doesn't have to have raised any red flags for you to be audited. Your return can also be randomly selected for audit.

reading. Just remember what topics were discussed. Then later when you're face to face with some recordkeeping problem, come back here to see if you can't find your answer.

****

Let's begin here with the records and documents that should be kept indefinitely.

Keep Indefinitely in a Safe Deposit Box or Home Safe

Here's a list, which is certainly not comprehensive, of documents that you need to retain *indefinitely* because at the very least they would be difficult to replace:

- Birth certificates
- Baptism certificates
- Social Security cards
- Marriage license/certificate
- Divorce papers
- Adoption papers
- Naturalization papers
- College transcripts
- High school and college diplomas
- Professional licenses and certificates (e.g., teaching, CPA)
- Papers related to military service (e.g., Honorable Discharge)
- Wills, if still in force
- Trust agreements, if still in force
- Retirement and pension records
- Life insurance policies, if still in force
- Promissory notes
- Deeds to property
- Title insurance policies
- Cancelled mortgages/releases of lien
- Stock and bond certificates, until the securities are sold
- Car titles, until transferred

Because these are documents that you need to retain indefinitely, it follows that you should keep them in a safe, secure place. For most people, that means a safe-deposit box at a bank. It's where we keep ours. Our box is a legal-size box about 5" deep, on which the annual rent is $40.

An alternative to a safe-deposit box is a fireproof, water-resistant home safe. These are sold by OfficeMax, Staples, Home Depot, Lowes, Walmart, and the like. The biggest problem I have with these safes, apart from the initial outlay—one that will hold what our safe-deposit box holds and protect the contents from a fire for up to an hour costs around $300, plus tax—is that we have no really satisfactory place to put one. If you do, you may wish to consider a safe.

Before leaving this particular topic, I should mention that there can be a problem with keeping your will in a safe-deposit box. That's because in some states banks may seal the box if the lessee, or one of the lessees, dies. To get into it to get the will, the executor has to get a court order instructing the bank to give him access. That's not mission impossible, but it takes time. If you have your will in a safe-deposit box, you should discuss with the bank what its policy is and then make provisions to deal with it accordingly. My bank's policy is to allow any surviving lessee, if there are two or more lessees on a box and one dies, unimpeded access, which means that if I suddenly pop off, there shouldn't be a problem with my executrix getting hold of my will. My executrix is my wife, and she and both of our sons are co-lessees.

Tax Records

I will begin here with a simple declarative sentence: Keep your *tax returns* forever. Why? Because all the experts say so. Personally, the only reason I can think of is to be able to prove to the IRS, should they ever come after you claiming that you hadn't filed for a certain year, that indeed you had. Other than that, I don't have a clue.[2]

With each *Form 1040* and its supporting schedules (*Schedules A, B, C, D* etc.), you should also keep copies of any tax statements, like *W-2s* and *1099s*, that you were

[2] If you don't have all your tax returns going back to the first one you ever filed forty-seven years ago, I wouldn't worry about it. Neither does anyone else I know.

required to mail in with your return when you filed. The experts also recommend that you keep with it the cancelled check(s) you used to pay your taxes.

The debate about how long you should keep tax records really has to do with all those *supporting tax records* that weren't mailed in with your return but underlie some of the numbers on it, like those on *Schedule A (Itemized Deductions), Schedule C (Profit or Loss from Business),* and *Schedule D (Capital Gains and Losses).* These records typically consist of documents like bills, invoices and statements (indicating how paid), receipts, cancelled checks, credit card receipts, acknowledgements from charities, buy and sell trade confirmations, realized gains & losses reports, real estate closing statements, and mileage records, which in the aggregate can fatten a tax file considerably.[3] Unless purged after a certain number of years, the extra space they take up can become a problem.

The general rule is that supporting records need to be kept for three (3) years, counting from the *later* of a) the tax return's *normal filing date*, which is always on or around April 15th, or b) its *actual filing date*, which, if the taxpayer filed for an extension, could be as late as October 15th. The three years comes from the fact that this is how long under normal circumstances the IRS has to audit a return and assess additional taxes. If a taxpayer who filed his 2015 return on, say, April 12, 2016, hasn't heard from the IRS by April 16, 2019, he can probably assume that he never will as regards that return.

He could, however, if the IRS had some reason to suspect that his return underreported *gross income* by 25% or more, or was in some way fraudulent. In the first instance, the IRS is allowed six (6) years to assess additional taxes, and in the second it has forever. The taxpayer who has committed fraud or didn't file can never rest easy.

I'm not sure what kinds of things would lead the IRS to suspect that someone had underreported his income, but I would advise anyone who has income from self-employment and/or income unsupported by a W-2 or 1099 to hang onto his supporting tax records for at least six years, and preferably seven, counting from when he *actually filed*. Why preferably seven? Because many tax advisors, erring on the side of caution, recommend seven. For the taxpayer above who filed his 2015 return on April 12, 2016, that means hanging onto his supporting records until at least April 16, 2023. This is what

[3] For a complete discussion of what your supporting tax records should consist of, I would refer you to *IRS Publication 552 ~ Recordkeeping for Individuals*, which you can pull up on the internet using that as your search term. Unlike some IRS publications, it's an easy read and mercifully brief—just nine pages.

we have always done, partly out of caution but also because *capital gains and losses* from securities transactions have sometimes had a very significant impact on our reported gross income, and until recently there was no official tax statement, like a 1099, on which the IRS was copied to support the numbers we reported on Schedule D.[4] If you're unsure whether you also could be vulnerable to the longer assessment period, you may wish to consult the person who does your taxes or, if you do them yourself, a professional tax preparer. Chances are he'll tell you that three years are enough. If you just want a hard and fast rule, go with seven years.

Regardless of whether you go with three years or seven, implementing this policy is quite simple. After you're done with your return every year, gather up all your supporting documents and stick them in a manila envelope, writing on the outside something along the lines of "Supporting records for 2015 tax return filed on April 12, 2016. Destroy after April 16, 2023." Then put the manila envelope, together with your copy of the return itself, in your tax folder.[5]

I suggest you have one file folder for each year's return and supporting records. I use the following labeling scheme: TAXES: 2009, TAXES: 2010, TAXES: 2011, TAXES: 2012, and so on. At this writing, I'm using a file labeled TAXES: 2016 to accumulate the supporting records that I'll need to prepare this year's return.

Concerning state income taxes, if you live in a state that has a state income tax, you may wish to make inquiries about how long you need to keep those returns and their supporting records. That said, I don't see how you can go very wrong keeping the returns themselves forever, just like you should your federal tax returns, and insofar as supporting records are concerned, my guess is that if you've got the IRS covered, you've got your state tax commission covered as well. It would be better, though, to check.

---

[4] Brokerage firms issue what is called a *1099B – Proceeds from Broker and Barter Exchange Transactions* in respect of securities sales, and a copy has always gone to the IRS, but until very recently (2011) this document only showed what you received for the securities you sold, not what your cost basis in them was. More about this later.

[5] Our supporting records typically consist of a little summary I always do of our medical expenses; our property tax statements with their tax office receipts; acknowledgements of charitable donations from our church, etc.; and 1099 Bs from our two brokerage firms. Not much, really.

Cancelled Checks, Credit Card Receipts, and Bank & Credit Card Statements

Most guidelines dealing with how long you should keep cancelled checks, credit card receipts, and bank and credit card statements will advise you to hold onto anything having any tax significance for as long as you are subject to audit, which to be on the safe side, as I just finished explaining, would be seven years beyond the date you filed your return for a particular year.

Many guidelines will also suggest that in any instance where a cancelled check or credit card receipt has tax significance, you staple it to whatever you paid, keeping the two documents together as supporting tax records. I do this with credit card receipts, but not with cancelled checks. On any bill or statement I pay by check, I write the date, amount, and number of my check, but I don't attach the cancelled check itself. That's because my bank doesn't return cancelled checks. Yours probably doesn't either. Nowadays what we get with our monthly bank statement, in lieu of cancelled checks, are "images" of our checks and deposit slips, ten or so to a page. My solution, then, to being able if required to document that I did in fact pay something with a particular check is to keep all my bank statements for as long as I can conceive being subject to audit. As a practical matter, this means keeping them going back to at least the January statement eight years ago. To understand where this comes from, see the footnote below.[6] In my case, eight (8) years of statements, with their images, fit into one three-ring binder with a 3" spine. It's not like they're crowding me out of house and home.

Nobody says you have to keep your bank statements as long as I do. Most guidelines, including ones put out by the Federal Deposit Insurance Corporation, suggest you destroy statements with no tax or other relevance after about a year.[7] Do what you want, but to me that's more trouble than simply keeping eight years of statements.

There are some things for which you should keep your proof of payment for not just eight years but indefinitely. One would be property you buy on a contract for sale or in a deal where the financing is being provided by an individual or company whose

---

[6] If you waited to pay your property taxes for, say, 2013 until January 2, 2014, in order to take it as a deduction that year instead and then waited until October 15, 2015, to file your 2014 return, your six-year assessment period wouldn't be up until October, 15, 2021, by which time 93 ½ months, or 7.79 years, would have elapsed from the date of your check. To keep the arithmetic simple, I call it eight years.

[7] "Your Financial Records: What to Toss and When." FDIC Federal Deposit Insurance Corporation, *www.fdic.gov/consumernews,* (June 13, 2014).

bookkeeping and back office capabilities might not be on the same level as that of a more established financial institution. Ditto for improvements to property that increase your cost basis. Ditto also for non-deductible IRA contributions. We'll get into property records a little later in this chapter and to non-deductible IRA contributions when we get to Chapter 5.

I see no reason to keep credit card *statements* as long as I do bank statements. I figure the *receipts* suffice to document anything I paid with a credit card. After a year or two, I shred or burn the statements. But if you want to hang onto them, there's certainly no harm in it. I just don't see that the statements tell you very much.

As for your receipts that have no tax relevance, you can destroy those after getting the monthly statement on which they appear and satisfying yourself that the charges agree. That is, unless there's some good reason, other than supporting a tax deduction, to hang onto them. One reason might be the possibility of your wanting to return or exchange the item purchased.[8] Another might be to document when and where you purchased something covered by a warranty.[9] A third reason could be that the receipt, like the check I mentioned earlier, helps to document some major improvement made to real property—for example, materials you purchased to add a deck off the back of your house.

Trade Confirmations & Brokerage Statements

Any time you buy or sell a security (e.g., stock, bond, CD, mutual fund), your brokerage firm will send you a *trade confirmation* showing (confirming) when you made the trade, when it settled, how many shares you bought or sold and at what price, the commission paid, and the net you paid or received. After looking these over, you're supposed to save them. Most guidance says to keep any "confirm" in respect of a purchase for as long as you own the security and, if and when you sell it, to remove its confirm from your file and staple it to the confirm covering the sale and put the two in your tax file as one of your supporting tax records. The difference between what you received for the security, net, and what you paid for it, total, is your capital gain or loss.

---

[8] If you return something to a store, they'll want to see your credit card receipt proving you purchased the item there.

[9] In this case, the best place to keep the receipt is stapled to your copy of the warranty.

Confirmations, however, won't tell the whole story where some of the shares sold were acquired through *dividend reinvestment*. Brokerage firms don't issue confirmations in respect of dividend reinvestments. They report this activity in their brokerage statements in those months or quarters that it occurs, and that's it. It used to be, then, back before brokerage firms were required to keep track of your cost basis, that in order to document your gain or loss on any shares acquired through dividend reinvestments, you'd have to save the *activity* pages from all your old statements showing what you had invested in those shares.[10]

Starting in 2011, brokerage firms have been required to keep track of your cost basis in the securities they hold for you and, when you sell something, to report your gain or loss on your year-end *1099 B (Proceeds from Broker and Barter Exchange)*. That's provided, however, that you acquired the securities subsequent to the rules change. If you acquired them before 2011, and particularly if you acquired them a long time ago from another firm from which you transferred them *in kind* to your present firm, they may not have your cost basis. In that case, you need to hang onto whatever you've got in the way of confirmations and other cost basis information until seven years beyond filing the return reporting their sale.

We have brokerage accounts with two different firms, and both have assured me that they have all our cost basis information for the securities they're holding, so that we don't need to worry with hanging onto any confirms in respect of pre-2011 purchases, not to mention anything subsequent. When we get a confirmation after doing a trade, all we need to do is look to see that everything looks in order. If it does, we should feel free to destroy it. If it doesn't—which has never happened—we'd need to call our broker to straighten things out.

These assurances notwithstanding, I'm still not comfortable discarding everything but my year-end account statements. I don't fully share my firms' confidence in today's digital record-keeping. So, besides our year-end brokerage statements in their entirety, I still keep the pages from interim month's statements that show activity, including dividend reinvestments. I don't keep confirmations, though.

[10] Even if not required to, some firms did keep track of their clients' cost basis anyway. Upon request, they'd give you at year end a *Realized Gains & Losses Report* providing all of the same information now reported on the 1099 B.

Every investor's situation is different. For many, dividend reinvestments will be a non-issue. Others have never moved their account, much less moved securities in kind from one firm to another. My advice to you, then, is that before adopting my policy or any other you have a conversation with your broker or investment advisor to see what he or she advises.

Property Records

Purchases of real estate are usually, though certainly not always, financed by some third party, like a bank, savings & loan association, or other mortgage lender. What you usually have, then, when you buy real estate is: 1) a *deed* from the seller to you (the buyer) conveying title to the property; 2) a *title insurance policy* issued by a third-party insurer, like Stewart Title, promising to stand behind the title you received from the seller should it ever be challenged and proved deficient; 3) a *note* from you (the buyer/borrower) to the mortgage lender promising to repay what you borrowed to buy the property, plus interest, in installments over some period of time; and 4) a *deed of trust* (aka *mortgage*) from you (the borrower) to a trustee (often an employee of the lender) conveying conditional title to the property until such time as you have fully complied with the terms and conditions of the note, so that if you don't the property can be sold and the proceeds used to pay off or pay down your loan. If everything proceeds happily and you pay off the note according to schedule, the trustee gives you a *release of lien.* The property is yours then, free and clear.

Different states may do things a little differently, and I know that even in Texas, where I live, there are different ways of buying property, different kinds of deeds, and so on. You can inherit property, you can buy it for cash, you can buy it on a contract for deed, you can acquire it in trade. But in my experience, these, or something very similar to them, are the documents you're most likely to see.

Whenever you buy or sell real estate, you also get a *closing statement*, which lays out the total due from the buyer and the net due to the seller. For the buyer, the closing statement documents his cost basis in the property, which he'll need to compute his gain or loss if he later sells it. Any additions or improvements made to property later will add to its cost basis and so should also be documented.

Whatever your documents are, you need to hang onto to them indefinitely, keeping them in a safe, secure, fireproof location, like a bank safe-deposit box. If, say, seven years after filing a return reporting the sale of property you want to get rid of all your documents associated with it, ask your attorney and your tax guy or gal if it's okay.

I put all legal documents for each property we've owned in a separate legal-size manila envelope, writing on the outside of the envelope what's in it. The one on our home reads along these lines:

Lot 47 Guadalupe River Estates

- Deed of Trust: Smith to Hill Country Savings
- Note: Smith to HC Savings
- Addendum to Note & Deed of Trust
- Assumption Deed, 9/27/1979
- Release of Lien, 2/6/1981
- Title insurance policy
- Closing Statement

(If you're mystified by the first four documents, that's because ours was not your typical house deal. We got our financing by assuming the sellers' indebtedness to the savings and loan that had financed them and were fortunate in being able to pay the note off early.)

I will also note, because it's relevant to what I just said earlier about documenting any additions or improvements to property, that some twenty years after buying our house we added onto it and otherwise extensively remodeled it. All of the invoices related to those improvements I keep in another big manila envelope labeled TAXES: Home Improvements. I keep that envelope in the same filing cabinet where I keep our last seven years of tax returns and supporting tax records. Again, that's because we will need this information, as well as our original closing statement, if and when we ever sell our home to compute our gain or loss.

Insurance Files

In Chapters 8 through 12, I discuss insurance. Here I'm just concerned with recordkeeping and records retention.

We have just about every kind of non-commercial kind of insurance they sell. That's not true, of course, but it feels that way. For each policy, I have a separate file folder. Here's how those folders are labeled:

- INS: Auto
- INS: Homeowners
- INS: Umbrella
- INS: Flood (We live on a creek)
- INS: Life
- INS: Long Term Care
- INS: Medicare Supplement
- INS: Prescription Drug Plan

I keep these files in a metal filing cabinet in our utility room. Except for the life insurance folder, they contain the policies themselves and any non-claim related correspondence. What the Life folder contains is a note saying that the policy itself is in our safe deposit box. I keep it there because if my wife and I were to die together in a common accident, our children would be sure at some point to examine the box's contents and find it.

Some advice I've read says that you should keep *all* insurance policies in a safe-deposit box or in a fireproof safe at home. Do what you want, but personally I don't see the need. I'm not worried that if a fire destroys our home and maybe our cars as well, we won't have coverage because we can't produce the policies owing to their having gone up in flames too. The insurance company itself has copies, as does the agency through which we purchased our policies, and I can't see either risking its reputation and punitive damages by trying to defraud me.

It probably goes without saying that insurance policies and related correspondence need to be retained for as long as the policies remain in force. Common sense would also tell you to hang onto any policy against which you've made a claim that's still unsettled.

Claims

We've never had a claim on our homeowners, flood and umbrella policies, I'm happy to say, and rarely one on our auto policy. Our most recent auto claim was several years ago when hail damaged my wife's car. Insurance covered everything but the deductible, and the paperwork was negligible, so what there was of it I just stuck in the file I keep on that particular vehicle (AUTO: Buick). Had the claim been long and drawn out, I would have opened a separate file on it (CLAIM: Hail Damage), and once the claim was settled, have closed the file, transferring its contents to the AUTO: Buick file. (I'll get to the auto files in a bit.)

What we nearly all of us have going on all the time are medical insurance claims. Because my wife and I are both on Medicare, our claims are always against it and/or our *Medicare Supplement,* or against our *Prescription Drug Plan.* For everyone else, meaning everyone not on Medicare, those claims will be against an individual policy or a group plan.

Health insurance is covered in Chapter 10. Suffice it to say here that nearly all medical insurance plans are based on one of four business models, each employing a different combination of measures to contain costs. These include coverage exclusions and restrictions on services from out-of-network providers, as well as cost-sharing in the form of deductibles, coinsurance, and co-payments. Understanding how your plan works is the first and most important thing you need to know in order to make sense of claims paperwork.

I suggest you accumulate this paperwork in a file labeled CLAIMS: Medical. The thing you need most to understand is the *Explanation of Benefits (EOB)* you'll get from your insurance company in respect of any services rendered to you that were billed to it. The EOB will briefly describe the service, give its date, and then show the total amount billed and how responsibility for that total has been apportioned in terms of what's your responsibility ("Amount not allowed," "Applied to deductible," "Coinsurance" and "Copayment amount") and what's theirs, the insurance company's. Anything that's your responsibility your health care provider will see to billing you. Managing your claims file mostly consists in stapling together the bills and statements to their relevant EOBs, and on any bill or statement you paid by check writing the number, date, and amount, and to any you paid with a credit card by attaching the credit card receipt.

You may be able, in some years at least, to use out-of-pocket medical expenses as an itemized deduction on Schedule A. In that case, the related paperwork would become supporting tax records, which you'd need to keep. What you don't need, either because it's tax-unrelated or unrelated to a claim that's still in progress, you can destroy.

That said, there's Plan B. This is to keep your medical claims paperwork, whether it has any tax significance or not, for as long as you do your supporting tax records. Again, implementing this policy is simple. At the same time, after doing your taxes, that you gather up all your supporting tax records and put them in a manila envelope, you do the same with your medical claims paperwork, writing on that particular envelope something along the lines of "Medical claims paperwork for 2015; destroy after April 16, 2023." Then file the two together behind your tax return, so that when the time comes that you can destroy your supporting tax records, you are reminded that you can destroy your medical claims paperwork for that year as well.

As we shall see, I do this with Medicare records. I like it because I don't have to think about what to keep and what not, and if I want to look back at something for other than a tax reason, I can. Anyone who thinks this is overkill is free to stick to Plan A.

Medicare-related Claims

This mostly applies to people 65 and older, so if you haven't gotten there yet you can skip to the next section.

Medicare is covered in Chapter 14. Here again I'm just going to discuss files and record retention as it relates to Medicare claims.

If you have Medicare, the *Centers for Medicare & Medicaid Services (CMS)* will send you a summary each quarter of any claims filed on your behalf. These are called *Medicare Summary Notices.* As you probably know if you have Medicare, like all other health care plans, it doesn't pay all of your medical expenses. There are deductibles and co-payments and coinsurance that apply and some services that Medicare simply does not cover. These are for your account and reported as such on your Summary Notices in the section where it shows what disposition Medicare made of each service provider's claim. It will be in the column headed "Maximum you may be billed."

To deal with this risk, many people carry some form of Medicare Supplement insurance. These so-called *Medigap* policies pick up all or some portion of what Medicare doesn't pay. How Medicare and your Medicare supplement coordinate the payment of benefits I'm not sure. I just know that when you go to a doctor and he bills out his services, your Medicare supplement insurance provider will know what Medicare accepts and agrees to pay and what that leaves them, or you, to pay. Then, eventually, just like Medicare, your insurance company lets you know what they did with the charges. They do this with an Explanation of Benefits that shows what your supplement paid and what, if anything, you'll have to pay. If you have to pay something, you'll be billed in due course by the health care provider. Check to see that the amount billed agrees with what the Explanation of Benefits says you owe. The two amounts should be the same.

You may also have enrolled in a Medicare-approved *prescription drug plan* that allows you to buy your meds at below-retail prices. Like a Medicare Supplement, these plans are sponsored by private health insurance companies. To the extent that you make use of your plan to fill your prescriptions—either through its mail-order service or a local pharmacy in its network—you'll get a monthly Explanation of Benefits from this plan provider too, recapping your purchases in terms of what each item cost at retail and how much of that price you actually paid and how much your plan paid. It tells you other things as well, which we'll save for Chapter 14.

We have five Medicare file folders—two for my wife, two for me, and one that we share:

- MED: CMS ~ This is the file we share. In it we keep all correspondence with Medicare (CMS), *except* their Medicare Summary Notices. To say that we keep all correspondence with Medicare in this file may imply that there's a lot. There's not. There's a copy of the completed questionnaire we each sent in when we became eligible for Medicare, a letter to each of us explaining how we can access our Medicare-related information on their website (MyMedicare.gov), copies of the Medicare cards we carry in our billfolds, and the latest edition of CMS's handbook "Medicare & You." It's a thin file.

- MED: Medicare/Medigap ~ These are the folders—I have one and my wife has one—where we keep CMS's Medicare Summary Notices, our Medicare supplement's Explanations of Benefits, and any bills we've had to pay. When a particular claim has been fully settled, we staple the relevant documents together. This is our eighth year on Medicare, and only once has one of us had to pay anything out-of-pocket.[11]
- MED: Prescriptions ~ Again, I have a file for my prescriptions and my wife has one for hers. Anytime we refill a prescription through our plan's mail order service, we get an invoice, and anytime we have a prescription filled at our local pharmacy, we get a little customer receipt with our credit card receipt attached. These go into this file. When we eventually get our monthly Explanation of Benefits, I pick out the invoices and customer receipts that pertain to it, staple them to the back, and put everything back in the file.

Every year when I do our taxes, I go through the motions of itemizing our deductions on Schedule A, which, among other things, involves toting up all of our medical and dental expenses, including the cost of Medicare Part B (which is subtracted from our Social Security); the premiums on our Medicare Supplements, Prescription Drug Plans and Long Term Care policies; as well as our out-of-pocket medical, dental and prescription drug costs. However, it is only to the extent that these costs exceed 7 ½% of our *adjusted gross income*[12] *and* that the sum of *all* our *itemized deductions* exceeds our *standard deduction* that we are able to claim anything. Most years we fail to clear both hurdles, so all this work goes for naught.

Even so, it has been my practice in recent years after doing my taxes to pull the contents of our Medicare/Medigap and Prescriptions files, whether or not they have any tax significance, and stick them behind our tax records as though they did. In seven years

[11] Ours is a Plan F supplement, which pretty much picks up any Medicare-approved service that Medicare doesn't owing to deductibles, co-pays and co-insurance.
[12] For anyone born on or after January 2, 1949, the hurdle is 10%.

when I destroy our supporting tax records, I'll destroy these too. Nobody says you have to do likewise. If a claim has no tax significance and you don't think you'll need to look at the paperwork again, you're free to destroy it whenever you like. My rationale for deciding to hang onto my claims paperwork for seven years is that it's simpler than having to think through what I need to keep and what I don't. Also, I occasionally want to look back at something for other than a tax reason.

Medical History Files

We have two files, one for my wife and one for me, where we keep documentation relevant to serious maladies we've been treated for, surgeries that we've undergone and things we've been vaccinated against. The files are labeled MED: History (Tony) and MED: History (Louise).

Estate Planning Documents

We keep the signed originals of our wills and other estate planning documents in our safe deposit box at the bank and a copy of everything at home. The copies are for quick reference. They're in a three-ring binder, which sits on the bookshelf in our office next to our bank and brokerage statements.

Utilities

I keep the file folders for utilities in our desk, where they're easy to reach, and as I explained in Chapter 1, I have all of our utilities either paid by bank draft or charged to a credit card. When we get these bills, they always say something like "Your credit card will be charged on 1/22/16 for $39.01." When a bill comes in, I'll look at it and then put it in its proper file. I've got the folders labeled as follows:

- UTIL: Water
- UTIL: Electricity
- UTIL: Tel, TV, DSL (Our telephone, satellite TV and DSL are "bundled.")
- UTIL: Cell Phone
- UTIL: Garbage

Some taxpayers are allowed to charge off all or some portion of their utilities on their tax return.[13] If you're a minister or you office out of your home, it might be worth your while to investigate this with a CPA or other tax expert. If you're not a minister and not officing out of your house, and you're not disputing a bill with the utility company, you may want to destroy paid bills after a year or so. Some guidelines say three (3) years, but why is unclear to me. The only purpose for keeping them, at least that I can see, is to be able to refer back to them if you need to. Most utility companies will allow you to do that online going back as many years as you would likely want to.

Autos

We have two cars, and I maintain a file folder for each. In these I keep the paperwork we received when we purchased the cars, as well as the invoices for all the repairs and maintenance we've had done since. I plan to keep these records for as long as we own the cars.

Here's how our auto files are labeled:

- AUTO: Buick
- AUTO: Honda

If you finance the purchase of a car, which is what most folks do, the bank or company that's providing the financing will keep the car's title in its possession until you have paid off your loan. When that happy day arrives and they send you the title, you should put it in a safe, secure place, like a safe-deposit box. You'll need it when the day comes that you sell the car and have to transfer title.

House Repairs

We have a file (MISC: House Repairs) where we keep invoices and the like related to anything we've had done to the house. The jobs run the gamut—everything from having the trim painted to pumping out the septic. Some years later when we wonder when we had something done, or last had it done, and what it cost, we can find the answer here.

---

[13] Also house repairs and maintenance.

Work Records

If you work, or ever did, you should keep any important documents relating to that employment. I worked for Chiquita Brands for thirty years and for A. G. Edwards for five, and I have a file for each company, one labeled WORK: Chiquita and the other WORK: A G Edwards. In them I keep papers documenting when I started, what I did, training I received, benefit plans I participated in, promotions I received—that kind of thing. I actually keep the stuff on Chiquita in a "wallet" folder because it's too voluminous for a file folder. That's out in our storehouse. All that the file folder in our utility room holds is a note to that effect.

Owner's Manuals & Equipment Warranties

These are for appliances and tools you own—things like your washer and dryer, vacuum cleaner, computer and peripheral equipment, lawn mower, and so on. Keep these manuals and warranties for as long as you own whatever they're for. My wife is in charge of keeping up with these at our house. She's got them in several accordion-like pocket files in a drawer in our filing cabinet.

Miscellaneous Stuff

This covers the multitude of personal stuff that we all tend to collect or inherit. In our case it includes newspaper and magazine clippings we thought worth keeping for whatever reason, letters from and between family members (including ours to our mothers that were in their things), my wife's old scrapbooks, our kids' report cards. As you will understand, as the years go by, these things take on a painful poignancy. I can't bear to look at the old letters, and I wouldn't think of getting rid of them.

All these things reside in file folders, with tabs like Family Letters, Interesting Articles, John's Wedding, and Doug's Wedding, in the same filing cabinet drawer where we keep the owner's manuals and warranties. I expect we'll keep them forever.

****

For file folders I have a little labeling scheme, which can be summarized as CATEGORY: Sub-category. Our insurance files, for example, are labeled INS: Auto,

INS: Homeowners, INS: Umbrella, INS: Flood, INS: Life, INS: LTC,[14] INS: Medigap and INS: Presc. Drug Plan.

File folders come in two sizes—letter-size (for documents that are 8 ½ × 11) and legal-size (for those 8 ½ × 14). I use the letter-size ones. Each folder is labeled and lives in its own file hanger, which has a tab that reads exactly like the file label. This avoids any confusion about where a particular file that's been removed is supposed to be put back.

In the same file hanger that holds each of our last seven years of tax returns and their supporting records, I also keep, as I explained a bit earlier, our Medicare/Medigap and Prescription Drug paperwork for the same years. That's whether or not any of it has any tax relevance, which it usually does not. But anything I might need is there in the event it *is* needed; I don't have to spend time sorting out what I might need from what I'm pretty sure I won't; it's fail-safe; and every year when I shred the supporting tax records from seven years ago, I can also shred a whole year's worth of these documents, which is more efficient than shredding them piecemeal.

Some kinds of records, like bank and brokerage statements, lend themselves better to being kept in 3-ring binders. If you get those with 3" spines, which will hold up to 650 pages of documents, you won't need too many. I put labels on the spines that read along the lines of BANK STMTS: Account #1 and BANK STMTS: Account #2.

A convenient way of keeping voluminous old files together—files like those for medical claims paperwork and old files from work and even old files on property you once owned—is in what are called "expandable wallets," which will hold a half-dozen or so very full letter-size file folders. We've got a number of these lying lengthwise at the back of the bottom drawer in our filing cabinet.

Another solution to keeping voluminous records may be to store them digitally in some way. I say "may be" because I have no experience with this kind of thing and am generally disinclined to rely very heavily on today's technology or tech companies being around years from now. But if space is at a premium in your house, you may want to look into digital storage.

[14] Long-Term Care

Lastly, as I mentioned at the outset, most of the documents we keep in our bank safe deposit box are in manila envelopes on which I've written what's in them.

As regards records retention, my policy is to err on the side of caution and keep things simple. Experience tells me that if I were to follow everybody else's advice by destroying any documents not needed for tax or other reasons after about a year, I'd no sooner do it than something would come up to make me sorry. And I'm also pretty sure that the space I sacrifice to caution, which I'd bet wouldn't take up more than half a file storage box, I more than recover by not having stuff lying around that I can't make up my mind what to do with.

I would not expect you necessarily to adopt my way of managing every kind of record discussed here. But think about what I've said on each topic, see how it compares to what other guidelines say and, then borrowing the most sensible ideas from everybody, come up with a regimen that works for you. The effort you put into this will be amply repaid. Nothing will give you a greater sense of having gotten control of your life than knowing what to with all that paperwork you've been uncertain about. It's a great feeling when you're done doing your mail to know where to put away all that stuff you know you need to keep. It's a greater feeling still, when you need something, to know where to find it.

THREE

Budgeting & Tracking Your Money

My definition of a household budget is that it's a plan for managing your spending in such a way as to enable you to meet your financial objectives. The budget process usually involves 1) setting limits on what you're going to spend over a month or a year on groceries, housing, transportation, clothing, dining out, travel & entertainment, and all the rest and then 2) monitoring afterwards how well you've done in terms of hewing to your plan. This second activity is often referred to as "tracking your money."

There are at least two problems with budgeting. One is that budgeting can be tedious, time-consuming work, at least the tracking your money part. The second is that saying you're going to stop throwing money away on stuff you don't need won't make it so. It's like dieting or quitting smoking: you've got to be really motivated to be successful. You've got to want to meet your financial objectives a whole lot more than you want the instant gratification you'll get from buying whatever's tempting you at the moment.

So what might your objectives be? Well, if you're retired, you might have just one, very simple, but super-important objective, which is not to outlive your money. If you're still young, you might have a number of objectives—things like buying a house, putting Junior through college and being able to retire at 67.

I won't say that if you don't budget, you won't reach your objectives, or that if you do, you surely will, but simply that a budget, like a map, can help you get to where you want to go.

****

So, assuming you *are* motivated, how do you proceed? Well, if you're computer literate, you might want to try a software package like *Quicken* or *Mint.com* that makes tracking your money, the more taxing part of budgeting, a snap. Given online access to your checking and credit card accounts, these programs will go into them, download all the posted activity for the period in question, classify each transaction by income and expense category, and then summarize it all. Besides supplying your online ID and occasionally having to correct how the software classified some transaction, you don't have to do anything; the program does it all. Over time it will build a budget for you based on your spending history, which up to a point is a pretty good approach.

For those who don't have a computer or just don't want to fool with the set-up and maintenance of a software system, there are various manual approaches to tracking your money, the simplest of which is to keep track of what you spend each day in a spiral notebook or in a ledger, where you have a column for each of your expense categories, and at the end of the month you tally the numbers in each column. All you need here, besides the notebook or columnar paper, is a little electronic calculator. You can buy both at Walmart, Office Depot or Staples for under $30.

What I'm going to lay out here is a third way to plan and track your spending. You don't need a PC to use it, and it will tell you at a glance every month, without your having to crunch any numbers, all you really need to know, which is: Is your plan realistic? Are you sticking to it? If not, where have you gotten off? And once you set the thing up, which is easy, it will pretty much run on its own. It's how I budget.

****

Let's begin with a conceptual framework and then consider some of the problems you may run up against in doing a budget.

Cash Flow Summary

Whether you're using a software program or doing everything by hand, what you're usually constructing is something called a *Cash Flow Summary*. You'll be familiar with this particular financial statement if you've ever tried to borrow a substantial sum of money because any lender will want to see one before committing to help you. It helps him gauge whether you have the free cash flow to repay the loan you're asking for. If you're not familiar with a Cash Flow Summary, Table 3.1 on the next page shows what one looks like. I warn you, though: it's more abbreviated than yours will be.

A Cash Flow Summary is for a household what an Earnings Statement is for a business. It provides a breakdown of Income and Expenses by category and tells you what the net of the two is, whether it's positive (a *Surplus*) or negative (a *Shortfall*).[1]

Necessary Spending versus Unnecesary

A business' Earnings Statement groups expenses under headings like *Cost of Goods Sold, Selling Expenses* and *General & Administrative Expenses*. We're going to group ours on our Cash Flow Summary under the headings of *Necessary Spending* and *Unnecessary Spending*.

Necessary Spending is spending on necessities, as well as on things you're required to do for contractual or other good reasons. The corollary is that if you don't deal with these things, you can expect to pay a higher price later in some other way. If you don't pay your mortgage, your lender will foreclose on you. If you don't pay your water bill, the utility company will shut your water off. If you don't pay your insurance premiums, your coverage will lapse. If you don't pay your taxes, Uncle Sam will garnish your wages. If you don't have your hair cut regularly and dress professionally, your employer may look for an excuse to let you go.

Unnecessary Spending is spending on things you don't have to have or do. If you renege on taking your wife on that European river cruise next spring that you had pro-

---

[1] The other personal financial statement you should be familiar with is the Net Worth Statement, which is discussed in Chapter 15. It corresponds to a business's Balance Sheet.

Table 3.1

Cash Flow Summary: April, 2015

	Month	Year to Date
INCOME		
Salaries & Wages, Net	$ 6,086	$ 24,344
Rental Income	$ 630	$ 2,520
Misc. Income	$ 4	$ 59
Total Income	$ 6,720	$ 26,923
EXPENSES		
Groceries & Household Supplies	$ 416	$ 1,668
House Pmts., incl Escrow for Ins & Taxes	$ 1,942	$ 7,769
Car Payments	$ 438	$ 1,752
Other Consumer Debt Payments	$ 110	$ 440
Preventive Mtce - House	$ -	$ -
Preventive Mtce & Tires - Car	$ 101	$ 101
Utilities	$ 461	$ 1,418
Gasoline	$ 226	$ 871
Insurance - Auto & Life	$ 217	$ 866
Medical - Deductible & Co-Payments	$ -	$ 228
Child Care	$ 725	$ 2,900
Clothing	$ 22	$ 424
Grooming & Personal Care	$ 75	$ 320
Dues & Subscriptions	$ 82	$ 117
Dining Out	$ 149	$ 486
Gifts	$ -	$ -
Travel & Entertainment	$ 11	$ 43
Charitable Contributions	$ 500	$ 2,000
Yard Care	$ 200	$ 800
ATM Withdrawals, incl. Fees	$ 204	$ 661
Other	$ 73	$ 377
Total Expenses	$ 5,951	$ 23,241
SURPLUS/(SHORTFALL)	$ 768	$ 3,682

mised, the worst that will happen is that you'll be in the doghouse for awhile. Viking River Cruises can't sue you.

Where you are in life, and if you're still working what you do for a living, will bear on the question of what's necessary and what's unnecessary, and some expense categories, like clothing, can be both. Back when I was working, my job required me to wear a coat and tie every day and look professional, and as fashions changed and dry cleaning took its toll, I was forever "having" to buy new clothes. But oftentimes I also bought things that just caught my eye or I thought were too cheap to pass up. Nowadays, being retired, any clothes I buy nearly always fall under the heading of Unnecessary Spending.

No budgeting software package that I'm familiar with makes any distinction between necessary and unnecessary spending. At least not in terms this plain. I think that's a mistake. Understanding that we're locked into some kinds of spending and not other kinds is critically important to how we manage our money. Our income isn't elastic, expanding to accommodate our spending needs and wants. It's inelastic—we've got only so much and that's it. We can only spend more by tapping our savings or taking on debt. I'll come back to these options later, but suffice it to say here that they have their limits and should be used cautiously. Leaving them aside, we must find a way to live within our means. Hopefully our means are at least adequate to dealing with the things we've got to spend money on in order to eat, keep a roof over our heads, get to and from work, pay our taxes and so on. Usually they are. But that's what the headings Necessary Spending and Unnecessary Spending are intended to remind us of. Income minus Necessary Spending equals what we have available to spend on unnecessary things and/or to invest. It's *all* we have.

Budgeting Necessary Expenses

Budgeting Necessary Spending is a piece of cake. That's chiefly because with only a few exceptions, which I'll get to in a bit, they come around regularly—which is to say, every week, every two weeks, every month, every quarter, every six months or once a year—and in amounts that are either exactly knowable in advance or reasonably predictable. The monthly payment on your 30-year fixed-rate mortgage isn't going to change until you've refinanced or paid the thing off. The premium on your homeowners policy won't change without your being given plenty of advance notice. Barring changes in your eating habits or the route you take to work or some seismic shift in the prices of their underlying commodities, groceries and gasoline will cost you about the same over each of the next twelve months as they cost you, average, over the past three.

Another thing that makes budgeting Necessary Spending a pretty certain undertaking is that, unlike Unnecessary Spending, it's not subject to impulse buying. You've got only so many expense categories to budget and no more. That's not to say that your obligations won't ever change, because of course over time they will. You may, for example, find yourself with another car payment because your old car became uneconomical to repair or in a moment of irrational exuberance you decided to indulge a lifelong desire to own a Corvette. These things happen. But they happen very infrequently, and when they do, it's no big deal. You make the required change to your budget and move on.

I said at the outset of this chapter that the budget process usually involves "setting limits on what you're going to spend on groceries, housing…and all the rest..," but that's not really how you should think about what you're doing when budgeting necessary things. You're not setting " limits" or " targets." You do that when you're budgeting the things you can live without, not the things you can't. There's not a whole you can do about what it costs you presently to service your debt, put food on the table, and pay your utilities, taxes, etc. These costs are knowable. It's just a matter of ferreting out the numbers and getting them down on paper. It may be that you're living beyond your means, but until you've done something about it, the facts are what they are.

Sinking Fund Accounts

If you pay the premium on your auto policy in semi-annual installments, your income taxes in quarterly installments, and your property taxes once a year, how do you deal with these spikes in your spending? What about the risk that the money you should be accumulating in your checking account to meet these more spaced-out obligations will burn a hole in your pocket before they come due?

One way of dealing with large quarterly, semi-annual, and annual obligations is to set aside money for them each month in a separate checking or money market account. I do this. I write a check each month on our primary checking account for one-twelfth of what we spent total last year on income taxes and property taxes, and I deposit this check into an account we have at another bank. When the time comes to pay these taxes, I pay them out of this *sinking fund*—our income taxes in quarterly installments and our property taxes in December (or the following January). In my budget, though, I'm showing that I'm paying these taxes monthly, which in a manner of speaking I am.

I could of course fritter away the money that accumulates in this sinking fund account as easily as that in my regular checking account, but its purpose is so unambiguous that until now the thought has never crossed my mind.

Monthly Budget vs. Annual Budget

If all your income is received monthly, which is usually the case with salary and always with Social Security and pensions and annuities, and you can use a stratagem like a sinking fund to level out your spending for things like quarterly tax payments, you could just do a monthly budget, since your income and expenses will always be about the same. It's every bit as easy, though, to do an annual budget, which will give you a much better sense as to whether you're on the right path or not. You can tell something from a year's worth of financial activity; you can't, really, from a month's.

Major Repairs and Major Unreimbursed Medical Expenses

In the business world, a *major repair* to a depreciable asset is one that extends its service life or improves the asset in some significant way. That's *not* what I mean here when I use the term. When I speak of a major repair in the context of a household budget, I'm talking about a repair that one couldn't pay for out of his normal monthly cash flow without impinging on other necessary things.

I don't fool with trying to budget major repairs. I don't see how you can. There are an almost limitless number of risks to your house and your car(s) that are either not covered by insurance or, if covered, are subject to policy deductibles, and in my opinion, at least, it's a waste of time to worry about them in a budget. You should have a plan, though, for what you'd do if unexpectedly faced with some huge repair. Mine is that I would deal with it out of savings. It's all I could do. Anyone who's still working would be wise to deal with it by socking away another 1% to 2% of his house's value in savings every year. The sooner he gets started the better.

Another big black hole is large unreimbursed medical expenses. This can be a problem for anyone who doesn't have health care insurance or has insurance but doesn't have a *health savings account (HSA)* with enough in it to deal with a big deductible. It can also be a problem for anyone who has any major dental work or orthodontia done because neither is covered by any health care plan that I know of. They're certainly not covered by Medicare.

Clothing

If your job requires you to stay abreast of changes in fashion and/or you have a young and growing family, buying new clothes is a periodic necessity. But budgeting clothing isn't as certain an undertaking as budgeting groceries, utilities, and most other necessities, which come around on some regular schedule and whose cost, if not known for certain, you can reasonably estimate by extrapolating from prior months' spending. What do you do, then? Well, if I were you, I'd figure that I'd spend about what the average American family spends, which is somewhere around 4% of annual income, and I'd divide whatever that number comes to by 12 and say that's what I'll spend per month. Then to make it so, I might get myself another credit card, which I'd use exclusively for buying clothes, and every month pay on it whatever I had budgeted, even if I owed nothing or had a credit balance.[2] If you think managing your spending for clothes with a special credit card is overkill and you have a better solution, go for it.

Preventive Maintenance & Minor Repairs

Preventive maintenance consists of those little things you can do or have done to avoid or delay all of a sudden having to deal with something major, like replacing your HVAC[3] system or rebuilding your car's engine. Twice a year I have the people who installed our HVAC system come service it, and every time the engine service light appears on my car's instrument panel telling me it's time to change the engine oil, rotate the tires or do anything else, I attend to it as soon as I can. I do other things as well with the house. We change the HVAC filters monthly. I have the gutters cleaned out every

---

[2] I know—this flies in the face of my earlier stern warning to pay off your credit card balance every month to avoid finance charges.

[3] Heating ventilation and air-conditioning.

spring. I water around the foundation every month or so because we're in a prolonged drought, and every 6 or 7 years I have the trim on our brick house power-washed and painted. All of these things I can pretty much do on my timetable and know in advance what I'll spend.

Stuff can still happen and sometimes does, usually with one of the cars. If it's something I can deal with without dipping into savings, great—it's a minor repair. If not, it's a major repair. In our budget for Necessary Spending, I have $300 a month allocated to a category described as Misc, incl. Minor Repairs. There's always something.

Tapping Your Savings

Financial planners speak of an investor being in either the *asset accumulation* phase of his life or the *asset distribution* phase. In the asset accumulation phase, you're setting aside a portion of your income and investing it; in the asset distribution phase, you're tapping what you've accumulated to help make ends meet. If you're in the asset accumulation phase, you should ignore investment income in doing your budget. That income should not be spent; it should be re-invested. If you're in the asset distribution phase, you may need the interest and dividends you earn on your investments to supplement your Social Security and any other sources of income, and accordingly have instructed your brokerage firm to cut you a check for them each month. In that case, you'll want to list this income.

But what if your interest and dividend income isn't enough? What then? What about dipping into your *principal*? To help answer this question, financial planners suggest adoption of *the 4% rule,* according to which the retiree should limit his withdrawal in the first year of retirement to 4% of principal and annual increases in this initial amount to the rate of inflation. To illustrate, suppose you retire with a $1 million nest egg. Applying the 4% rule, you could pull $40,000 from your nest egg in Year 1, and assuming a 3% bump in the Consumer Price Index over each of the next two years, you could pull out $41,200 ($40,000 × 1.03) in Year 2 and $42,436 ($41,200 × 1.03) in Year 3. I pass this on with two caveats: The first is that, like all rules of thumb, it's not foolproof and isn't going to be as safe for someone retiring early as for someone retiring late. The second caveat is that such withdrawals are *not*, repeat *not*, in addition to any interest and dividends or *required minimum distributions (RMDs)* taken; these are to be counted as part of the 4% and should make up the lion's share of it, if not all. Thus, if the rule allowed you to pull out $42,436, but you were planning to take your interest, dividends and RMD anyway and they totaled, say, $31,000, you wouldn't want to tap your principal for more than about $11,400 ($42,426 – $31,000 = $11,426).

Tapping the Equity in Your House

When I speak of tapping the equity in your house, I'm talking about taking out a *reverse mortgage*. That said, I have no experience with reverse mortgages beyond having looked at the paperwork a friend sent me on one he was considering taking out on his home. That was several years back. As I recall, the financial institution he was dealing with had appraised his house for around $270,000, and on this amount, they would lend roughly 63% based on his age (late 70s) and their actuarial tables. Sixty-three percent of $270,000 comes to about $170,000. That's what he would be borrowing. However, the lion's share of this—$110,000 or so— would go to paying off his existing mortgage, such that what would be available to him—as a lump sum, in monthly payments, or as a line of credit—would only be $60,000. Still, he would be out from under monthly mortgage payments and have some extra income besides, and during his lifetime, he'd never have to repay the $170,000 provided that he continued to occupy his house, keep it in good repair, and pay his property taxes on time. Upon his death, the house would be sold to satisfy the indebtedness on it, and anything it brought in excess of that would pass to his estate. I think for some people, and particularly those without children or dependents, a reverse mortgage can be very useful. My main concern would be my ability to stay in my house if I were to become incapacitated. My understanding is that if you stop occupying your home, that's a basis for the lender to accelerate your note.

If you'd like to know whether a reverse mortgage might help you deal with a cash flow issue, you might begin by talking to an FHA Home Equity Conversion Mortgage (HECM) specialist. You can reach one at (800) 510-0303.

****

With all of that out the way, let's begin. But as we do, let me invite you first to jump ahead to Table 3.3 beginning on Page 51 and study it for a minute or two. Everything I will try to explain about how I construct a budget is illustrated there. If you refer back to it frequently as we progress through the 6-step process, it will help bring everything into better focus.

Preparing Your Budget

I do my budget using a Microsoft spreadsheet program called Excel, but pencil, paper, and any calculator that adds, subtracts, multiplies, and divides will serve nearly as well. It's just easier to edit with a spreadsheet program and the math is quicker.

Whether or not you use a spreadsheet program, you'll need five or six columns for numbers. If you get paid every two weeks, head the columns as follows: Bi-Weekly, Monthly, Quarterly, Semi-annually, Annually, and Total Year. If you don't get paid every two weeks, you don't need the Bi-Weekly column.

Step 1 – Down the left side of the paper, list each of your sources of Income and beside each item, in the appropriate column, enter the amount you get per pay period; then annualize the numbers and total.

So let's say, keeping things simple, that you're a retired widow(er) and have four sources of income: Social Security ($2,000 monthly), stock dividends ($5,000 quarterly), bond interest ($2,000 semi-annually), and the Required Minimum Distribution on your IRA ($6,000 annually). Your annual income from Social Security would be $24,000 ($2,000 × 12), from dividends $20,000 ($5,000 × 4), from interest $5,000 ($2,500 × 2), and from your RMD $6,000. Summing these numbers, your total year income would be $55,000.

Now let's say that you know—because for the past two years you've had to tap your investments—that you can't live on $55,000 a year. In that case, you'd want to insert another line before your Total Income line, which you'd call From Savings, If Needed/As Needed, or words to that effect, and beside which, in the column headed Total Year, you'd enter the amount you're prepared to further pull from your investments. How much is that? Apply the 4% rule. Going back to the example I gave a few pages back, if the rule allows you to pull out $42,436 total and you're already planning to take your dividends, interest, and RMD totaling $31,000, you're good for another $11,436.

Step 2 – Repeat with Necessary Spending what you just did with Income.

Table 3.2 on the next page offers a menu of income and expense categories and sub-categories that you may find helpful. Add sub-categories as needed. The more granular your budget is, the better your numbers will be, and the easier you'll find it every month to match your actual spending, as per your bank and credit card statements, to what you have said here you will spend. Do not think that this will make your form go on forever. It won't. Unlike unnecessary things, as I noted earlier, you have a finite number of necessary things on which to spend your money. Thus, if you want a sub-category for each kind of preventive maintenance you do, that's fine. I do. Under Housing this year I have sub-categories for PM – HVAC System, PM – HVAC Filters, PM – RO System and PM – Carpet Cleaning. Some years, depending on what I've got in mind to do, I need more of these preventive maintenance sub-accounts.

If you have a mortgage, your monthly payment probably includes escrow for property taxes and insurance. Do not break this out. You want your budget to reflect the exact same numbers you'll see on your bank statement each month.

That said, if you don't get paid bi-weekly but, like us, have certain expenses that come around every two weeks, convert these expenses to monthly expenses by multiplying them by 2.167 (52 ÷ 2 = 26; 26 ÷ 12 = 2.167). You can do the same with weekly expenses using 4.333 as your factor. You'll sacrifice very little and have a more manageable spreadsheet.

Step 3 – Subtract Total Year Necessary Spending from Total Year Income, bracketing the result if it's negative; describe as Available for Savings & Unnecessary Spending.

If you have a surplus, great—you can go on to the next step, which for those in the asset accumulation phase is Step 4 and for those in the asset distribution phase Step 5. If not, meaning you have a shortfall, you're at a stopping point. It makes no difference whether you're retired or still working, a shortfall at the Necessary Spending level calls for making major lifestyle adjustments—going back to work or, if you're still working,

Table 3.2

INCOME & EXPENSE CATEGORIES & SUB-CATEGORIES		
INCOME	NECESSARY EXPENSES	NECESSARY EXPENSES
Salaries & Wages, Net	Transportation (continued)	Other Non-discretionary
Net Business Income	Preventive Maintenance (PM)	Birthday Gifts
Social Security, Net	Minor Repairs	Christmas Gifts
Pension, Net		Dues & Renewal Fees (Detail)
Annuity	Grooming & Personal Care	Misc., incl Minor Repairs
Rental Income	Barber/Hairdresser	
Royalties	Cosmetics	UNNECESSARY EXPENSES
Investment Income		Dues & Subscriptions
Dividends	Insurance	Local Newspaper
Interest	Life Insurance	Other (List)
Capital Gains	Air Rescue Insurance	
IRA RMDs (Req'd Min Distrib)		Charitable Contributions
Miscellaneous Income	Health Care	Church
	Insurance (Med, Dental, etc)	Other (List)
NECESSARY EXPENSES	Health Savings Account Contrib.	
Groceries & Household Supplies	Long Term Care	Clothing
	Medicare Supplement	
Housing	Prescription Drug Plan	Yard & Garden
Mortgage Payments	Unreimbursed Medical & Dental	Lawn Care
Rent		Professional Landscaping
Homeowners Ins (or Renter's Ins)	Child Care/ Day Care	Nursery & Garden Ctr Purch
Umbrella Liability		
Flood Insuance	Clothing	Travel
Property Taxes		Airfares
Preventive Maintenance	Taxes	Lodging
Minor Repairs	Income Taxes	Meals
Homeowners Association Fees	Property Taxes	
	Personal Property Taxes	Dining Out
Utilities	Professional Services	
Electricity	Tax Preparation Software	Beer, Wine & Spirits
Gas		
Heating Oil	Loan Repayments	Entertainment
Water	Educ. Loan Payments	
Telephone	Installment Loan Payments	Major Purchases
DSL		List
Cell Phone	Pets	
Cable/Satellite TV	Grooming	Home Improvement Projects
Garbage Collection	Vet	List
	Boarding	
Transportation		Other Discretionary
Car Payments	Church	Books
Auto Insurance		House Cleaning
Gasoline		ATM Withdrawals
Tolls & Parking		Gifts

getting a second job; selling the house and moving into something more affordable; persuading Mom to move to Dallas from Des Moines to look after the kids so you can take them out of daycare; moving in with a child; something. I'm not being facetious. I understand lots of people find themselves with not enough income through no fault of their own. Their spouse died, they got a divorce, they got sick, they got laid off, something. But whatever led to their predicament, they've got to find a way out of it, and soon. Until they do, they must put on hold any savings and unnecessary spending.

Step 4 – List any savings/investment plans you have and what you will invest in each and how often (monthly, quarterly etc.); annualize the numbers and sum.

This is basically for those in the *asset accumulation phase*, but nothing says retirees whose income exceeds what they need to live on can't have things they're saving and investing for—a grandchild's college education, for example. It's just that young people, generally, have more things that they need to put money away for. Among them: a down payment on a home, retirement, putting their children through college.

If you need help quantifying what you need to be investing on some periodic basis to meet an objective, a broker can help. He's got tools and resources at his disposal designed just for this purpose, and his help is free.

Step 5 – Repeat with Unnecessary Spending what you did in Step 2 with Necessary.

I suggest that you begin here with the things to which you have become habituated. For us, that is dues and subscriptions to different organizations and periodicals; birthday and Christmas gifts for children and grandchildren; contributions to our schools and favorite charities; dining out with friends after church every Sunday; and having a lady come every two weeks for three hours to clean the house. Also, during those months when the grass needs mowing, a yardman for two hours every Saturday. Like Necessary Spending, all of these things are easy to budget because they come around like clockwork so many times a year and always cost about the same.

I also budget something to cover the miscellaneous inessentials on which we fritter away money every month. We buy this stuff mostly on impulse, so the number I use is simply a target. It's what I'd like to hold this kind of spending to. If that makes it sound like I'm not always successful, that's because I'm not.

At this point I'm done, even though I still have some money left over. This left-over money is my surplus. If I didn't have a surplus, and indeed a good-sized one, I'd know to expect trouble later on. Budgeting is not an exact science, prices are always inching up, and we all share a tendency to lowball what we'll spend on things whose costs must be estimated.

So, what do you do about budgeting any unnecessary, out-of-the ordinary things you might want to do, like taking a European vacation or installing granite counter-tops, that you can't do out of your monthly cash flow? Speaking for myself, I don't do anything about budgeting such things. We just decide whether the thing is worth pulling money out of savings to do or it's not. If the decision is yes, we do it; if not, we don't. Anyone who can't do this needs another plan. One of our daughters-in-law has one. In her budget she sets aside a certain amount of money every month for a family vacation and anything else special they want to do or get. That money goes into a special savings or checking account to accumulate until it can be used for its intended purposes. This is similar, of course, to how I manage our income and property taxes.

Step 6 ~ Subtract Total Year Savings and Total Year Unnecessary Spending from the sub-total in Step 3; describe as Surplus/(Shortfall).

Needless to say, a shortfall won't do and neither, as I just finished explaining, will a surplus that doesn't provide ample wiggle room.

Before we leave Table 3.3, there are several things I'd call to your attention. First, note that there are no sub-totals for Available for Savings & Unnecessary Spending and Surplus/(Shortfall) *except* in the Total Year column. Sub-totaling the other columns (Monthly, Quarterly etc.) would serve no purpose. Income and expenses that recur quarterly don't necessarily do so in the same month. Ditto for those that recur semi-annually and annually.

Second, your budget can go on for a number of pages. Therefore, if you're not doing your budget using a spreadsheet program, which makes editing easy, I'd recommend that you use a pencil instead of a ballpoint and that you leave three or four blank lines in the Income and Necessary Spending sections to allow adding something later that you forgot or purposefully didn't include, like Major Repairs.

Third, don't worry too much about getting your schedule of Unnecessary Spending exactly right. The important thing to know about this kind of spending is how much of it you can afford to do. Deal with the little stuff that will come up by having a catch-all account (Misc, incl. ATM[4]) with a budget that you think you can live with. Deal with anything big that you want to do but cannot out of your monthly cash flow either as an off-budget item, as I do, or by socking away money for it each month, as my daughter-in-law does.

****

We come at last to the all-important subject of tracking your money.

Let's begin by considering why it is so important. There are a number of reasons. The first is that you can't even do a budget unless you've got some spending history. Absent some history, how could you know what to budget for groceries, gas, utilities and anything else where you can only extrapolate from the average of past spending? You couldn't. Second, tracking your actual income and expenses serves as a reality check. It's the only way you can confirm that your budget—and how faithfully you're executing it—actually has you on the path to achieving your financial objectives, which is the whole point. Third, if your actual results aren't very close to what you budgeted, which will be the case some months, particularly in the early ones after you've just gotten started, tracking your spending will tell you why. If you have a significant variance in Necessary Spending, it will tell you that you overlooked something that you should have budgeted and/or you did a sloppy job of estimating and/or something random but unavoidable came up that you had to deal with, like repairs or major medical expenses. If you're way over your budget for Unnecessary Spending, it will point the finger at you for having rationalized buying or doing something that you didn't have to buy or do.

As I explained at the outset, software like Quicken or Mint.com makes tracking your money easy. I just have one objection to them and that is that they want to tell me far, far more than I'm interested in knowing. I don't need graphs and pie charts—I'm not

[4] Automatic Teller Machine withdrawals.

Table 3.3

Income	Monthly	Quarterly	Semi-Ann	Annually	Total Year
Social Security	**$ 2,000.00**				**$ 24,000.00**
Investment Income & RMDs					
Dividends		$ 5,000.00			$ 20,000.00
Interest			$ 2,500.00		$ 5,000.00
RMDs from IRAs				$ 6,000.00	$ 6,000.00
Sub-total	**$ -**	**$ 5,000.00**	**$ 2,500.00**	**$ 6,000.00**	**$ 31,000.00**
Total Inc before W/Ds from Svgs	**$ 2,000.00**	**$ 5,000.00**	**$ 2,500.00**	**$ 6,000.00**	**$ 55,000.00**
From savings, if needed/as needed					**$ 11,436.00**
Total Income	**$ 2,000.00**	**$ 5,000.00**	**$ 2,500.00**	**$ 6,000.00**	**$ 66,436.00**

Necessary Spending	Monthly	Quarterly	Semi-Ann	Annually	Total Year
Groceries & Household Supplies	**$ 550.00**	**$ -**	**$ -**	**$ -**	**$ 6,600.00**
Housing					
Mortgage Pmts, incl Taxes & Ins	$ 830.85	$ -	$ -	$ -	$ 9,970.20
PM - HVAC System		$ 55.00	$ 160.00		$ 540.00
Homeowner Association Fees				$ 100.00	$ 100.00
Sub-total	**$ 830.85**	**$ 55.00**	**$ 160.00**	**$ 100.00**	**$ 10,610.20**
Utilities					
Water	$ 150.00	$ -	$ -	$ -	$ 1,800.00
Electricity	$ 192.00				$ 2,304.00
Tel, TV & DSL	$ 161.00				$ 1,932.00
Sub-total	**$ 503.00**	**$ -**	**$ -**	**$ -**	**$ 6,036.00**
Transportation					
Car Payments	$ 429.17	$ -	$ -	$ -	$ 5,150.04
Auto Insurance	$ 89.30				$ 1,071.60
Gas	$ 250.00				$ 3,000.00
Vehicle Registration				$ 62.50	$ 62.50
Preventive Maintenance				$ 1,200.00	$ 1,200.00
Sub-total	**$ 768.47**	**$ -**	**$ -**	**$ 1,262.50**	**$ 10,484.14**
Grooming & Personal Care					
Hairdresser (Cut/Perm)	$ 45.00	$ 40.00	$ -	$ -	$ 700.00
Cosmetics , etc.			$ 100.00		$ 200.00
Sub-total	**$ 45.00**	**$ 40.00**	**$ 100.00**	**$ -**	**$ 900.00**
Health Care					
Medigap Insurance	$ 167.28	$ -	$ -	$ -	$ 2,007.36
Presc. Drug Plan	$ 54.20				$ 650.40
Unreimbursed Med & Presc Drugs				$ 300.00	$ 300.00
Other Dental (Teeth cleaning)				$ 100.00	$ 100.00
Sub-total	**$ 221.48**	**$ -**	**$ -**	**$ 400.00**	**$ 3,057.76**

Table 3.3 Continued

Necessary (Cont'd)	Monthly	Quarterly	Semi-Ann	Annually	Total Year
Clothing					**$ -**
Insurance					
Air Rescue Insurance				$ 65.00	$ 65.00
Sub-total	**$ -**	**$ -**	**$ -**	**$ 65.00**	**$ 65.00**
Taxes (Tax Preparation)					
Income Taxes (Sinking Fund)	$ 325.00	$ -	$ -	$ -	$ 3,900.00
TurboTax				$ 65.00	$ 65.00
Sub-total	**$ 325.00**	**$ -**	**$ -**	**$ 65.00**	**$ 3,965.00**
Church	**$ 500.00**	**$ -**	**$ -**	**$ -**	**$ 6,000.00**
Other					
Pet Care	$ 19.00			$ 100.00	$ 328.00
Birthday Gifts				$ 150.00	$ 150.00
Xmas Gifts				$ 250.00	$ 250.00
Misc, incl Minor Repairs	$ 300.00				$ 3,600.00
Sub-total	**$ 319.00**	**$ -**	**$ -**	**$ 500.00**	**$ 4,328.00**
Total Necessary Spending	**$ 4,062.80**	**$ 95.00**	**$ 260.00**	**$ 2,392.50**	**$ 52,046.10**

Available for Savings & Unnecessary Spending	
	$ 14,389.90

Savings/Investments	Monthly	Quarterly	Semi-Ann	Annually	Total Year
Grandson's 529	$ -	$ -	$ -	$ 500.00	**$ 500.00**
Sub-total	**$ -**	**$ -**	**$ -**	**$ 500.00**	**$ 500.00**

Unnecessary Spending	Monthly	Quarterly	Semi-Ann	Annually	Total Year
Dues & Subscriptions					
Herald Tribune	$ -	$ 37.50	$ -	$ -	$ 150.00
Better Homes				$ 22.00	$ 22.00
Sub-total	**$ -**	**$ 37.50**	**$ -**	**$ 22.00**	**$ 172.00**
Charitable & Other Contributions					
Salvation Army	$ 25.00	$ -	$ -	$ -	$ 300.00
Am. Cancer Society				$ 100.00	$ 100.00
W. Texas State				$ 100.00	$ 100.00
McAdoodle for President				$ 100.00	$ 100.00
Sub-total	**$ 25.00**	**$ -**	**$ -**	**$ 300.00**	**$ 600.00**
Dining Out & Entertainment					
Symphony Tickets	$ -	$ -	$ -	$ 200.00	$ 200.00
Dining Out	$ 50.00				$ 600.00
Other				$ 600.00	$ 600.00
Sub-total	**$ 50.00**	**$ -**	**$ -**	**$ 800.00**	**$ 1,400.00**

Table 3.3 Continued

Unnecessary (Cont'd)	Monthly	Quarterly	Semi-Ann	Annually	Total Year
Yard & Garden					
Yardman ($30/wk for 26 wks)	$ 130.00				$ 780.00
Lawn & Garden Ctr.				$ 200.00	$ 200.00
Other	$ 25.00				$ 300.00
Sub-total	**$ 155.00**	**$ -**	**$ -**	**$ 200.00**	**$ 1,280.00**
Other					
House Cleaning ($60 every 2 wks)	$ 130.00				$ 1,560.00
Other, incl ATMs	$ 300.00				$ 3,600.00
Sub-total	**$ 430.00**	**$ -**	**$ -**	**$ -**	**$ 5,160.00**
Total Unnecessary Spending	**$ 660.00**	**$ 37.50**	**$ -**	**$ 1,322.00**	**$ 8,612.00**
Surplus/(Shortfall)					**$ 5,277.90**

making a PowerPoint presentation to anybody about where our money goes—and I don't need reminders of upcoming bills and alerts that what we've spent this month on utilities, say, is abnormally high compared to what we've spent in prior months. Having said this, I must confess that it's been years since I used Quicken, and I have only the most superficial acquaintance with Mint, which lots of people apparently really like.

Of course, as you may know, Quicken and Mint are not your only software solutions to tracking your money. Many, if not most, banks nowadays also provide their clients with online tools for tracking their money. Both of the banks I use do, and the tools work fine. They are easy to learn to use, too, which is a great virtue.

My problem is that although I have a personal computer and all the rest, plus the leisure time to devote to it, I just don't have the patience for even the little bit of effort that tracking my money online involves. That's not likely ever to be more than just looking at how the program categorized every bank and credit card transaction and occasionally having to correct something, but even that little bit is more trouble than I want to be put to every month. I just want to be able to look at my bank statements and credit card statements when they come in the mail every month and before I file them away and see that everything on them tracks pretty well with my budget. Happily, I've come up with a very simple way of doing that.

Here's how it works: We have three checking accounts and three credit cards (Visa, MasterCard and American Express). One of the checking accounts (I'll refer to it as Checking Account #1) and one of the credit cards (Visa) are used exclusively for Necessary Spending, while another checking account (Checking Account #2) and the MasterCard are used exclusively for Unnecessary Spending. The third checking account, which is at another bank, is the sinking fund account into which we transfer money every month for our taxes and out of which we pay them when they come due. The American Express card is used exclusively for those unusual situations where that's the only credit card a merchant will accept. Our monthly car payment, most of our utility bills, and all our insurance premiums, except the flood insurance premium,[5] are set up to be drafted against Checking Account #1 every month. So is the balance on our Visa and American Express cards. Most months the only checks we'll write are to our church and my wife's hairdresser. We put all our groceries and gas on Visa, plus pretty much everything else that's necessary. We've also authorized our telephone/DSL/satellite TV provider and the people who collect our garbage to collect from us monthly by debiting this card. In any given month, our Visa statement will only show three to five charges that aren't for groceries, gas, telephone/DSL/TV, and garbage collection, and they're nearly always for just three things—prescription drug co-pays, office supplies, and preventive maintenance/minor repairs. I will occasionally sum the groceries and gas charges to see how they compare to what I've budgeted. Other than that, I can tell at a glance, because I do it every month, whether what I'm seeing on our credit card statement and bank statement is what I'm expecting to see. If it is, good, I can move on to something else. In the rare instances, when it is not, I look to see why. Usually it has to do with repairs or some medical or dental expense. Once in a great while, it's because one of us used the wrong account or card to pay for something. That will happen, and I don't worry about it. I'm not looking for perfection; I'm looking for a practical way to see how well I'm managing, that's all.

There is nothing set up to be drafted against Checking Account #2 except the balance on our MasterCard, and we don't write many checks on it either (maybe five or six in a month). We do most of our unnecessary spending using our MasterCard. Most

[5] Our flood insurance premium can't be paid in monthly installments.

months more than half of those charges will be in respect of eating out, which we do most Sundays after church. This is in my budget. So too is anything we spend on dues and subscriptions, charitable contributions, and gifts. I do less well on the miscellaneous stuff budgeted as Misc., incl. ATM. If there is occasionally a check or credit card charge for something pricey that's not in my budget, it will come as no surprise. It will be for something we weighed beforehand against the reality that it will ultimately have to be paid for from savings.

Checking Account #1 is funded by our Social Security, my pension, my wife's royalty checks, certain income from one of our two brokerage accounts, and occasionally a transfer from savings, with nearly everything going in by direct deposit. Checking Account #2 is funded by transferring money over from Checking Account #1. I make this transfer about five days before the balance on the MasterCard is scheduled to be drafted and generally for the sum of it and the checks I've written on Account #2 since the last transfer. I monitor what's going on in all these accounts by looking at them online every week or so. If I see that the balance in Checking Account #1 is getting too low for comfort, I'll move money to it from savings. The balance in Checking Account #2 is rarely if ever a problem because we keep a pretty good-sized cushion in it to avoid overdrafts.

****

If we don't have financial objectives and realistic strategies for achieving them, which we then faithfully see to completion, we set ourselves up for a lot of regret later. Imagine your friends, one by one, starting to retire and realizing that you'll never be able to because you didn't save and invest enough when you could. Or imagine, having retired, that you're running out of money. These are common predicaments.

But even people who *do* have clearly stated objectives[6] and understand perfectly what is required to meet them don't always achieve success. Chief among the reasons why, I suspect, is that they can never effectively manage their spending. Whether they buy a bigger house and/or a fancier car than their circumstances warrant or they can't get control of their wasteful spending or are guilty of all these things, their first mistake

[6] I discuss goals, objectives and strategies at some length in Chapter 15.

is not having a budget and living by it. Doing a budget the way I've laid out here will bring you face to face with the reality of what you can and cannot afford.

I explained first how to do a yearly budget, then how to track your spending using separate checking accounts and credit cards for necessary and unnecessary spending. This isn't to suggest that you can't just as well go about these things in reverse order. If you want to start tracking expenses for a while before tackling your budget, that's fine. Maybe better.

Also, if you don't care for the terms Necessary Spending and Unnecessary Spending, by all means use other terms (e.g., Necessary/Discretionary, Essential/Non-essential, Required/Wasteful). The important thing is that you see your spending in terms of what you're locked into and what you're not. When it comes to managing your money, that's the beginning of wisdom.

Lastly, I would strongly encourage you to adopt my suggestion of doing your necessary spending in one set of checking and credit card accounts and your unnecessary spending in another. Not only does this make tracking your money all but effortless (when it's otherwise so tiresome as to be ultimately unsustainable), it will curb your impulse buying. That's because it requires you every time you're about to buy something to ask yourself, "Which checkbook or credit card do I use for this? Is this something I really need or is it something I can get by without?" If the answer is "something I can get by without," chances are you'll opt to save your money.

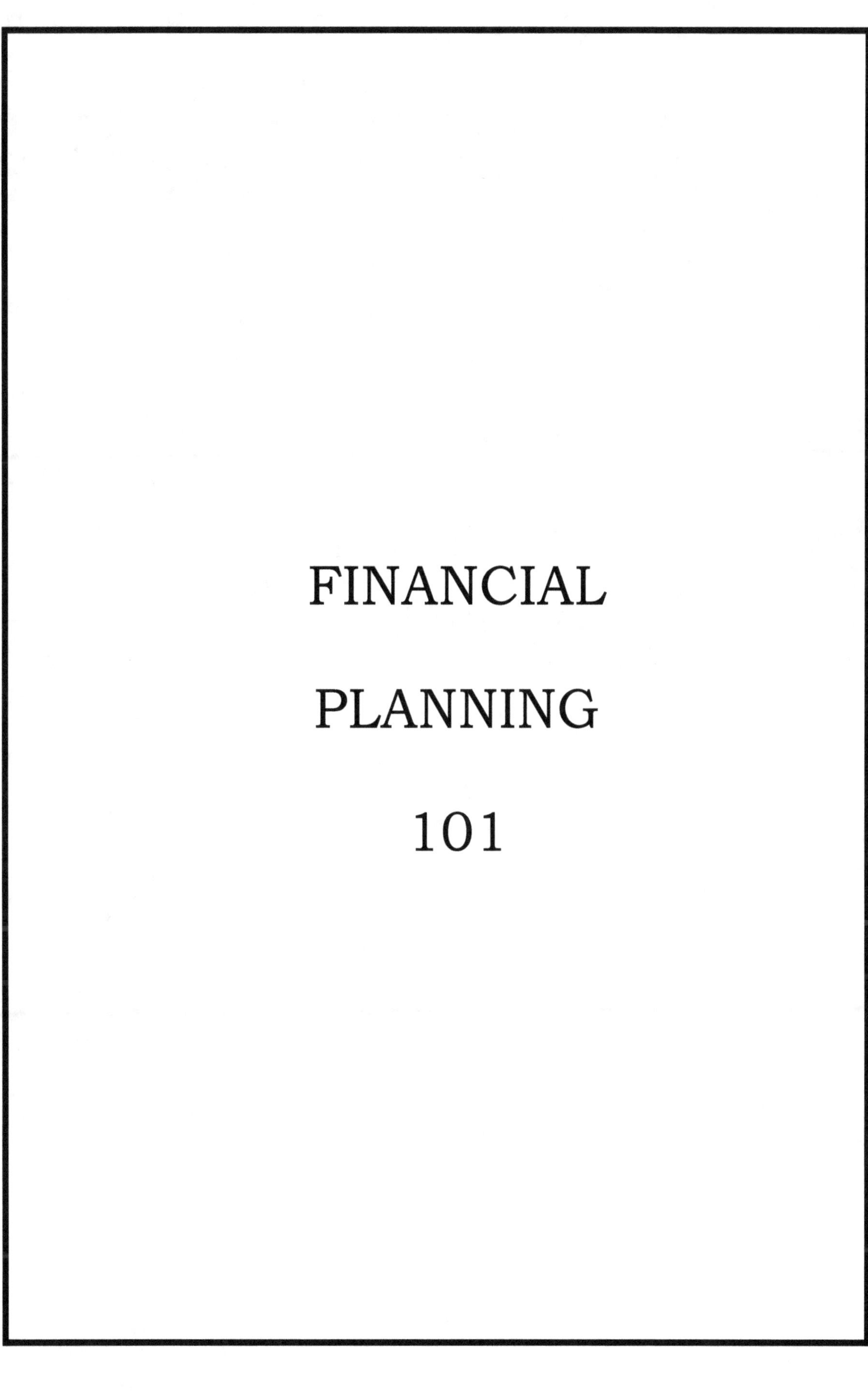

FINANCIAL

PLANNING

101

FOUR

Estate Planning

Few things will compound the new widow's emotional distress like the sudden realization that she doesn't understand the first thing about her financial situation.[1] Sadly, lots of women find themselves in this predicament. That may be because their husbands, regardless of what paragons they may otherwise have been, for whatever reason never got around to doing any kind of estate planning nor sharing much about their financial affairs and arrangements. But lots of these women also have themselves partly to blame because they never bothered to ask questions.

To avoid being in this pickle yourself someday, take an interest now in understanding your family's finances—what you own and what you owe, what you've

---

[1] As explained in the Preface, I started out to write a book for new widows and soon-to-be widows, having been led to do so by my experience helping a friend organize her affairs after the sudden death of her husband who until then had always handled their affairs. My first chapter in that book was this one, exactly as it is presented here. Rather than re-work it for a general audience, I will just say here that I know a new widower can find himself in the predicament I describe just as easily as a new widow. That's because in many families—and for all I know, most—it's the wife who manages the money, who has seen to the couple having wills prepared, and who knows where all the important documents are.

got coming in and what you've got going out—and at least the basics of estate planning. Also make it your business to know where all of the important documents are.

Other chapters deal with family finances; this one deals with estate planning. It won't make you an expert—I'm certainly not an expert—but it should equip you with a good general understanding of the subject, enabling you to make sense of your own situation and then to have an intelligent conversation with an estate planning attorney if that seems advisable.

****

Estate planning has basically to do with organizing your affairs before death so that when you do depart this world as much of your property as possible goes to those you'd like to receive it with the least delay. This implies minimizing legal expenses and, if your estate is sizeable, estate taxes. There are strategies for accomplishing both of these objectives.

Let's start by understanding that the ownership of most types of property, other than the contents of your house and your personal effects, is a matter of public record. When you die, your ownership interest in such property—your house, your car, your checking account, your stocks and bonds, and virtually everything else of significant value—must be transferred to someone else. This can only be accomplished in one of two ways—through probate proceedings or by will substitute.[2]

Probate

Probate is a court supervised legal process whereby a *personal representative* appointed by the court gains control of a deceased person's assets, settles any taxes and debts he owed, transfers titles and deeds, and distributes what's left (*the residue*) to his heirs. It involves an actual court and a judge and usually, but not necessarily, an attorney. If the deceased left a valid will, it will express his wishes insofar as who should inherit his property and who he wishes to be his *executor*. If he died intestate—i.e., without leaving a valid will—the court will determine, according to the state's intestacy statutes,

---

[2] Actually, household contents and personal effects, which rarely have title documents, often just get carried off by family members.

who gets what, and will appoint an *administrator*. How the terms personal representative, executor, and administrator are used depends on the state, but all three people do the same thing. I'll mostly refer to the personal representative as the executor.[3]

According to something I read a while back, seven out of 10 people die intestate. That's more than I would have thought. My guess is that a good many of these people intended to have a will prepared someday—they just never got around to it. One reason might be their reluctance to getting involved with a lawyer, who they fear will charge a small fortune for doing one. But for the average person, whose estate will be rather modest and uncomplicated, that shouldn't be the case. Any attorney who's keeping up with the times will have estate planning software that can take the client's answers to a series of questions and spit out a will lickety-split. The time and work required of the attorney should be minimal. He also understands that people now have alternatives. For under $100 you can use an online resource, such as *LegalZoom* or *Quicken WillMaker Plus*, to do a will for you. It will satisfy your state's legal requirements just as well as the attorney's.[4]

The legal requirements of a will may vary a bit from state to state, but are basically the following: First, the *testator* (the person making the will) must have reached the age of majority, which in most states is 18, and be mentally competent ("of sound mind"). Second, the document needs to name *beneficiaries* who'll get what's left in the testator's estate after any indebtedness has been paid off. Third, the document needs to name a personal representative (aka executor/executrix) who, under the probate court's supervision, will see to doing all of the things that have to be done to settle the testator's estate. Fourth, the will needs to be in writing. Fifth, the testator needs to sign it in front of at least two disinterested individuals. Sixth, the witnesses must sign attesting to having seen the testator sign.

Typically, a husband and wife will both have a will in which each leaves to the other all of his or her worldly goods, provided that the other is still living. Against the

---

[3] A lady executor is an *executrix*.

[4] I'm not advocating that you use an inexpensive software package instead of an attorney. A software package may satisfy your state's legal requirements just fine; it may not suit your purposes so well. I'm just saying that it's an option to doing nothing. Personally, I would much prefer spending hundreds of dollars more to use an attorney.

eventuality that he or she has not survived, one or more contingent beneficiaries are named. If the couple has had children, they're usually named as the contingent beneficiaries. If there are extenuating circumstances—an estate valued above the estate tax exemption or a second marriage for one or both—they may wish to consider a revocable living trust of some sort. More about that in a bit.

I am not going to go into probate except to note that the process can take a long time and in some states be very costly. If the deceased died intestate (or even if he didn't but his will is contested or can't be found), it will take even more time and cost even more money. The proceedings are also open to the public, which can be a concern. To the extent that probate can be avoided, that's generally a good thing.

Will Substitute

The way to avoid probate is to transfer property to one's heirs by means of a *will substitute***.** There are a number of these will substitutes, but they all vest ownership in one of two ways: 1) by right of survivorship or 2) by beneficiary designation.

Right of Survivorship

Right of survivorship refers to a form of joint property ownership where, when one of the owners (joint tenants) dies, his or her interest automatically vests in the surviving owner(s), avoiding the need for probate. This form of property ownership is called *joint tenancy with right of survivorship*, abbreviated *JTWROS*. In roughly half the states where both tenants in this arrangement are spouses, it's called *tenancy by the entirety (TBE).*

Besides joint tenancy with right of survivorship and tenancy by the entirety, there are three other ways you can own property. You can be a *sole owner*, where there's no one else you share title with; you can be a *tenant in common*, where you and your two neighbors, say, each have an undivided one-third interest in the wooded lot behind your houses; and, finally, depending on where you live, you and your spouse might own just about everything as *community property*, each of you having an undivided one-half interest. Title held in any of these ways will be subject to probate when the owner dies, unless it's covered by a beneficiary designation.

It is common—maybe even the norm—for couples living in non-community property states to hold most of their significant assets acquired during their marriage either as joint tenants with right of survivorship or as tenants by the entirety. When that's the case and one of them dies, his or her half interest in the assets automatically vests in the surviving spouse, who then becomes the sole owner.

In nine states[5] any property that a couple acquires during their marriage, regardless of whose name or names may appear on the title, is presumed to be community property. Community property is based on the idea that each spouse, regardless of whether he or she works outside the home, makes an equal contribution to the couple's economic partnership and so should share equally in its material achievements. Husband and wife each has a half interest in everything the couple has. The only exceptions are property that one or the other of them received by gift or inheritance, or purchased with separate property funds, including monies brought into the marriage. Community property is joint tenancy, but it's not the same as JTWROS or TBE because it doesn't carry with it a right of survivorship. Under community property laws, each spouse retains *testamentary control* over his or her interest, meaning he or she can will it to someone other than the surviving spouse. They probably wouldn't do this, but the point is they could.

Arizona and California allow couples to hold property as *community property with right of survivorship (CPWROS)*. Five other community property states, including Texas, allow couples to execute a separate agreement creating a right of survivorship in community property. We've done this. If you live in a community property state, you might want to look into it.

It should be noted that joint tenancy with right of survivorship is not limited to married couples, as is tenancy by the entirety and community property with right of survivorship. For example, three unmarried brothers living anywhere could pool their resources to buy a bass boat together, agreeing that if any one of them should die his interest would go in equal measure to each of his two surviving siblings. To this end they would hold the boat as JTWROS.

---

[5] The nine community property states are Arizona, California, Louisiana, Idaho, Nevada, New Mexico, Texas, Washington and Wisconsin.

Beneficiary Designation

Some kinds of assets *permit* the owner to designate a beneficiary who'll get the property on his death, while other kinds may *require* it.

If you have a checking account, you can sign what is called a *Payable-on-Death (POD) agreement*, where you name one or more people to get whatever you've got in the account when you die. If you've got a non-qualified[6] brokerage account, you can do the same, only in this case it's called a *Transfer-on-Death (TOD) agreement*. You don't have to sign one of these agreements if you don't want to—it's entirely up to you. It's just a device for avoiding probate.

Life insurance policies, variable annuity contracts, and retirement savings plans, like 401(k)s, 403(b)s, 457s and IRAs, all require, or at least call for, the owner to name a beneficiary. To collect the death benefit or whatever is in the account, the beneficiary only has to provide the insurance company or trustee with a copy of the owner's death certificate and his (the beneficiary's) personal identification. There's no need to go through probate.

The most useful all-round will substitute has got to be the *revocable living trust*. It not only avoids probate (passing property by beneficiary designation) but can be used to minimize estate taxes. I will have more to say about revocable living trusts in a minute, but first I need to say something about estate taxes. No discussion of revocable living trusts can be very meaningful if you don't understand something about estate taxes.

Estate Taxes

The first thing you need to know about estate taxes (aka "death taxes"), if you don't already, is that estates valued above a certain amount are taxed by the federal government and in some states by the state government as well. You may wish to look into whether your state has an estate tax or an inheritance tax.[7] I'm only going to discuss the federal estate tax here.

A *federal estate tax return* (*IRS Form 706)* must be filed within 9 months of someone's death if his *gross estate* plus *adjusted taxable gifts* exceed the *federal estate*

[6] In other words not an IRA of some sort where the earnings grow "tax-deferred."
[7] An estate tax is levied on the estate, an inheritance tax on the heirs.

tax exemption (exclusion amount), which was raised in 2011 from $3.5 million to $5 million and, with annual adjustments for inflation since, is now (in 2016) $5,450,000. That's whether or not any tax is owed.

Think of a decedent's gross estate as being basically comprised of his separately-owned property, *plus* his fractional interest in anything jointly owned with somebody else (like his wife[8]), *plus* the death benefit from any life insurance policy on which he was both the owner and the insured. It can include some other things too, but they're too esoteric to spend time on here.

The term "adjusted taxable gifts" refers to any gifts that the decedent might have made over his lifetime (actually since 1976) that in the year he made them exceeded the *annual gift tax exclusion*. To briefly explain, one way an affluent person can minimize the bite that estate taxes will take out of what he leaves to his heirs is to gift money or assets to them while he's still alive, because so long as he keeps his annual gifts to each donee under a stipulated amount, the tax code allows him to do that and not report it. But if for some reason he makes a gift to someone of more than the annual gift tax exclusion, which presently is $14,000, he must report it by filing a *gift tax return* (*IRS Form 709*) by April 15th of the following year. And on Schedule B of that return, he is required to recap all prior years' taxable gifts so that both he and the IRS are kept abreast of what the running total is. When he dies, this running total is added to his gross estate to see if the two amounts together exceed the exclusion. If they do, as I said, an estate tax return will have to be filed.

But the fact that a return has to be filed doesn't necessarily mean that there's a tax to be paid. That's because the decedent's gross estate is not the same thing as his *taxable estate*. A person's debts aren't extinguished when he dies; they simply become obligations of his estate. So to get to what's available to be taxed—to what the IRS calls the decedent's *adjusted gross estate*—it is necessary to subtract from his gross estate his debts, and also his funeral expenses and the expenses incurred in administering his estate, like attorney and CPA fees, as well as any theft and casualty losses. Then from his adjusted gross estate, two other deductions are allowed—the *marital deduction* and the

---

[8] His fractional interest in property held with his wife as JTWROS or TBE or in community property would be one-half.

charitable deduction—that either singly or together can be used to reduce his taxable estate to zero. Both are unlimited. Often, however, these deductions are not used, because the decedent either was not married or he chose not to leave everything to charity, preferring instead to leave his heirs his estate net of taxes to leaving them nothing at all. Thus, if neither of these deductions is taken, the taxable estate will be the same as the adjusted gross estate. But whether it is or it isn't, it's the decedent's taxable estate *plus* his adjusted taxable gifts that come together as his *tax base* and determine whether any tax is due. If the tax base is greater than the exclusion ($5,450,000), there's a tax liability; if it's less, there isn't. If there is a tax liability, it will be figured using a 40% tax rate. Table 4.1 below will give you a flavor of how this works.

Table 4.1 ~ Federal Estate Tax Worksheet

Decedent's property	
- Separately owned property	$5,527,000
- Interest in jointly-owned property	$0
- Life insurance	$1,000,000
Decedent's gross estate	$6,527,000
Less:	
- Funeral & administrative expenses	-$13,000
- Debts of the decedent	-$3,278
- Mortgages & liens	-$8,436
- Theft & casualty losses	-$2,000
Adjusted gross estate	$6,500,286
Less:	
- Marital deduction	-$2,000,000
- Charitable deduction	-$50,000
Taxable estate	$4,450,286
Plus:	
- Adjusted taxable gifts	$1,500,000
Tax base	$5,950,286
Less:	
- Estate tax exclusion	-$5,450,000
Tentative tax base	$500,286
- Tax rate	40%
Tentative tax	$200,114
Less:	
- Credits	$0
Estate tax	$200,114

Revocable Living Trusts/AB Trust

Many well-to-do couples avoid estate taxes, or at least minimize and postpone them, by use of some type of revocable living trust. Perhaps the most common of these is the *family trust, credit shelter trust,* or as it's commonly and helpfully called, an *AB trust*.

This is a trust in which a husband and wife (the *grantors* or *settlors*) transfer ownership of their property—their house, their checking account, their investment accounts, whatever—from themselves to the trust, naming themselves as the primary beneficiaries and someone else, usually their children, as secondary beneficiaries. Having done that they cease to be the legal owners of those assets; their trust is. However, the trust is usually set up so that they're its co-trustees, meaning that they retain control over the assets in it, and as the trust beneficiaries, they get to use the assets like the house and the car and spend the income generated by any investment assets. They can also sell any assets they like, using the proceeds as they see fit. If they want to while they're both still alive, they can even undo the trust, transferring everything in it back to themselves. In a practical sense, having your property in an AB trust changes almost nothing. The trust even uses the husband's social security number as its tax ID.

But things get interesting when one of the spouses dies. Let's say it's the husband. On his death, the trust splits into two trusts, into an *A trust* (for the "above-ground" spouse) and a *B trust* (for the "beneath-ground" spouse).[9] The trusts are then funded. Into the B trust goes all of the decedent's separately-owned property, plus one half of the couple's jointly owned property, provided that the total here does not exceed the estate tax exclusion amount. What doesn't go into the B trust then ordinarily goes into the A trust. If what goes into the A trust is valued at more than the current estate tax exemption, that's something for the surviving spouse's heirs to worry about when she dies, which could be many years later, by which time Congress may have raised the exemption.

The A trust is actually a continuation of the living trust, and the surviving spouse can do with it as she likes, including changing the beneficiaries who will inherit

---

[9] Sometimes the A trust is referred to as the *survivor's trust* and the B trust as the *decedent's trust, by-pass trust* or *family trust*. I'll stick to A and B here, because it's simpler.

what's in it on her death. The B trust, however, is a new, *irrevocable* trust that requires its own tax ID.[10] None of its terms can be changed. The surviving spouse can, and should, withdraw all of its income for her use every year, and she can if she likes invade the principal every year for some modest amount.[11] Finally, if absolutely necessary for her "health, education, maintenance and support," she can invade it for even more.[12]

Before 2011 a marital trust, like an AB trust, was one of the few ways an affluent couple could make use of each spouse's personal estate tax exclusion amount to eliminate or minimize the taxes on what they wished to leave to their heirs. If a couple had only a simple will in which each left to the other all of his or her worldly possessions, there would be no estate tax due on the passing of the first spouse—again, let's say, the husband—no matter how large his estate, thanks to the unlimited marital deduction; but on the death of his widow, there would be if her estate exceeded the estate tax exemption. To understand how the AB trust solved this problem, let's consider a couple with a $9 million estate who own everything jointly (as JTWROS, TBE or community property).

Scenario #1: Husband and wife each have a *will* bequeathing all their worldly possessions to the other. The husband dies. His half of everything passes intact to his widow either by right of survivorship or through probate. No estate tax return claiming the marital deduction is *required* inasmuch as his estate is under $5,450,000. Sadly, just a year later, she dies. As the sole owner of everything she and her husband had once owned jointly, her estate has ballooned from $4.5 million to $9 million. Of that $9 million, only $5,450,000 is shielded from taxes; $3,550,000 isn't, and the estate taxes on that come to $1,420,000![13]

Scenario # 2: Instead of wills our couple has an *AB trust* into which they have transferred ownership of all their property. The husband dies. Instead of his half of everything ($4,500,000) passing to his wife by right of survivorship, it goes into the B trust where it is more than amply sheltered by the $5,450,000 exemption. The other

---

[10] The survivor's trust will usually employ her Social Security number as its tax ID.

[11] Which used to be, and maybe still is, the greater of $5,000 or 5% of the value of the trust assets.

[12] By pulling out a significant sum for her "maintenance," the surviving spouse risks having the B trust included in her estate when she dies, which would defeat what she and her husband were trying to accomplish with the AB trust in the first place.

[13] $3,550,000 × 40% = $1,420,000

half, of course, goes into the A trust where, when the wife dies, it is sheltered by her $5,450,000 exemption. Savings to the heirs? You guessed it: $1,420,000.

Depending on circumstances, the AB trust may still be the best way for a couple to make use of each spouse's exclusion, but it is no longer the only way.

Portability of Deceased Spouse's Unused Exemption Amount

Since 2011 Federal law has allowed a surviving spouse to make use of the *deceased spouse's unused exclusion (DSUE)* amount. In Scenario # 1 above, no use whatsoever was made of the husband's $5,450,000 exclusion because everything that might otherwise have comprised his taxable estate was left to his widow, qualifying it for the unlimited marital deduction. His exclusion, then, was said to be "wasted." Nowadays any unused exclusion can be "ported" to the surviving spouse, to be added to his or her exclusion when he or she dies. For this to happen, all the executor of the first-to-die's estate has to do is complete Form 706 and claim it.

In Scenario # 2, the "DSUE amount" that could be "ported" to the surviving spouse would be $950,000, representing the difference between the exclusion ($5,450,000) and the amount used to shelter what went into the B trust ($4,500,000).

Bypass Trust and Qualified Terminable Interest Property (QTIP) Trust

It is not uncommon in second marriages for one spouse to bring a lot of money into it and the other spouse not so much. Frequently, too, one or both will have children from a first marriage. This presents a dilemma for the spouse with the money. Let's say it's the husband and let's give him a name, George. Once a highly compensated business executive, George married an old girlfriend, Georgia, after it happened that both of them lost their first spouse to illness. Both have grown children. George's dilemma is that he wants, if he predeceases Georgia, for her to receive the income from his estate, but when she dies, for the property itself (the *corpus*) to go to his children. How can this be accomplished? Answer: With a *bypass trust*. In addition to giving Georgia the income from it during her lifetime and George's children its corpus when she's gone, the bypass trust takes advantage of the estate tax exemption to avoid death taxes.

A *Qualified Terminable Interest Property (QTIP)* trust can be used to accomplish the same objectives of giving the surviving spouse a life estate in the income from an estate while leaving the corpus to the decedent's children (or other beneficiary), but it differs from the bypass trust in that it makes use of the marital deduction, not the estate tax exemption, to avoid death taxes. And actually it doesn't really avoid them; it merely postpones them, because when the surviving spouse dies, what's left in the QTIP trust gets figured into his or her gross estate. But if the inclusion of the QTIP in the last-to-die spouse's estate pushes it over the estate tax exemption, giving rise to estate taxes, those can be recovered from the QTIP. After all, the last-to-die spouse's estate wasn't the beneficiary of the QTIP. Typically, somebody like George would arrange his affairs so that after funding his bypass trust with assets up to the exclusion amount, his executor would put any excess assets into a QTIP for his wife. If the wife's estate were modest like Georgia's, her exclusion amount might suffice to shelter everything.

Other Estate Planning Documents

There are a number of other documents that are usually, though not always, included in an estate plan. Each is discussed very briefly here.

Durable Power of Attorney

A *durable power of attorney* is a document in which you appoint one or more people, acting jointly or severally, to act in your place and on your behalf in managing your affairs. It's basically good until you rescind it or you die, but you can be very specific in terms of what powers you're giving and under what conditions they may be exercised. When we lived out of the country, we gave my mother such a power because we had several pieces of rental property that needed to be managed by someone close-by who could deal face-to-face with our tenants, repair people, and so on. Later, when my mother began having age-related problems herself, she gave my sister and me a durable power of attorney to act for her. It's a good thing she did because within a couple of years she descended into Alzheimer's, never to resurface. When she died, those powers became null.

As opposed to a regular power of attorney, which becomes null if the grantor becomes incapacitated, a durable power of attorney remains in force. That's why it's called durable.

If you become physically or mentally incapable of managing your affairs and you have never given anyone a durable power of attorney, someone (usually a friend or a relative) will likely petition the court to appoint a guardian for you. That person could be a close relative if one's nearby, but if one's not, it could be someone you don't even know who will need to be compensated for his time. I have no first-hand experience with a court-appointed guardianship, but it's my understanding that the process involves lots of expensive and time-consuming legal folderol. And if you recover your faculties, you will have to convince the court of that before it will put you back in charge of your life.

If you have a revocable living trust, it will allow for your co-trustee (likely your spouse) or a successor trustee to manage the property owned by the trust if you can't, but he or she may be powerless to do anything about any property that for whatever reason is held outside the trust.

Durable Power of Attorney for Health Care

This is sometimes called a *medical power of attorney,* and it's altogether different from the document discussed above, although I understand that the two can be combined. With this one, you're appointing someone to make health care decisions for you in the event you're unable to make them for yourself. This person can admit you to a hospital, rehab center, nursing home, or other medical facility, and can authorize whatever medical care your health care providers recommend, including surgery. But, again, he or she can only do this if you're "out of it," so to speak. That would be your condition if you had been in a bad car wreck and were unconscious, or if you had been diagnosed with Alzheimer's. When my mother's condition got to the stage eventually where she could no longer be cared for at home, my sister and I had her admitted to a long-term care facility using the health care power of attorney she had given my sister some years before. We used that same power of attorney nearly three years later to authorize her health care providers to put her on palliative care after it became clear that the antibiotics she was being given would not cure her condition but merely prolong her suffering. This was in keeping with her *living will.*

Living Will

A *living will* and *directive to physicians, family or surrogates* are the same thing: a document in which you express your wishes insofar as what life-sustaining measures, if any, should be taken to keep you alive if you're unable to make decisions for yourself due to injury (maybe you're in a coma) or illness (like Alzheimer's), and in your physician's judgment, your condition is either a) terminal, such that you're expected to die within 6 months, or b) irreversible, so that you'll never again be able to care for yourself or make decisions for yourself. This, at least, is how the one approved for use in Texas reads.[14] For both conditions described, it gives you the choice of saying, in effect, "don't use any life-sustaining procedures on me—just keep me pain- and anxiety-free," or "use all available life-sustaining treatments to keep me alive as long as possible."

The living will approved for your state may read a little different from this. You can almost certainly get a blank one from your nearest hospital because nearly all hospitals will ask anyone they schedule for serious surgery if he or she would like to execute a living will. But don't wait until then to do one; it'll be tricky scheduling your surgery if you're unconscious.

Pour-over Will

A *pour-over will* is used with a living trust to deal with any property that the decedent, for whatever reason, never put into the trust. The one I had, back when we had a family trust,[15] stated that anything I owned outside our trust was to go to my wife and, in the event she was no longer living, to go into my trust, there to be distributed according to its terms. It's important to note here that such property is subject to probate.

****

---

[14] Every state has its own prescribed form, which cannot be toyed with.

[15] When it became possible to port the "deceased spouse's unused exclusion," we revoked our family trust and went back to wills. When one of us goes, it will make things simpler for the surviving spouse.

So, where do you go from here?

A good place to start, I believe, is by preparing an inventory that lists everything of value that you, or you and your spouse, own. Indeed, if you're a married woman facing the prospect of soon being widowed, you probably ought to get started today. Table 4.2 below is a sample inventory that you can use as a guide. Note that it indicates in respect of each asset, which is briefly described, how title is held (sole ownership, joint tenancy with right of survivorship, tenancy in common, community property, etc.) and, if applicable, where its deed or title can be found.

This inventory will serve two broad purposes: The first is to expose any weaknesses in your current estate plan or, worse, the fact that you have no estate plan. If there is something that needs to be done, you want to deal with it while there's still time. The other thing it does is tell the person charged with settling your estate, or your husband's, what it is that you, or he, owned so that no time and money is wasted trying to figure this out. I would add that if the deceased is your husband, there's a good chance that you're the executrix or trustee.

Table 4.2 ~ Inventory of Titled Property

Property Description	**Owner-ship**	**Comments**
Real Estate		
- House @ 212 Elm Street	JTWROS	Deed is in safe deposit box at BofA
- Cabin on Beaver Lake	A's trust	Kids are beneficiaries; David has life estate
Brokerage & Retirement Accounts		
- # 277-35679 Joint acct @ Edward Jones	JTWROS	TOD to kids
- # 999-24698 David's traditional IRA	David	Anne is beneficiary; kids are contingents
- # 995-79433 David's Roth IRA	David	Anne is beneficiary; kids are contingents
- # 999-24701 Anne's traditional IRA	Anne	David is beneficiary; kids are contingents
Checking Accounts		
- 577-1853-8 Account #1 @ BofA	JTWROS	POD to kids
- 244-7655-9 Account #2 @ BofA	JTWROS	POD to kids
- 3774-9898 Sinking Fund @ Union Bank	JTWROS	POD to kids
Cars		
- Honda Pilot	JTWROS	Title in safe deposit box @ BofA
- Buick Enclave	JTWROS	Title held by BofA pending loan pay-off
Life Insurance		
- $1 million whole life policy	David	Policy in safe deposit box
(Lincoln Liberty Life ~ Tel (321) 683-2345)		Anne is beneficiary; kids are contingents

Not being an attorney, I'm not qualified to give legal advice, but I can't believe that anyone would challenge my saying that to the extent that you can minimize the assets that must be probated, that's a good thing. It will mean less expense. The way to avoid probate, as we've seen, is through the use of will substitutes. Just be careful.

Be *very* careful about using joint tenancy with right of survivorship as a strategy. Once you put someone on a title as a joint tenant, you can't just remove him if later your expansiveness seems to have been a bad idea. You'll have to go through some legal rigmarole to get him off, and he'll have to agree to it.

Other bad things can result. For example, if you and your husband both have children from a previous marriage and you make him a joint tenant on something you own and then you die, it'll be his to do with as he wishes, and if he's stinker or just thoughtless, he can leave it all in his will to his children, leaving yours out in the cold. It happens. Likewise, if you put *one* of your children on your brokerage account as a joint tenant, as I once had a client insist on doing, that child will become the sole owner of the account if you die first. It won't make any difference what your will says; your other children won't have any share in it.

If you live in a community property state as I do and, like me, have been married forever and your will and your spouse's both leave everything to the other, I cannot see any reason *not* to avail yourselves of any and every opportunity to convert plain-vanilla community property into community property with rights of survivorship. As I mentioned earlier, we've done this. The particular document we executed consists of just one page and is called a *Survivorship Agreement for Community Property*.

Consider using POD and TOD agreements on bank and brokerage accounts held in your name only. They allow you to name primary and secondary beneficiaries. You could name your husband, say, as your primary beneficiary on a brokerage account that is your separate property and your two children as contingents. If you later separate from your husband, you can revoke the agreement. PODs and TODs are the easiest things in the world to undo. You just have to remember to do it.

Remember that trusts can offer satisfactory solutions to lots of problematic situations. If you and your husband have a joint estate in excess of the federal estate tax exclusion, you might consider putting your property into an AB trust, which may still be a more sure way of sheltering it with two exclusions than relying on the portability of the deceased spouse's unused exclusion amount. If you're in a second marriage and one of you has a substantial separate property estate that underwrites a lifestyle that the other could not maintain on his or her own, the spouse with the money—let's say it's you—might consider putting it into a bypass trust, so that if you predecease your husband, the income from the trust will go to him for the rest of his life, but upon his death, the corpus will go to your children, or anyone else you chose. There are other kinds of trusts I've not previously touched on but will mention here, just briefly. If they strike a chord, you will need to make further inquiries. If you have a handicapped child who depends on you for support, consult an estate planning attorney about setting up a *special needs trust* to provide for the child after you're gone. If you want to leave money to your church or some other charity, ask an attorney about setting up a *charitable trust*. There are a several kinds of charitable trusts. All can provide significant tax benefits.

Finally, don't forget those other estate planning documents that I talked about—the durable power of attorney, the durable power of attorney for health care and the living will. These really don't have anything to do with your estate, of course, but they are no less important for that if you're ever incapacitated and need someone you love and trust to make decisions for you.

FIVE

Saving for Retirement

A few years back I had a once-a-week volunteer gig at a local alcohol and drug rehab center where I talked to the guys in the program there about money matters. I don't recall for sure how long the program was from start to finish for the guys cycling through, but it seems like it was eleven weeks, which meant that I needed that many different one-hour talks if I was to avoid repeating myself to the rare individual who stayed the course and "graduated." Coming up with that many talks that were relevant to men whose minds always seemed otherwise occupied presented a challenge that I never quite overcame. However, I did have one talk that always succeeded in at least stimulating a lot of discussion. Quoting from my original notes, it began as follows:

> Yesterday my wife and I ate at Whataburger, something we almost never do. I noted that the 'meal deal,' which includes their regular hamburger, medium fries, and a 32-ounce fountain drink, costs $5.49, not including tax, which adds 45¢, bringing the total to $5.94. I would guess that the

meal deals at McDonald's, Wendy's, and Sonic run about the same. After lunch we went to HEB, and at the checkout I happened to notice that a carton of Marlboro Lights, which I used to smoke, costs $50.29. I assume that sales tax gets added to that as well, such that the total is more like $54.44. After we got home, I did some arithmetic. I figured that if I ate at Whataburger every day—which my plumber had once told me he did—and I still had my two pack-a-day cigarette habit, I'd be spending at least $5,595[1] a year killing myself with fast food and nicotine. That same $5,595 per year invested in an IRA returning an average 8% per year, *tax-deferred,* would grow to over $87,000 in 10 years. In fifteen years to $164,000. In twenty years to $276,000. In thirty years to $684,000. In forty to over $1.5 million ($1,565,374).[2]

I then went on to explain that accumulating a substantial sum of money for retirement isn't rocket science. It doesn't require that you be able to divine what the stock market is going to do. Nobody can do that. What it does require is that you be a saver rather than a spender, and that you not delay in exploiting the power of *compound interest,*[3] which Albert Einstein, no less, said was the greatest mathematical discovery of all times.

It also requires—the tax-deferred part does—that the money you save be invested in an IRA of some sort or in a *qualified* employer-sponsored retirement account. Anyone who can—and doesn't—exploit the opportunity of investing in an IRA, 401(k), or the like to the fullest of his ability needs to have his head examined.

****

An IRA is an Individual Retirement Plan, of which there are four kinds—*traditional, Roth*, *SEP,* and *SIMPLE*. The traditional and the Roth are accounts you

---

[1] I explained that in coming up with this number I had reduced the cost of the Whataburger meal by $1.50, which I estimated to be the cost of a ham and cheese sandwich or some similar sack lunch.

[2] The most you can contribute to an IRA presently is a bit less than $5,595— it's $5,500 a year—and an 8% return might be too much to expect. Most illustrations of tax-deferred growth will use 7%.

[3] Compound interest is simply interest on interest.

would see yourself to opening and funding. The SEP and the SIMPLE, on the other hand, are both set up at the initiative of a business, which contributes to each employee's account. Other company-sponsored qualified retirement plans include *defined benefit pension plans, money purchase plans,* and *401(k) plans.*

Non-profits, like schools, universities, charities, churches, hospitals, and other tax-exempt institutions, may also sponsor retirement plans. These include defined benefit plans and *403(b)* and *457* plans.

The discussion here will be mostly concerned with the traditional IRA, the Roth IRA, the SIMPLE IRA, and the 401(k). If you work for a company offering a SEP IRA, you'll get some free money once a year, but there's nothing much you have to do other than open an account to receive the money and decide how to invest it. As for 403(b) and 457 plans, they are enough like the 401(k) that if you understand how the 401(k) works, you should understand how they work. I'm going to stay away from money purchase plans because I have no experience with them and from defined benefit plans, which I do know something about, because no one except the government and non-profits offers these plans anymore.

Traditional IRA

The traditional IRA was created by Congress back in 1974 to encourage anyone who isn't covered by a company-sponsored retirement plan to build a retirement nest egg of his own by providing him with two significant tax incentives. The first is that he is allowed to deduct his IRA contributions in the year for which he makes them from his taxable income *(Form 1040, line 32).* The second is that he pays no taxes on the investment earnings inside his IRA until he withdraws them. Another way of expressing this is to say that contributions to a traditional IRA go in "pre-tax" and "grow tax-deferred."

To discourage the account owner from pulling money out of his IRA before attaining the age of 59 ½, he is subject to a 10% penalty to the extent that he does *(Form 1040, line 59).* That is, unless one of the following four exceptions apply: 1) the withdrawal was made owing to the death or disability of the owner, 2) to deal with unreimbursed medical expenses exceeding 10%[4] of adjusted gross income, 3) to help with the purchase of a first home,[5] or 4) to pay qualified post-secondary schooling expenses. But regardless of whether one of these exceptions applies, *any* withdrawal from a traditional IRA must be reported as taxable income in the year made *(Form 1040, line 15)*.

Upon reaching age 70 ½, the account holder *must* begin taking *distributions* every year by December 31. These are referred to as *required minimum distributions*, *RMDs* for short. The *first* RMD—and that one only—can be delayed until April 1 of the year following the year the owner becomes 70 ½. However, if he does that, he will have to take two RMDs that year, one pertaining to the prior year when he turned 70 ½ and one for the current year.[6] Failure to take an RMD in full by the required due date will result in the shortfall being slapped with a 50% penalty. This means that if your RMD was supposed to be, say, $3,000 and for whatever reason you only took $1,200, you'd end up having to pay a $900 penalty on the $1,800 you failed to take. Normally your IRA custodian—the brokerage firm, bank, or other financial services institution holding your account—will see to your taking your RMD by its due date.[7] They'll also calculate how much it should be.

The amount of your annual RMD is figured by taking your prior December 31 account balance and dividing it by a factor corresponding to your age taken from the *Uniform Lifetime Table* shown on the next page.[8] Note that for someone my age, 74, the factor is 23.8. Thus, if my IRA account balance at the close of last year was, say, $100,000, the distribution I'd be required to take this year would be $4, 202 ($100,000 ÷ 23.8).

The amount you can contribute to an IRA in any one year is all of your *earned* income up to the *contribution limit*, which is presently (2016) $5,500. But that's only the limit if you're under age 50. If you're 50 or over, you can contribute up to $6,500, the extra $1,000 being treated as a *catch-up contribution*. You can go right on contributing up to the magical age of 70 ½.

---

[4] 7 ½% for anyone born before Jan 2, 1949.
[5] Limit $10,000.
[6] Which could increase his income enough to throw him into a higher marginal tax bracket.
[7] To be safe, make a point of requesting that they do this.
[8] The table actually goes out to age 115 & older.

Table 5.1 ~ RMD Table

Age	Divisor	Age	Divisor	Age	Divisor
70	27.4	80	18.7	90	11.4
71	26.5	81	17.9	91	10.8
72	25.6	82	17.1	92	10.2
73	24.7	83	16.3	93	9.6
74	23.8	84	15.5	94	9.1
75	22.9	85	14.8	95	8.6
76	22.0	86	14.1	96	8.1
77	21.2	87	13.4	97	7.6
78	20.3	88	12.7	98	7.1
79	19.5	89	12	99	6.7

You can also make a *spousal contribution* on behalf of your non-working husband or wife provided you have earned income equal to what you're putting into both accounts—yours and your spouse's. To do this, you must file a joint return.

Not all contributions to a traditional IRA are necessarily tax-deductible. If you happen to be an *active participant* in a qualified plan at work—a 401(k), say—your contribution, as well as any contribution you might make to your non-working spouse's IRA, may not be fully deductible or even partially deductible. It will depend on your tax *filing status* (*single, married filing jointly* etc.) and *modified adjusted gross income (MAGI)*. This can get a little confusing, so take your time with the following explanation.

To determine how large a deductible contribution *you*, as an active participant, can make to *your* traditional IRA, you must consult the table below[9] and maybe do a little math.

Table 5.2 ~ Ded. Allowed When Owner is Active Participant (2016)

Filing Status	**Modified AGI**	**Deduction**
Single	$61,000 or less	Full deduction
	$61,001 to $70,999	Partial deduction
	$71,000 or more	No deduction
Married Filing	$98,000 or less	Full deduction
Jointly	$98,001 to $117,999	Partial deduction
	$118,000 or more	No deduction
Married Filing	$1 to $9,999	Partial deduction
Separately	$10,000 or more	No deduction

[9] These tables change every year or so, depending on the prior year's inflation rate.

So, let's say that you're 30, married and filing jointly, your earned income for the year was $83,000, and your modified adjusted gross income was $111,350. There's certainly no problem with your making a full $5,500 contribution, as your earned income is many multiples of that. Instead, the question is: how much of that $5,500 will be deductible? It clearly won't be all because your modified adjusted gross income (MAGI) is greater than $98,000. And it won't be zero because your MAGI is less than $118,000. Which means that it will be a number in between, requiring that you interpolate. Doing that, you will find that the maximum deductible contribution you can make to a traditional IRA is only $1,829.[10] Any contribution in excess of that will be treated as a non-deductible contribution. More about this in a minute.

First, though, let's consider your spouse, who we'll say is your wife. If she had earned income and was also an active participant, she could make exactly the same deductible and non-deductible contributions to a traditional IRA that you could make yourself. As an active participant, she would be bound by the same rules. It's worth pointing out, though, that even if her earned income were less than $5,500 she could still contribute that much provided your combined earnings sufficed to cover both contributions.

What if she had earned income but was *not* an active participant? In that case, any contribution to her IRA would be *fully* deductible. And, again, she could contribute the full $5,500, even if her earnings were less, so long as your combined earnings sufficed to cover both contributions.

The third possibility here is that your wife had *no* earned income—you did, but she didn't, and you participated in your employer's 401(k). In that case, to know how large a deductible spousal contribution you could make to her IRA, we would have to go to another table, which is Table 5.2a, shown on the next page.

According to it, if the MAGI per your joint return were, as we assumed above, $111,350, you could make a fully-deductible $5,500 contribution to her IRA since you're far below the $184,000 threshold.

[10] $5,500 – (($111,350 – $98,000) × ($5,500 ÷ ($118,000 – $98,000))) = $1,829

Table 5.2a ~ Deduction Allowed for Contribution to Non-Working Spouse's IRA when Other Spouse is an Active Participant (Year 2016)		
Filing Status	**Modified AGI**	**Deduction**
Married Filing Jointly	$184,000 or less	Full deduction
	From $184,001 to $193,999	Partial deduction
	$194,000 or more	No deduction
Married Filing Separately	From $1 to $9,999	Partial deduction
	$10,000 or more	No deduction

The deadline for contributing to an IRA and taking it as a deduction in that year's tax return is April 15 of the following year, which of course is also the filing deadline. That doesn't mean that you cannot make contributions before if you wish. But if you or your spouse participates in a plan at work, and your income could present a deductibility problem and you would rather contribute to a Roth, if you can, than make a non-deductible IRA contribution to a traditional IRA, you should probably hold off until just before finalizing your return.

If you do have a deductibility problem but cannot contribute to a Roth, it probably makes sense to make a non-deductible contribution to your traditional IRA versus investing in a regular brokerage account or doing nothing. Why? Because your account will still enjoy tax-deferred growth.

If you do make a non-deductible contribution, you will need to file a *Form 8606* with your return and keep a copy. You'll need this paperwork when you eventually pull money from your IRA to avoid paying taxes on the pro-rata share of your withdrawal that represents non-deductible contributions. The fact that those contributions were non-deductible means you've already paid taxes on them. You don't want to pay taxes on them again.

Roth IRA

It is always said that the main difference between a traditional IRA and a Roth is that money goes into a traditional before-tax and is taxed when it comes out, whereas it goes into a Roth after-tax but is *not* taxed when it comes out. Which is true, at least up to a point, but it's certainly not the whole story. Here's how I would compare the two IRAs.

First, the things they have in common: Both IRAs have the same contribution limits (the lesser of $5,500/$6,500 and total earned income), the same deadline for making those contributions (April 15th of the following year), the same flexibility in making spousal contributions, the same kind of account custodian (brokerage firm, bank, or other financial services institution), and the same restrictions on how the money can be invested (only in publicly-traded securities, money market funds, CDs, precious metals, coins, and real estate).[11]

Now, how they're different: Contributions to a Roth are *never* tax-deductible; income by itself *is* an issue, but participation in a qualified plan at work is not; the account grows *tax-free*, not tax-deferred; distributions are *tax-exempt*; you do *not* have to begin taking distributions upon reaching age of 70 ½; and if you are still working then, you can go right on making contributions.

Some of these differences may warrant a bit more explanation. Some people are confused by the terms "pre-tax' and "after-tax" as used to describe IRA contributions. It's pretty simple, though. Pre-tax contributions are contributions you made that you were allowed on your tax return to deduct from income. After-tax contributions are any contributions you made that you couldn't deduct.

Income by itself is never an impediment to making a contribution to a traditional IRA. It is, however, with a Roth. As shown below, your ability to contribute to a Roth may be limited or non-existent depending on your MAGI and filing status.

Table 5.3 ~ Roth Contribution Limits (2016)

Filing Status	Modified AGI	Contrib. Limit
Single	Less than $117,000	Up to the limit
	From $117,000 to $131,999	A reduced amount
	$132,000 and over	Zero
Married Filing Jointly	Less than $184,000	Up to the limit
	From $184,000 to $193,999	A reduced amount
	$194,000 and over	Zero
Married Filing Separately	Less than $10,000	A reduced amount
	$10,000 and over	Zero

With a traditional IRA, your MAGI only affects your ability to *deduct* your contribution and then *only if* you or your spouse is an *active participant* in an employer-

[11] I can't think who would invest their IRAs in precious coins and real estate.

sponsored retirement plan. With a Roth, it makes no difference at all if one of you is an active participant. The only thing that matters is your MAGI.

So, let's go back to our earlier example where we said that you're age 30, married filing jointly, participate in a qualified plan at work, and your MAGI is $111,350. Can you make a fully deductible $5,500 contribution to a traditional IRA? No, because your MAGI is more than $98,000. We figured that the most you can deduct is $1,829, such that if you make a $5,500 contribution to a traditional the other $3,671 will be non-deductible. Can you contribute to a Roth? Yes, up to the $5,500 limit because your MAGI is less than $184,000. Would contributing to a Roth make more sense than making a largely non-deductible contribution to a traditional? It does to me. Distributions from a Roth would be completely tax-free, whereas distributions from a traditional to which non-deductible contributions had been made would only partially be,[12] and you'd have to bother with some paperwork.

Let's assume the same facts as above, except that your MAGI is $97,000 instead of $111,350, allowing you to make a fully deductible $5,500 contribution to a traditional. Would that make more sense than contributing the same amount to a Roth? The theoretically correct answer is that it would if you can be reasonably sure that you're in a higher tax bracket now than you will be when you retire and begin taking distributions. As a practical matter most folks would opt to contribute to a traditional in order to reduce their taxes. There have been years when we've done both, funded my wife's traditional and my Roth.

If you do that—that is contribute the same amount to both a traditional and a Roth—and invest in the identical same securities, the two accounts will grow to the exact same amount over time. You'll pay no taxes on the earnings in either so long as the earnings are left to compound.

After the age of 70 ½, provided you don't pull the same amount from your Roth as you are required to pull from your traditional, the Roth will obviously become the bigger account.

---

[12] The pro-rata part of your distribution that was attributed to non-deductible contributions would not be taxable, while the other part, which would be attributed to earnings, would be.

There are conditions attached to the Roth's tax-free distributions. While you can always withdraw your *contributions* from a Roth without incurring any tax or penalty, *earnings* are a different matter. For earnings to come out tax- and penalty-free, you must have had your Roth IRA for at least five years *and* be at least 59 ½. If you pull money from a Roth while failing to meet both conditions, you'll be hit with a 10% penalty on your earnings, *in addition* to paying taxes on them. The same exceptions that apply to early withdrawals from a traditional IRA (death, disability, first-time home purchase etc.) also apply to a Roth.

SIMPLE IRAs

SIMPLE here stands for *Savings Incentive Match PLan for Employees.* Like SEPs,[13] they are established by small businesses because they are relatively easy to set up and administer. But a SIMPLE IRA isn't as simple as a SEP. With a SEP, only the employer contributes to the employee's IRA. With a SIMPLE, the employee may contribute as well through *salary deferrals,* which are excluded from his W-2 earnings. The employer, for its part, can make either matching contributions (up to 3% of compensation) or, in the case of employees who opt not to contribute, non-matching contributions. The employer's contribution is tax-deductible.

To be eligible to participate in the company's SIMPLE plan, the employee must have earned at least $5,000 working for the company during any preceding two years and be expected to earn at least that much during the current plan year. If he wants, he can elect to defer 100% of his earnings, but not more than $12,500, unless he's over 50, in which case he can defer another $3,000 as a catch-up contribution.[14] Whatever is withheld from his earnings each pay period as a contribution to his SIMPLE the employer is responsible for depositing into his account, wherever held, within the following 30 days.

The employer can hold off making its contribution until it has filed its taxes, which, if it files for an extension, might not be until mid-October of the following year. As to what it contributes, it has a choice—match each eligible employee's elective deferral, dollar for dollar, up to 3% of compensation, or make a 2% non-matching

[13] SEP stands for *Simplified Employer Plan.*
[14] These are the limits for 2015. Every year or two they are adjusted upwards for inflation.

contribution to all eligible employees irrespective of whether they make elective deferrals. There are exceptions to this norm, which in the interest of staying out of the weeds I won't go into.

As far as early withdrawals and distributions are concerned, they are the same as those for the traditional IRA, with one significant exception. If you're under 59 ½, any withdrawal you make within *two years* of the first contribution made to your SIMPLE will be subject to a penalty of 25%, not 10%.

Compared to other retirement savings accounts, there is a lot to like about a SIMPLE IRA. You can save more than twice as much in a SIMPLE as you can in either a traditional or a Roth, and you have the added bonus of the company contribution. You can save more in a 401(k), 403(b), and 457,[15] as you'll see, but you won't necessarily be the beneficiary of a company contribution, and if you are, you'll be subject to vesting. With a SIMPLE IRA, once the company's money is in your account, it's 100% yours.

401(k) Plans

Most large corporations have long since replaced their *defined benefit* pension plan with a *defined contribution* plan of some sort, usually a 401(k).

Under a defined *benefit* plan, like Chiquita's Tropical Retirement Plan to which I belonged and from which I receive a monthly pension, the employer bore full responsibility for seeing to it that when an employee retired it could provide him for the remainder of his life with the monthly pension to which his salary and years of service entitled him. Needless to say, when a corporation cannot be sure of future investment returns and has hundreds, or even thousands, of employees, a high percentage of whom likely will not remain in company service long enough to be vested in the plan, much less retire under it, it is faced with a very big challenge every year determining its funding requirements and how to put idle money to work. Even with help from outside actuaries and plan administrators and guidance from the government, it is a challenge that ever since the advent of the 401(k) in 1984 most companies have been unwilling to take on. I think Chiquita may be typical. It replaced its old defined benefit plan roughly twenty years ago with a 401(k).

---

[15] It's likely that you'll have a matching company contribution of some sort if you participate in a 401(k), but *unlikely* if you are in a 403(b) or 457.

A defined *contribution* plan, like a 401(k,) stipulates how much employer and employee can each contribute annually to the employee's retirement account, but it says nothing about what those contributions will grow to. How the employee chooses from among his choices to invest his contributions is his business, and how his investments perform is his worry, not the company's.

401(k) plans may vary somewhat from company to company, but all allow employee salary deferrals and most provide for some sort of employer-match. The law permits the employee to defer up to 100% of compensation but not more than $18,000 (2016), unless he is age 50 or older, in which case he can defer another $6,000 as a catch-up contribution, raising his total deferral to $24,000. As for the employer's contribution, most plans provide for the employer to match the employee deferral up to some percent of compensation. Fifty-cents on the dollar up to 3% of compensation may be typical. Some examples may be helpful to understanding how such a match would work.

First, let's suppose that your salary is $75,000, you're 51, you elect to defer 6%, plus another $6,000 as a catch-up contribution, and your employer does a 3% match. In that case you'd be contributing $10,500 yourself over the year ($75,000 × .06 = $4,500; $4,500 + $6,000 = $10,500), and the company's match would be $2,250 ($75,000 × .03 = $2,250). The total, then, contributed to your 401(k) for that particular year would be $12,750. It probably wouldn't all go to work at the same time, however. That's because you likely would be contributing monthly, whereas your employer might hold off making its contribution until the following year, after doing its taxes but before filing.

Now let's look at a somewhat more complicated situation. Let's say that your salary is $300,000 a year. Provided your plan allowed it (which is likely), you could elect to have $2,000 (($18,000 + $6,000) ÷ 12) withheld from your pay every month to go into your 401(k). Your employer's match, however, whenever it was made, would not be, as you might expect, half of $18,000 (which is $9,000) because there happens to be a cap on how much compensation can be considered for 401(k) calculations. Presently (2016) that cap is $265,000. As a consequence, your company's matching contribution would be limited to $7,950 ($265,000 × .03). Even so, that's a nice chunk of free money.

Roth 401(k) plans allow employees to contribute after-tax dollars to their 401(k)s. In other words, their contributions are not excluded from their W-2 earnings as they would be if they were tax-deferred. The same contribution limits still apply.

The employee's investment choices with a 401(k) are not as broad as they are with an IRA. With an IRA, the account owner can invest in all the publicly-traded securities (stocks, bonds, ETFs, mutual funds, CDs, etc.) that the plan provider has on offer. With a 401(k) his choices are much more limited. There will be a menu of mutual funds from which the employee can select the ones to which he wishes to allocate the money in his account, and there's not much he can do if he's unimpressed with his choices except to complain to the plan administrator. The plan provider is often a mutual fund company, and the plan administrator is often the company's human resources department.

I have mentioned *vesting* several times. Vesting refers to how many years the employee must work for the company before the contributions it makes to his 401(k) become his. This is to discourage employees from taking their free money as soon as it's in their account and waving goodbye. Often there is a vesting schedule, whereby, for example, after only one year of service, you're 0% vested; after 2 years 20% vested; after 3 years 40%; and so on out to six years, when you become 100% vested.

If you leave company service and the company's plan allows it, you may be allowed to leave your 401(k) there. A wiser choice might be to move the money and/or securities in it to an IRA, where you would have more investment options. Against that, though, you would have to weigh any reinvestment costs, which could be significant.[16] If you go to work for another company having its own 401(k) and they'll let you move your 401(k) over to theirs, you might want to consider that. If you do move your account to an IRA or to another 401(k), just be sure to do a *trustee-to-trustee transfer*.[17] If you do not, you will have 20% of your account withheld and sent to the IRS as an advance payment on any taxes and early withdrawal penalty to which you may be subject. To get this money back after doing your taxes, you would have to be able to show that within 60

[16] The next chapter covers investments. Suffice it to say here, mutual funds sold by *full-service* brokerage firms are almost always *load funds*, meaning they have sales charges. And on any security you buy or sell through a brokerage firm, you'll pay a commission.

[17] When the trustee-to-trustee transfer is to an IRA, it is often referred to as a *direct rollover transfer*.

days of your withdrawal you had put all the money back into an IRA or another company's 401(k). Besides being a lot of trouble, this would require you to borrow from somewhere, perhaps other savings, the 20% that the IRS was holding.

Someone who retires before he's 59 ½, possibly as a result of being laid off and not being able to find another job, can take penalty-free *periodic* distributions from his 401(k) under IRS rule 72t. As usual there are some conditions. In this case, it is that the distributions must be taken in substantially equal payments and continue for the longer of 5 years or the owner turning age 59 ½. There are two or three formulas accepted by the IRS for calculating the periodic distribution.

As with the owner of a traditional, SEP, or SIMPLE IRA, upon reaching age 70 ½, anyone who has a 401(k) must begin taking RMDs.

Solo 401(k)

It is possible now if you're self-employed and have no employees, except perhaps your spouse, to set up a 401(k) covering just you or the two of you. Such a 401(k) is referred to as a Solo 401(k) or Individual 401(k), and what's noteworthy about it is that it will permit you, provided you've got the earnings to swing it, to boost your 401(k) contributions—employee deferrals and company contributions combined—to a total of $53,000. This is done through profit-sharing, as the employee deferral limits are the same $18,000/$24,000.

****

If you began this chapter not knowing much about IRAs and employer-sponsored qualified plans like the 401(k), I hope the foregoing was helpful. As I will show in just a bit, the tax-deferred growth you get in these accounts will over time make a huge difference in the size of your retirement nest egg compared to what you'd have in a non-qualified brokerage account invested in the exact same securities.

First, though, let's look at compounding, which is the magic by which your nest egg can grow over time at an accelerating rate to a number many multiples of what you put into it. Consider Table 5.4 on the next page depicting the growth of an IRA to which you annually contribute $5,500, investing it always in a bond paying 7%. Do not worry

Table 5.4 ~ Growth of $5,500 Invested at Start of Every Year & Compounded at 7%

Yr	Bal @ Start	Invested	Interest Earned	Bal @ Close	Accum Investments	Accum Interest	Bal @ Close
1	$0	$5,500	$385	$5,885	$5,500	$385	$5,885
2	$5,885	$5,500	$797	$12,182	$11,000	$1,182	$12,182
3	$12,182	$5,500	$1,238	$18,920	$16,500	$2,420	$18,920
4	$18,920	$5,500	$1,709	$26,129	$22,000	$4,129	$26,129
5	$26,129	$5,500	$2,214	$33,843	$27,500	$6,343	$33,843
6	$33,843	$5,500	$2,754	$42,097	$33,000	$9,097	$42,097
7	$42,097	$5,500	$3,332	$50,929	$38,500	$12,429	$50,929
8	$50,929	$5,500	$3,950	$60,379	$44,000	$16,379	$60,379
9	$60,379	$5,500	$4,612	$70,490	$49,500	$20,990	$70,490
10	$70,490	$5,500	$5,319	$81,310	$55,000	$26,310	$81,310
11	$81,310	$5,500	$6,077	$92,886	$60,500	$32,386	$92,886
12	$92,886	$5,500	$6,887	$105,274	$66,000	$39,274	$105,274
13	$105,274	$5,500	$7,754	$118,528	$71,500	$47,028	$118,528
14	$118,528	$5,500	$8,682	$132,710	$77,000	$55,710	$132,710
15	$132,710	$5,500	$9,675	$147,884	$82,500	$65,384	$147,884
16	$147,884	$5,500	$10,737	$164,121	$88,000	$76,121	$164,121
17	$164,121	$5,500	$11,873	$181,495	$93,500	$87,995	$181,495
18	$181,495	$5,500	$13,090	$200,084	$99,000	$101,084	$200,084
19	$200,084	$5,500	$14,391	$219,975	$104,500	$115,475	$219,975
20	$219,975	$5,500	$15,783	$241,258	$110,000	$131,258	$241,258
21	$241,258	$5,500	$17,273	$264,032	$115,500	$148,532	$264,032
22	$264,032	$5,500	$18,867	$288,399	$121,000	$167,399	$288,399
23	$288,399	$5,500	$20,573	$314,472	$126,500	$187,972	$314,472
24	$314,472	$5,500	$22,398	$342,370	$132,000	$210,370	$342,370
25	$342,370	$5,500	$24,351	$372,221	$137,500	$234,721	$372,221
26	$372,221	$5,500	$26,440	$404,161	$143,000	$261,161	$404,161
27	$404,161	$5,500	$28,676	$438,337	$148,500	$289,837	$438,337
28	$438,337	$5,500	$31,069	$474,906	$154,000	$320,906	$474,906
29	$474,906	$5,500	$33,628	$514,034	$159,500	$354,534	$514,034
30	$514,034	$5,500	$36,367	$555,902	$165,000	$390,902	$555,902
31	$555,902	$5,500	$39,298	$600,700	$170,500	$430,200	$600,700
32	$600,700	$5,500	$42,434	$648,634	$176,000	$472,634	$648,634
33	$648,634	$5,500	$45,789	$699,923	$181,500	$518,423	$699,923
34	$699,923	$5,500	$49,380	$754,803	$187,000	$567,803	$754,803
35	$754,803	$5,500	$53,221	$813,524	$192,500	$621,024	$813,524
36	$813,524	$5,500	$57,332	$876,356	$198,000	$678,356	$876,356
37	$876,356	$5,500	$61,730	$943,586	$203,500	$740,086	$943,586
38	$943,586	$5,500	$66,436	$1,015,522	$209,000	$806,522	$1,015,522
39	$1,015,522	$5,500	$71,472	$1,092,493	$214,500	$877,993	$1,092,493
40	$1,092,493	$5,500	$76,860	$1,174,853	$220,000	$954,853	$1,174,853

that in today's interest rate environment no such investment exists. We're just looking at how compounding works.

Here are our assumptions: You open and fund the account on, say, April 10, 2016, after doing your taxes for 2015, the year for which you're making your contribution. Year 1, then, ends on April 9, 2017, and Year 2 begins the next day, April 10, 2017, when you make another $5,500 contribution, investing it the same way. You hold to this regimen for the rest of your working career.

At the end of Year 1, your account balance will stand at $5,885, of which your contribution will account for $5,500 and interest earned $385. All of that $385 will have been earned on your contribution.

Fast forward to Year 10. The year-end balance stands at $81,310, of which $55,000 ($5,500 × 10) comes from contributions and $26,310 from interest. Of that $26,310, $21,175 would be interest earned on contributions and $5,135 interest earned on interest (which is compound interest). Note that in Year 10 your account grew nearly as much from interest as from contributions. You contributed $5,500 as usual and earned $5,319 in interest.

Jump ahead to Year 20, where your year-end balance now is $241,258, of which $110,000 ($5,500 × 20) comes from contributions and $131,258 from interest. Note that accumulated *contributions* have doubled, which is exactly what you would expect, but accumulated *interest* has quintupled ($131,258 ÷ $26,310 = 4.99). A big part of that $131,258— $50,408—is interest on interest. Note, too, that in Year 20 what you earned in interest ($15,783) was nearly three times the $5,500 that you contributed out-of-pocket. Your account is growing at gathering speed, all thanks to compounding. Nothing is required on your part but to keep on keeping on.

Look now at Year 30. Your year-end balance is $555,902, of which accumulated contributions account for $165,000 and accumulated interest $390,902 (70.3%). Of that $390,902, $211,876 (or 2/3rds) is compound interest. Notice too that your $5,500 contribution was dwarfed by interest earnings of $36,367.

Finally, let's look at Year 40, at what we'll assume is the culmination of your scrimping and saving. Your continued patience and discipline have not gone unrewarded. In the ten years since we last looked, your account has more than doubled, growing from

$555,902 to a whopping $1,174,853. Of that, forty years of contributions account for just $220,000, or 18.7%. The other $954,853, or 81.3%, is interest, and most of that—$639,153 to be exact—is interest on interest.

****

Three questions remain to be answered. One, how much would you have in forty years if you saved your money in a regular brokerage account, where your earnings weren't growing tax-deferred? Where are you going to find $5,500 to save when you're already barely making it? Where in today's low interest rate environment can you find something safe that will return 7% a year?

Here's my answer to each of these questions.

Savings in a non-qualified account versus in an IRA (versus in a 401(k))

Table 5.5 below summarizes, in five-year increments, the growth of $5,500 invested every year in a non-qualified brokerage account and compares the results to the IRA numbers we just looked at in Table 5.4, as well as to what you'd have in a 401(k) where your employer matched your $5,500 elective deferral with a 50¢ on the dollar match, raising your total yearly contribution to $8,250.

Table 5.5 ~ Growth of $5,500 Invested Every Year Compounded at 7%: Non-qualified vs IRA vs 401(k) w/ Match

Yr	Non-Qualified	Trad or Roth IRA	401(k) w/ Match
5	$32,147	$33,843	$50,765
10	$73,666	$81,310	$121,965
15	$127,289	$147,884	$221,826
20	$196,547	$241,258	$361,888
25	$285,997	$372,221	$558,331
30	$401,524	$555,902	$833,853
35	$550,735	$813,524	$1,220,286
40	$743,447	$1,174,853	$1,762,279

The tax rate used for the non-qualified account is 25%. That may be too high for young people just starting out whose accounts and investment earnings are modest and too low for older people whose accounts and earnings in the fullness of time have grown large. As an average, it seems reasonable.

After spending a few minutes mulling the differences in the three account balances, you will understand why I said at the outset that anyone who can and doesn't exploit the opportunity of investing in an IRA, 401(k) or the like to the fullest of his ability should have his head examined.

Where to find that $5,500

Chances are you don't eat a Whataburger Meal every day and have a two-pack-a-day cigarette habit that you're wasting $5,500 a year on. Chances are, however, that you're spending that much and more on other things you could do without. If you cannot think what, I suggest you go back and read the chapter on Budgeting, and then do a budget in the way I lay out there, analyzing your spending between what is necessary and what is unnecessary. I feel pretty sure that if you do this, you'll find at least $5,500 in annual unnecessary spending that you could be saving.

I would also add that there is general agreement among financial planners that people in the asset accumulation stage of their lives should be saving at least 10% of their income. If you're not, consider the possibility that you're living beyond your means.

What you can safely invest in that pays 7%

The very short answer to this question is: nothing. There is not now, nor has there ever been, anything safe that you could invest in year after year that would *guarantee* you a 7% return. The 7% is a purely hypothetical number.

It isn't entirely without basis, though. It's a number that is commonly used in illustrations of this nature. I think of it as the return you might have on a balanced portfolio of 60% equities and 40% bonds, where the *compounded average annual return* on equities has been on the order of 10% for the past forty years and that on a big bond fund, like the *Pimco Total Return Bond Fund*, maybe half of that over the past 10 years.[18] That would actually work out to around 8%. Never mind, though—7% is a safer number.

[18] This is not a plug for the PIMCO Total Return Fund. It's just that PTTAX is a large, well-known bond fund that's been around for a good while. As reported today (2/22/2016) on PIMCO's website (http://www.pimco.com) , the fund's 10-year average annual return as of 1/31/2016 was 5.4%.

As to whether it makes any difference whether your account compounds at a steady 7% year after year or it compounds at an average of 7% a year, it doesn't. A steady 7% is much easier on the nerves is all.

****

It is always a good idea, if you can, to spend less than you take in and to invest the surplus. However, if you're going to make compounding work its magic, you must start early. If you wait till you're twenty years away from retirement to accumulate that same $1,174,853 that you'd have after investing $5,500 a year for forty years, your task becomes formidable, to say the least. Remember that all you can invest in an IRA is $5,500 a year, at least until age 50, and that doing that resulted in a balance after twenty years of just $241,258. That leaves $933,595 to be made up by investing in a non-qualified brokerage account, where earnings are taxed. Assuming the same 7% average return and a 25% tax rate, you would have to invest $26,125 *every year* to accumulate that much money. And do not forget, that would be in addition to the $5,500 you put in your IRA.

Will you really need a million dollar nest egg to enjoy a comfortable retirement? No, you likely will need more. A million dollars is what someone like you might need today to maintain a comfortable standard of living. In twenty, thirty, or forty years, thanks to inflation, it will be more—a lot more.

But if you're young, inflation isn't what you need to worry about so much, because your earnings and the contribution limits to IRAs and the like should keep up. What you need to worry about, I think, is the possibility that Social Security won't be there for you as it has been for your parents, grandparents and great-grandparents. This is a whole other subject, but one that you should be following closely as someone vitally concerned.

SIX

Investing

About three years after retiring from Chiquita Brands, having by then concluded that retirement didn't pay worth a damn, I got a job with A.G. Edwards as a financial consultant, aka financial advisor, aka stock broker.

I must say that I never did anything professionally that I enjoyed more, not that I set the world on fire. I began this second career at age 60, and foolishly rejecting the tried-and-true methods of building a client base through cold calling, networking, and direct marketing, I decided—preposterously, I see now—to base my success squarely on being the most knowledgeable broker in our small town, a fact that I hoped would spread quickly by word of mouth. I set out immediately to obtain the Certified Financial Planner™ (CFP®) designation and to read every book on investing I could lay my hands on. But just after passing the CFP examination, I had an abdominal aortic aneurysm repair, which very nearly did me in, and after that my ambition deserted me. So did my patience. Two years later I decided that it was time I retired, and I did. The world is not the poorer for it, I'm sure.

Looking back, I realize that my strategy for success was flawed from the start. There may be a few very savvy people out there who can read the tea leaves, divine where the market is going, and position their clients accordingly, but I wasn't ever going to be in that league, and frankly I never knew anyone personally who was. That's not because brokers are dumb, though as in any profession some are; it's because the market is extraordinarily unpredictable. In my opinion, most successful brokers aren't successful because they're good at picking stocks or know (or even have a clue) whether the Dow will be up or down six months from now; they're successful because they're good salesmen and skilled at managing relationships.

A big chunk of what your broker knows is presented in this chapter. You may still need him or her, but reading this should help you to better understand what for.

****

Let's begin with *asset classes.* The three basic asset classes traditionally have been *stocks, bonds,* and *cash.* In recent years, *real estate* and *commodities* have also gained acceptance as asset classes that may belong in your portfolio. Many investment strategists say that we should all own a bit of gold or other precious metals as a hedge against inflation. Just as many strongly disagree.

Stocks

Issuing stock is one of three ways corporations have to raise capital for their various needs. Issuing bonds and borrowing from banks are the two other ways. We'll get to bonds next.

There are two types of stocks—*common stock* and *preferred stock.* I am not going to spend time on preferred stock, except to say that a) it entitles the holder to a fixed dividend and b) most of it is held by other corporations. Corporations are able to exempt much of their dividend income from taxes. Individuals cannot. Henceforth, when I talk about stock, I'm talking about common stock.

When you buy common stock, you acquire a fractional interest in the *ownership* of a corporation. That's why it's sometimes called *equity capital.* You could acquire your stock during the company's *initial public offering (IPO)***,** but it's far more likely that you'd buy it indirectly from someone else in the *secondary market*, on a *public stock exchange*, like the *New York Stock Exchange (NYSE)* or *NASDAQ*, through a brokerage firm. If the company is profitable, you may receive a *dividend*, which is a distribution of earnings, and over time see the stock go up in value. Some companies, though, don't pay a dividend, and if earnings disappoint, the stock will probably perform poorly. You buy a stock hoping that its value will go up. You can never be sure that it will. Indeed, you can be sure that sometimes it won't. Your *total return* on a stock is the dividend you receive on some periodic basis (like once a quarter) plus the *appreciation* (you hope) in its market value. Total return is usually expressed as a percentage of the stock's market value at the start of the holding period. If, for example, you buy 100 shares of AT&T today at $31.75/share and, after receiving four 47¢ dividend payments, sell your shares a year later for $38.23, your total return will be 15.41%—5.41% from dividends and 10% from the *capital gain* you realized. Doing an internet search today (at www.moneychimp.com), I learned that the *S&P 500's* average annualized total return, from January 1, 1970, through December 31, 2015, was 10.28%. (The S&P 500 is an index that serves as a proxy for large company stocks.)

You have to be careful when thinking about stock market returns that you don't expect something around 10% every year. The average for the past forty-five years may be on that order, but when you look at the yearly numbers, they're all over the place, up 21% one year, down 9% the next. On average, about one out of every 5 years has been a down year. What's very interesting, though, is that the risk of losing money is attenuated the longer you're in the market. If you look at rolling five-year periods since 1970—e.g., 1970-1974, 1971-1975, 1972-1976, and so on—you'll see that negative returns are fairly rare. Look at rolling ten-year periods, and they are rarer still. Look at rolling fifteen-year periods, and there are none; all are profitable. The moral here is that stocks should be a long-term investment. Ten years at least.

Stocks can be sliced and diced all kinds of ways. Investment professionals talk about *domestic stocks* and *foreign stocks*, distinguishing in the case of the latter between *developed markets* and *emerging markets*. They talk about *large cap, mid cap,* and *small cap stocks*. And they talk about *growth stocks and value stocks*. I'll get into this in a bit when we get to the all-important subject of asset allocation.

For the moment, the only other thing I want to say here before moving on to bonds is that there are a number of ways you can own stocks. You can own them as individual securities, where, for example, you own 100 shares of Microsoft; you can own them through *mutual funds*, like the *American Growth Fund*; and you can own them through *exchange traded funds*, so called *ETFs*, like the *i-Shares S&P 500*. I'll discuss these options when we get to the subject of diversification.

Bonds

Bonds are generally thought to be less risky than stocks, but that's not because they're easier to understand. They can involve a little math, some of it complicated.

When you buy a bond, you get a piece of paper issued by a corporation (or bank or some government entity) acknowledging that it owes you a sum of money, almost always some multiple of a thousand dollars, which it promises to repay, together with *interest*, at some specified date in the future, known as the *maturity* date.[1] Think of interest as rent on the use of your money. If you buy a bond at *par* (i.e., face value) on the day that it's issued and hold it to maturity, your *yield* (return) will be exactly equal to the bond's *coupon* interest rate.[2] If the par value is $10,000 and the coupon 5%, you will receive $500 in interest every year.

Most bonds pay interest *twice a year*. In my example above, your $500 would probably be paid to you in two semi-annual payments of $250 each. Exceptions to this general rule include *T-bills, zero coupon bonds,* and *strips*. A T-bill is a bond issued by the U.S. Treasury maturing in a year or less and having no coupon; a zero-coupon bond is like a T-bill in that it has no coupon, but its issuer isn't the Treasury and its maturity is longer than a year; and a strip is a coupon bond whose coupons have been stripped off to be sold separately. None pays semi-annual interest. Instead all are sold at discount to face value, such that the interest you earn is the difference between what you paid for the bond and what you receive when it matures. If you paid $950 for a bond that will pay you

[1] Actually, you won't normally get a piece of paper and the bond won't be in your name; it will be in *street name.* More on this later.

[2] Bonds used to have cupons attached to them that the bondholder would clip off and send to the issuer to claim his semi-annual interest payment. The sum of those cupons (i.e., interest payments) divided by the amount at which the bond would be redeemed at maturity was the cupon rate.

$1,000 when it is redeemed in one year, your *yield to maturity* will be 5.263% ($1,000 - $950 = $50; $50 ÷ $950 = 5.263%).

Depending on prevailing interest rates, bonds that mature more than one year into the future can be priced above or below the bonds' par value. Those that trade above par value are referred to as *premium bonds* and those below as *discount bonds*. The premium or discount affects the yield to maturity, lowering it (vis-à-vis the coupon rate) in the case of a premium bond and increasing it in the case of a discount bond.

There are a number of ways of measuring yield. There is *current yield, yield to maturity,* and *yield to call.* Current yield is the return you get by dividing the interest the bond pays annually by its current price. If you buy a $10,000 face value bond paying $600 a year in interest for $9,500, your current yield will be 6.316% ($600 ÷ $9,500), which, needless to say, is higher than the coupon rate of 6% ($600 ÷ $10,000). Yield to maturity differs from current yield by taking into account two other factors, namely the price at which the bond will be redeemed at maturity and the time remaining to maturity. That may not sound like much, but it complicates the dickens out of the math. It complicates it to such an extent that the only practicable way of figuring a bond's yield to maturity is by using a programmable calculator or computer program. Fortunately, your broker has instant access to this number and, for that matter, any of the other yields. In comparing bonds with similar maturities and of the same credit quality, the yardstick you want to use is yield to maturity (YTM). All other things being equal, you want the one with the highest YTM. But before buying that bond, ask if it's *callable*. This refers to a provision in some bonds that allows the issuer to redeem them (i.e., return your principal) before the bonds mature. A company or municipality may exercise its right to call a bond if market interest rates have gone down significantly, allowing the issuer to replace that bond with a new bond issue paying a lower rate. A bond's *yield to call* can be significantly lower than its yield to maturity, enough so that you might decide to opt for a bond whose YTM is slightly lower because it's not callable.

Generally speaking, the longer a bond has till maturity, the higher its yield. This is because the future is uncertain. If you can't be absolutely certain that a bond issuer will still be in business in two years, how much more uncertain must you be that it will be around in ten years, or in twenty-five? To be induced to take on the increasing uncertainty of a longer maturity, you will require a higher rate of interest. When you hear people talk about *yield curves*, this is what they're referring to.

Credit quality is a major consideration when buying bonds. This refers to the issuer's ability to pay interest and principal when due. There are three main independent rating agencies that assign credit ratings—*Standard & Poor's (S&P), Moody's Investor Service,* and *Fitch Ratings*. Their top four ratings (essentially AAA, AA, A, BBB) are assigned in descending order to *investment grade* paper—i.e., bonds suitable for investment by banks—and their bottom five (BB, B, CCC, CC, C) to speculative grade. Stay away from any individual bond that's not investment grade.

The safest bonds are issued by the U.S. government. These are called *Treasuries.* Treasuries are issued for terms ranging from 4 weeks to thirty (30) years. Anything with a maturity under one (1) year is, as you would expect, called a *Treasury bill* (*T-bill* for short). Presently, T-bills come with maturities of 4 weeks, 13 weeks, 26 weeks, and 52 weeks. Beyond 52 weeks, the maturities on Treasuries jump to 2 years, then to 3, then to 5, then to 7, then to 10, and finally to 30. The 2, 3, 5, 7, and 10-year paper are called *Treasury notes*, while the 30-year paper is called a *Treasury bond.* T-bills are issued in very large denominations ($10,000 to $1,000,000), whereas notes and bonds are normally issued in $1,000 denominations and multiples thereof. However, the latter can also be purchased at auction directly from the U.S. Treasury with as little as $100. You'd do this online at www.treasurydirect.gov.

There is a huge market in Treasuries. Corporations, banks, pension funds, foreign central banks, and individuals all own Treasuries. They're popular because the holder of a Treasury doesn't have to worry about default. Even if the government owes trillions, running astronomical deficits year after year, it will never run out of money because if push comes to shove it can print the stuff. Because they're considered risk-free, the yield on a Treasury is always lower than that on a triple-A rated corporate bond with the same maturity.

States, counties, cities, and publicly-owned entities, like regional hospitals and airports, also raise money for public works by issuing bonds. These are called *municipal bonds*, or *munis* for short. Munis are usually issued in $5 thousand increments. People in high tax brackets are attracted to them because the semi-annual interest paid on munis is usually exempt from Federal income taxes and state income taxes as well where the issuer is in-state. As I write this, the municipal bond market is still being roiled by a number of factors, resulting in nominal yields comparable to or better than what you can get on Treasuries with similar maturities. For someone in the 33% tax bracket who is deliberating between buying a ten-year Treasury and a ten-year, triple-A rated muni, both paying 2.25%, the smarter choice is obvious. His after-tax yield on the Treasury would only be about 1.5% (2.5% × (1 – .33)), while on the muni it would still be 2.25%.

The safest municipal bonds are *general obligation* (*GO*) bonds, which are backed by the full faith and credit of a taxing authority. School bonds are GO bonds—the money to make the semi-annual interest payments and to repay the principal when the bonds mature comes from school taxes. *Revenue bonds*, on the other hand, depend on the income generated by the issuing entities—a regional hospital or airport, for example—to meet their interest and principal repayment obligations. There are other types of munis besides GO and revenue bonds, and it's important when shopping for munis to understand what you're looking at. I said munis are "usually" tax-exempt. *Private activity* munis, issued to finance projects benefiting private parties, like sports stadiums, often are not. You need to know, of course, the muni's credit rating and whether it owes its triple-A rating (the highest rating) to the fact that it's *insured.* Some of the bond insurers may not really deserve the AAA rating they confer on the paper they're insuring. You also need to know if the bond is subject to the *alternative minimum tax (AMT).* If it is, its interest could be taxable to you, which would likely defeat your purpose in buying the bond in the first place.

Government-sponsored entities (GSEs), like *Fannie Mae* and *Freddie Mac,* also issue bonds, known in the investment business as *agency bonds*, which carry a triple-A rating due to the implied backing of the Federal government. The GSEs are chartered by the government to promote home ownership, which they do by providing mortgage lenders with liquidity. It used to be, before the GSEs, that banks kept the home loans they made on their books and made their money on the difference between the interest they earned on those loans and the little bit of interest they paid on the deposits that provided the wherewithal to make the loans. The problem with this arrangement, from the standpoint of expanding home ownership, is that the banks are constrained by their deposits and reserve requirements in making additional loans. Fannie and Freddie solve this problem by buying the loans from the mortgage lenders, enabling them with the funds thus obtained to make new loans.[3] For their part, Fannie and Freddie "bundle" the loans they buy into what are called *mortgage-backed securities* for sale to mostly institutional investors, and with the monies from these sales, they buy more mortgages. It's a cycle that in theory can go on endlessly. I mention agency bonds and mortgage-backed securities only because they made sensational headlines back in 2008 when, as a result of the housing market crash, their market value plummeted, which in turn threatened the stability of our financial system because so many big banks and hedge funds had bought huge amounts of them using short-term borrowings.

Bonds issued by corporations, which are called *corporates*, are normally issued in $5,000 denominations and increments thereof. Some corporates are secured against default by a mortgage on property, the way home loans are; others are not. Those that aren't secured are referred to as *debentures*. All other things being equal, a secured bond is obviously safer than an unsecured one. Again, corporate bonds rated BBB to AAA are considered investment grade. Anything below BBB is considered speculative, aka *junk*. Do not buy *individual* junk bonds.[4] The risk of default on junk bonds is too high.

Certificates of deposit (CDs), which are issued by banks, are very similar to bonds. They are popular because they are insured by the *Federal Deposit Insurance Corporation (FDIC)* for up to $250,000 ($500,000 if in a joint account).

As I said at the outset, bonds are generally thought to be safer than stocks for several reasons. One is that provided the issuer doesn't default and you hold your bond till maturity, your return is certain and you get your principal back.[5] Stocks don't come with such a promise. Second, in the event of bankruptcy liquidation, bondholders will get paid off before stockholders get anything.

---

[3] Banks now make their money on home loans from mortgage origination fees, loan servicing fees and the like.

[4] This is not to say that you shouldn't have any of your money in a mutual fund or ETF that owns junk bonds. Such funds are euphemistically referred to as *high yield* bond funds. They wring a lot of the risk out of their portfolios by careful security selection and avoiding over-exposure to any one issuer.

[5] Actually, what you get is the bond's face value, which would be less than what you paid for it if you had purchased it at a premium to face value, and more if you had purchased it at a discount.

This is not to say that bonds don't carry some risks. Besides credit risk, which we've already discussed, there is what is called *interest rate risk.* That is the risk that interest rates will rise, making your bond less valuable than when you bought it. If you bought a $10,000 bond paying 5% ($500/year) and a year later needed to sell it, you wouldn't get your $10,000 back if similar bonds—same credit rating, same maturity—were paying 6% ($600/year). The market value of your bond would be discounted to make its yield to maturity comparable to the six-percenter. By the same token, if interest rates fall, the value of your bond will go up. The longer the maturity on a bond, the more sensitive its market price is to changes in interest rates. If you hold your bond to maturity, the fluctuations in its value as market interest rates rise and fall are neither here nor there. That said, it will never put a smile on your face to see on your statement that the 10-year Treasury you paid $10,000 for is now valued at $9,750.

Bonds are also not as liquid and transparent as stocks. They do not trade on a public exchange all day long where you can see the *bid* and *ask* prices in real time.[6] Chances are that if you buy a bond you'll buy it second-hand, so to speak, from your brokerage firm's bond inventory, and if you sell one, it will be sold through your brokerage firm to a bond dealer. The brokerage firm will earn a commission on the sale, which will be imbedded in the price you pay or receive. Do not sell a bond without getting a bid on it first.

As with stocks, you can own bonds in the form of individual securities or through mutual funds and ETFs.

Cash

Cash includes the money you have in your pocket or under your mattress, plus the money you have in your checking account, plus whatever you have in money market accounts, whether at the bank or in your brokerage account.

There's not a lot to say about cash, other than a word or two about money market accounts. Money markets are mutual funds that are invested in very safe, short-term bonds or IOUs, like commercial paper and T-bills. These funds are designed to maintain

[6] The *bid* is the price at which a market specialist will purchase a particular stock; the *ask* is the price at which he will sell you that stock. The bid is always somewhat lower than the ask. The difference between the bid and the ask is called the *bid/ask spread*, or just the *spread.*

a $1 a share value, and their yield is pretty modest. Even so, it's at least better than what you'll get on any other kind of cash account. Most brokerage accounts are set to *sweep* any money from a security sale or redemption that isn't reinvested within 24 hours into a money market to earn something.

Real Estate

For the individual investor, a practical way of owning prime real estate is through *real estate investment trusts*, or *REITS*, as they're called. These are companies that own commercial property, like office buildings, shopping malls, and apartment buildings. Some own mortgages instead. Whatever they own, they are required to distribute 90% of their earnings to their shareholders. In return, they don't pay corporate income taxes like most public companies.

REITs are attractive for two reasons. One, the fact that they're required to pay out 90% of their net earnings means they may throw off a lot of dividend income. Two, they are the most liquid form of real estate ownership and the most trouble-free. If you've ever owned a rent house or a little office building, as we have, you know that selling them can take forever and dealing with tenants can be a pain in the neck.

Commodities

I'm not going to go into commodities in any depth for the very simple reasons that a) I know next to nothing on the subject and b) know no one who ever traded commodities regularly who came out ahead. That includes a close friend who parlayed a dream and a $26 thousand bet on coffee futures into $1.4 million. Emboldened by this success, he kept trading. Coffee, corn, soybeans, wheat, you name it. Sometimes he was lucky, sometimes he was not, but I'm doubtful that his successes and failures evened out. He might be better off had he stopped while he was ahead.

When I talk about commodities, I'm not even thinking about buying and selling commodity futures. I'm just talking about owning some *precious metals*, like gold, silver, platinum, and palladium. The reason for having these in your portfolio is to hedge against inflation and/or dollar devaluation.

You can own these metals three different ways. You can own gold and silver in the form of coins, like South African *Kruggerands* or Canadian *Maple Leafs*, or any of them as bullion; you can own any of the metals through an exchange-traded fund (ETF) that in turn holds the real deal in a bank vault somewhere; and you can own the companies that mine the metals. I prefer the ETFs. The problem with owning coins and bullion is storage. Where are you going to store your Maple Leafs or gold bars that is safe? The problem with owning mining companies is that many of the countries where they operate are politically unstable.

I would not allocate a very big portion of my portfolio to precious metals—certainly not more than 5%—no matter how concerned I was about the likelihood of runaway inflation or some act of terrorism. This is a very speculative asset class.

Asset Allocation

This is the thing you need to try to get right. According to some academic studies, 90% of investment performance is determined by *asset allocation. Security selection* and *market timing*, which we all tend to obsess over, are in the long run comparatively unimportant.

Asset allocation has to do with how you divide up your investment pie among the different asset classes just described. What percent of your total portfolio should be allocated to equities (stocks), what percent to bonds (fixed income), what percent to cash, what percent to real estate, and what percent, if any, to commodities, like precious metals?

The answer to these questions, at least theoretically, lies in finding that combination of asset classes that is likely, based on past performance, to provide the best overall return consistent with the individual's expressed *risk tolerance*. Risk tolerance refers to how much of a downswing in the value of his portfolio an investor can stomach before selling.

Brokers all have a little software program that will tell you, based on your answers to a series of questions dealing with your *investment objectives* (*income, capital appreciation, capital preservation*, etc.), *risk tolerance,* and *investment time horizon,*[7] what their firm believes is the appropriate asset allocation for your portfolio. You can find these asset allocators on the internet as well.

[7] Investment time horizon refers to the number of years an investor expects to hold an investment or portfolio.

As you grow older and have less time to recover from a severe market correction, your asset allocation should change, taking on a more conservative hue, which translates to less equities and more fixed income. More about this later.

The asset allocation pie chart in Figure 6.1 below is purely for illustration purposes.

Figure 6.1 ~ Asset Allocation Model

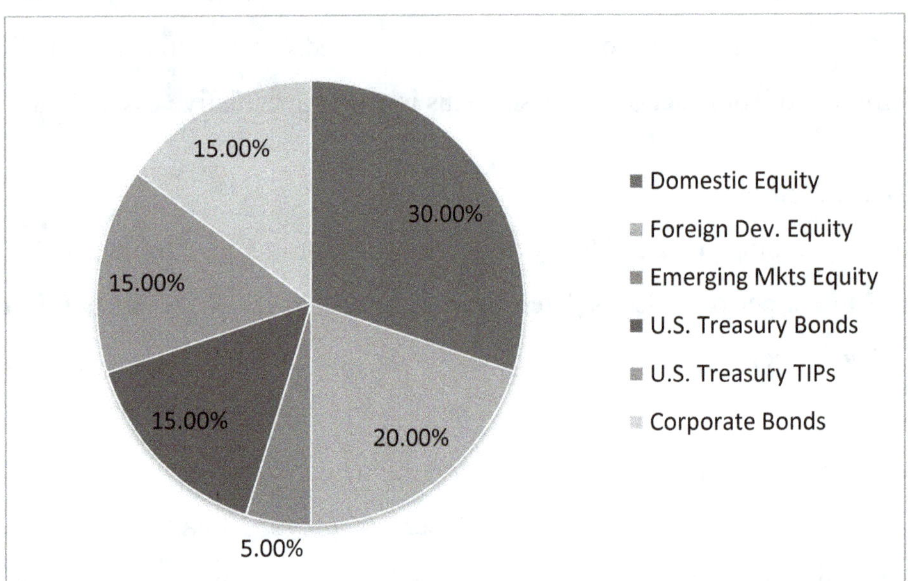

How equities are sliced and diced

As you study this pie chart, you may be asking yourself, "What are domestic equities, foreign developed equities, and emerging markets equities?" A *domestic equity* refers to stock in a company domiciled in the U.S. A *foreign equity* refers to one domiciled outside the U.S. Some of these foreign countries have very developed industrialized economies, while others are just emerging from economic backwardness—hence the terms *foreign developed markets equities* and *emerging markets equities*. Australia, Japan, South Korea, and the Western European countries are all foreign developed markets. Brazil, Russia, India, China (collectively dubbed the "BRIC" countries), the rest of Latin America, much of Asia, Eastern Europe, and all of Africa are emerging markets. Obviously some are more economically developed than others.

Any really well-balanced portfolio of equities will include domestic stocks and foreign developed markets stocks, plus some emerging markets stocks. That's because markets everywhere do not go up and down in tandem and/or to the same degree. The more *uncorrelated* markets are—that is to say, the less they move in tandem—the better the *diversification.* By having some stocks that zig when others stocks zag, you reduce the risk of your portfolio having a disastrous year. As markets around the globe become more integrated, however, they are also becoming more correlated.

On some asset allocation models, you will see the domestic equity piece further divided into slivers that say, *large-cap, mid-cap,* and *small-cap*. "Cap" here is short for *market capitalization.* Market capitalization is simply the product of multiplying a stock's market value by the total number of publicly traded shares outstanding. Presently, small-cap stocks are defined as having a market capitalization of under $2 billion, mid-cap stocks between $2 billion and $10 billion, and large-cap stocks over $10 billion. The people who decide where to draw these lines have their reasons I'm sure, but what those might be I can't imagine. Two billion doesn't sound small, and ten billion doesn't even begin to capture the size of some of these behemoths. Take Apple Inc. (AAPL). As I write this, Apple has a market capitalization of nearly $536 billion!

In any case, size is important to the extent that large-cap stocks tend not to have as many bad years as small- and mid-cap stocks, but paradoxically over time do not, on average, appreciate as much. If you're young and have a long investment time horizon, you might want to over-weight small-cap stocks. Just be prepared, if you do, for dramatic ups and downs in their performance. For the same reason, if you're not so young, you should probably go light on them.

You'll also hear stocks referred to as *growth* stocks or *value* stocks. *Growth* stocks are called that because they're experiencing very rapid growth. They tend to be expensive as measured by their *price/earnings (P/E) ratios***.** (A company's P/E is calculated by dividing the price of its stock by its *earnings per share*.) Classic examples of growth stocks would be the rapidly expanding information technology companies of the 1980s and 1990s, like Microsoft, Apple, Cisco, and Oracle. *Value* is a more subjective term. Some analyst will say that Company XYZ is a value stock because he believes it's under-priced relative to its good fundamentals. That is clearly not a consensus opinion or the stock would be trading higher. As you would expect, value stocks tend to have low P/Es.

Growth versus value is a big deal in some people's minds. Not in mine. From what I know, neither style has been shown to outperform the other over long periods. Suffice it to say, some money managers specialize in identifying stocks with great growth prospects and get good at that art; other money managers specialize in looking for stocks that are under-valued and get good at that.

Diversification

Diversification is all about having your eggs in more than one basket.

You want not only to be diversified across asset classes, which is what asset allocation is all about, but you need to be diversified within asset classes. If you invest in an index fund that tracks the S&P 500, you know to expect the market to have good years and bad but over time to reward you, probably pretty handsomely. If, however, you buy just one stock, you not only have the risk that your stock will follow the market down in any general downdraft, you have a multitude of other risks besides. The company could be threatened by some new technology; it could become the subject of some investigation; its products could be pulled from store shelves because of some safety issue; it could lose money; its CEO could unexpectedly die; it could go broke. Any of these and an endless number of other not improbable eventualities could cause the stock to plummet. The same goes for investing in sectors. Just ask the folks who put all their eggs into the technology sector back in the late 90's.

For your equity portfolio to be diversified enough to eliminate all but *market risk*, you need to own at least thirty individual securities spread across most *sectors* – consumer staples, consumer discretionary, financials, information technology, energy, etc. You can do this by buying individual stocks or by buying *mutual funds* or *exchange traded index funds (ETFs).* Since most mortals cannot pick winners, nor successfully time the market, we should forget about assembling our own stock portfolio. Our only sensible choices are to invest in mutual funds or ETFs or turn our investments over to a *registered investment advisor (RIA)* to manage.

You can also use mutual funds and ETFs to diversify your bond holdings. I do that, but I also own individual bonds that I bought when I thought they were attractive. I've tried to *ladder* the maturities on these, so that I've got more or less the same amount maturing every couple of years out to about fifteen (15) years. I also avoid being overly exposed to any one issuer's paper.

Mutual funds and ETFs

What's a mutual fund and what's an ETF?

Without putting too fine a point on it, a *mutual fund* is an investment company that owns a large portfolio of stocks or bonds or both selected to achieve some stated objective, like long-term capital appreciation. By buying into a mutual fund, you acquire an undivided interest in all the securities the fund owns. The fund may focus on large-cap U.S. growth stocks, or small-cap emerging markets stocks, or high-yield (junk) bonds, or whatever.

Mutual funds come in two flavors—as *open-end* funds and *closed-end* funds. The key difference between the two is that an open-end fund will keep taking in new investors, putting new money to work by adding to its portfolio of securities, whereas a closed-end fund issues a certain number of shares and that's it. If you didn't get in on the fund's IPO and you want to own it, you'll have to buy your shares from somebody else on the stock exchange. Closed-end funds trade just like any other kind of stock, and the price at which they trade can be more or less than the market value of the securities they own. When you buy or sell shares in an open-end fund, you're dealing directly with the fund itself, and what you pay or what you receive is a function of the *net asset value (NAV)* per share of the underlying portfolio of securities.

Some open-end funds charge a sales charge, or *load*, when you buy them, and others do not. The latter are referred to as *no-load* funds. The sales charge on a load fund can be quite hefty, depending on how much you're investing. For an investment of up to $25,000 in an equity fund, the load might be 5.75%, stepping down from there and disappearing altogether with an investment of $1 million. In a bond fund, the load might start at around 3%. There's no evidence that load funds outperform no-loads, but be warned: full-service brokerage firms do not sell no-loads.

All open-end mutual funds[8] have *operating expenses*, which the mutual fund investor never sees but have a negative impact on his fund's performance. These fees range from around 0.4% on an *index fund* to around 1.5% on an *actively managed* fund. An index fund is comparatively inexpensive to operate because, unlike an actively managed fund, it doesn't require a stable of MBAs doing securities analysis; an index fund simply owns whatever securities are in the index it is trying to mimic.

There is also little evidence that all that securities analysis with its attendant expense ultimately buys you anything. In any given year, roughly 75% of actively-managed equity mutual funds under-perform the market. That's not because the guys who run these funds aren't smart—they're very smart. It's because they and other professionals—the hedge fund managers, pension fund managers, and the traders who work on the big banks' proprietary trading desks—dominate trading and they're competing against each other. Half, perforce, will do better than the market (the average) and half worse. And from the above-par performance of the half who did better, you have to deduct expenses and fees. When you do that, only a quarter of the funds still outperform. Those that outperform over extended periods are fewer still. So, more and more, people are asking why bother with actively managed mutual funds. Just buy the market using index funds or index ETFs.

Which brings us to ETFs. An ETF is an *exchange traded fund*, of course. The overwhelming majority of ETFs track some index (e.g., the *S&P 500*; the *MSCI Europe, Australasia & Far East;* the *MSCI Emerging Markets Free*). They've been around for a comparatively short time and have a more complex structure than mutual funds. They also have a number of virtues vis-à-vis mutual funds. When you buy or sell an open-end mutual fund, you don't get priced till the end of the day. ETFs trade just like stocks, so you get priced then and there (as you would with a closed-end fund). Also, because of the way they're structured, ETFs are more tax-efficient and may have somewhat lower operating expenses than index mutual funds. For all of these reasons, ETFs are my preferred way of holding stocks in a brokerage account.

---

[8] Closed-end funds have operating expenses as well, though their fees tend to be lower than the open-end funds' fees.

The building blocks of a stock portfolio consisting of ETFs would be those that track either the *S&P 500* (large-cap U.S. stocks) or the *Wilshire 5000* (the total U.S. stock market, including large-cap, mid-cap and small-cap stocks), plus the *MSCI EAFE* (Europe, Australasia & Far East foreign developed markets), and the *MSCI EMF* (foreign Emerging Markets Free).

Taxation of investment income

As we've seen, investment income consists of dividends, which are a distribution of corporate earnings to shareholders; interest, which is rent on the use of your money; and capital gains, which is the profit you have when you sell a security for more than you paid for it. (If you sell it for less, you have a capital loss.)

Most dividends paid by U.S. corporations are what are called *qualified dividends*, meaning "qualified" to receive the same preferential tax treatment under current federal tax law[9] that is accorded to *long-term capital gains*. A long-term capital gain (or loss) is distinguished from a *short-term capital gain* (or loss) by how long the security sold had been held. If the holding period was a year or longer, the gain (or loss) on the sale is considered long-term for tax purposes. If the holding period was less than a year, the gain (or loss) is short-term.

There is nothing exceptional about the tax treatment accorded to interest (provided it's not tax-exempt municipal bond interest), non-qualified dividends and short-term capital gains. All get taxed at *ordinary rates*, the same as salary and wages.

Tax-exempt interest and qualified dividends and long-term capital gains are a different story. Tax-exempt interest, as you might expect, is excluded from *taxable income* altogether. Qualified dividends and long-term capital gains *are* included in *taxable income* but taxed preferentially. Rates of 0%, 15%, or 20% apply to both, which rate depending on the individual taxpayer's marginal tax rate. It's 0% for the taxpayer whose marginal rate is either 10% or 15%; it's 15% for the taxpayer whose marginal rate is between 25% and 35%; and it's 20% for the taxpayer whose marginal rate is 39.6%,

[9] State tax laws are beyond the scope of this discussion.

which is the top rate. Your marginal tax rate here is the rate at which an additional dollar of income would be taxed to you.[10]

Capital losses can be used to offset capital gains. If the net result is a loss, the taxpayer may deduct up to $3,000 of such loss from his taxable income that year. Anything in excess of $3,000 may be *carried forward* to offset gains in future years, with anything left over, up to $3,000 a year, used to reduce ordinary income.

Because stocks are overwhelmingly in the hands of the well to do, the special tax treatment given to qualified dividends and long-term capital gains leads some people to complain that our tax code favors the rich. Defenders of the special treatment justify it on the grounds that it incentivizes people to invest in business, which is the wellspring of our prosperity.

IRAs and Qualified Accounts

The discussion above on taxes is only relevant to your garden variety brokerage account, savings accounts, and such. Taxes on earnings are a non-issue as regards *individual retirement accounts (IRAs)* and *qualified* employer-sponsored retirement plan accounts like *401(k)s, 403(b)s* and *457s*. The money that goes into these accounts, as well as the earnings on the investments made in them, aren't taxed until money comes out.[11] Then whatever the individual withdraws, for whatever reason, is subject to taxation at ordinary rates.

Annuities

Annuities are insurance products sold by insurance companies. That said, they are often sold through financial advisors at brokerage firms. The basic idea with an annuity is that you trade a sum of money for an income stream, like a pension. The simplest annuities are the *immediate annuities*, where, in effect, you say to the insurance company something like, "I'm a female, age 67. What will a $1,000 a month income stream for life

---

[10] If this is a bit confusing, remember that our tax rates are progressive. That is to say that they step up as income rises. Up to a certain level of income, you pay no taxes, but on any income above that level up to some second level you pay 10%, and on any excess above this second level up to a third level, you pay 15%. This stair-stepping goes on till you reach a certain income threshold, which presently is $250,000 in the case of married couples filing jointly, at which point the tax rate maxes out at 39.6%.

[11] When it comes to taxes, there is always an exception. Roth IRA and 401Roth (k) contributions go in after-tax and come out tax free, as explained in Chapter 5.

cost me?" Or you ask, "I've got an extra $100,000 sitting around, but I need more income; what kind of monthly income stream will $100,000 buy me?" If you agree to the company's terms, they take your money and you get the income.

A *variable annuity (VA)* is quite a different product. With a variable annuity, the money you invest goes into mutual funds (*separate accounts* in variable annuity parlance) where it grows tax-deferred, just as it would in an IRA. After a certain number of years, you can annuitize if you wish. It used to be, and maybe still is the case, that most people who owned variable annuities never did annuitize. They just liked the tax-deferred growth and the protection from creditors that variable annuities provide.

Nowadays, there's renewed interest in annuities because of their ability to do what no other investment can do, which is to provide a person with income that he can't outlive. If you're like a lot of retirees whose savings suffered huge losses in 2008, and now owing to ultra-low interest rates, you find yourself unable to earn enough on safe fixed income investments to make ends meet, you may wish to talk to a financial consultant about an annuity. He'll be happy to explain his best VA products to you. That's because the commissions on them are big. And because they're big, you will get hit with a large back-end sales charge if you buy a variable annuity, and then repenting of your decision, decide to get out of it.

Understand, too, that variable annuities can be very complex and hard to understand. Many offer riders that you can buy to enhance their product and differentiate it from other VAs, but conditions always apply. I never was comfortable selling VA's, given the potential for misunderstanding.

If you annuitize, a portion of your annual income stream will be treated as a return of principal, which is non-taxable, and a portion as taxable income.

Options

Options are a form of *derivative*, in fact the most common one. A derivative is simply a security that derives its value from the value of some other security.

A *call option* gives the owner the right to buy a security, usually a stock, at some specified price, called the *strike price*, on or before some specified future date. A *put option* gives the owner the right to sell a security, usually a stock, at some specified price, again called the strike price, on or before some specified future date. You can buy or sell either kind of option.

Options are beyond the scope of this book. I have touched on them here only because you've heard of them, I'm sure, and may wonder what they are. I don't do options now for the very simple reasons that we don't own many individual stocks[12] and I'm too lazy to fool with them anymore.

Brokerages Firms versus Investment Advisors

Keeping things simple, there are three approaches to investing. There's the do-it-yourself approach, where you open an account with an online discount brokerage firm, like *Scottrade* or *Charles Schwab*, and based on your own research decide what to invest in. The second approach is to open an account at a full-service brokerage firm, like *Morgan Stanley* or *Wells Fargo Advisors*, where you work with a *financial advisor* who can help you develop an investment plan and implement it. The third approach is to turn your money over to an independent *registered investment advisor*, like *Fisher Investments*, to manage for you.

Unless you know what you're doing by either having worked in the investment business or done extensive reading, I'd be reluctant to recommend you take the do-it-yourself approach. I would be afraid that what you would save on commissions you would more than lose in under-performance as a result of poor asset allocation and exiting the market every time it corrects. I say this in spite of the fact that most of the online brokers have tools you can use to help with asset allocation and other planning issues. I just question whether many people actually use them.

Most investors, conscious of their lack of expertise, work with a *financial advisor*, aka *broker*, at a full-service brokerage firm. He has the expertise and the tools and resources needed to help his clients with all aspects of financial planning. He can tell you, based on your investment objectives, time horizon, and tolerance for risk, what's a suitable asset allocation model for you. He can tell you, based on your age and the

[12] The only kind of options I ever did was sell *covered calls*, where my downside risk was limited to losing out on the gain if a stock I owned and on which I had written an option rose above the strike price and was called away. I would never sell a *naked call*, where I didn't own the stock on which I was selling a call option. My loss potential in that case would be unlimited.

expected return on your asset allocation mix, what you'll need to invest on some periodic basis to meet your various financial objectives—for example, retiring at 67 with a nest egg big enough that you can tap it every year till you're 100 for the inflation-adjusted equivalent of, say, $50,000 today. He can also run Monte Carlo simulations that attempt to tell you how likely that plan is to be successful. All that help with planning is a great bargain, seeing as how it's free. What is not a bargain is the help with implementation. That's because implementing an investment plan necessarily involves buying and selling securities, and the commissions you'll pay on broker-assisted trades at a full-service brokerage firm are many multiples of the commissions you'll pay if you trade through one of the online discount brokers. The other thing you need to be aware of is that your broker doesn't earn a salary. His income is more often than not 100% commission-based. That can lead to an unscrupulous broker *churning* your account, where he gets you to trade a lot in the belief that you can achieve above-average returns if you're nimble and know which stocks are poised to take off and which have peaked or are headed down.

If you have financial assets in excess of, say, $500,000 but don't feel up to making any investment decisions, you might want to consider delegating that responsibility to an *investment advisor*. He's different from a *financial advisor*, which I've been referring to as a broker. The investment advisor who's managing money has carte blanche to buy and sell securities in his clients' accounts any time he sees fit. A broker does not. Before he can do a trade, a broker must have the client's approval. But because the investment advisor can act on his own, he's held to a higher standard than the broker in terms of acting in the client's best interests. He's also compensated differently. A broker's earnings are mostly *commission-based;* an investment advisor's are *fee-based.* Typically that fee is somewhere between 1% to 1 ½% annually on *assets under management (AUM).* The only investment advisory firm I have had any dealings with charges me 1 ¼%, which it collects in quarterly installments. It earns no commissions on the trades it makes. Another large unaffiliated financial services company has custody of clients' accounts and handles trade executions. Its commissions are on the order of $15 a trade, which is almost double what an online discount broker would charge, but much less than the $108 or so that you might expect to pay a full-service brokerage firm on the typical $5,000 buy or sell transaction.

An investment advisor's interests are said to be aligned with his clients' because to make more *off* them he's got to make more money *for* them. The investment advisor who charges one and a quarter percent (1 ¼%) for managing a $500,000 account is on track to earn an annual fee of $6,250. But if the account grows by, say, 10%, so will the advisor's income. In the same way, if the client's account value drops, so too will the advisor's income, and by the exact same percentage. This gives the investment advisor an incentive to do the best he can by his clients, including keeping their trading costs low.

****

I've come now to the end of my discussion of investing. I'd like to close by highlighting what I think is important to remember, including a few things that I've not yet talked about.

Even though, as I suggested at the outset, many brokers tend to be better salesmen than knowledgeable investment advisors, they have their uses. Just remember that they are commission agents whose livelihood depends on selling stuff to you, or for you, and that their commissions are outrageous compared to what the discount brokers charge. Remember, too, that they cannot pick stocks nearly as well as they might have you believe, and they definitely cannot time the market.[13]

So what are they useful for? First and foremost, they have tools. They have clever little software programs that, as I said earlier, will tell you, based on your responses to a series of questions, what their firm suggests is the appropriate asset allocation for your portfolio.[14]

As explained in Chapter 3 on Budgeting, they have tools, too, to tell you how much you need to be investing each month or every year to fund a child's college education. Just tell your advisor what university and when Junior will be matriculating. If you want to know how much you need to be investing every year to accumulate a certain amount by the time you retire, they can prepare a financial plan for you. If you want to

[13] That I know of, and in spite of all the market forecasters out there, no one has ever been able to consistently time the market's ups and downs.

[14] Although all the experts agree that there is no absolutely right answer to the question of what someone's asset allocation should be, you can be sure that these programs will do a far better job of suggesting how your portfolio should be positioned, given your investor profile, than anything you or your broker could come up with on your own.

know how likely it is that you won't outlive your retirement nest egg, they can run Monte Carlo simulations that will attempt to answer that. They've got lots of financial planning tools that can help you plan your future. And this help is free.

They can explain investment products to you and answer questions. Don't understand what is meant by *laddering bonds* or why you should have your securities held at your brokerage firm in *street name*, as opposed to having them registered in *your* name and keeping them in *your* possession?[15] Ask your broker. He can explain.

They can keep you from running afoul of the rules governing IRAs, which are hard for most people to keep straight in their heads. Because brokers deal with these all the time, they stay conversant on the subject. And if they don't have the answer to a question, they can call their back office and get it. If you are 70 ½ or older, they'll see to it that you don't fail to take your *required minimum distributions* in a timely manner.

Financial advisors are also useful if you want to buy or sell a bond. Indeed, I don't know how you'd go about doing either without a broker, although I'm sure you can. Just be sure when you buy a bond to ask lots of questions and, before selling one, to ask for a bid.

As you get older, begin to pull in your horns. Reduce your exposure to risk. This is particularly advisable if you're retired and must tap your investments to supplement your Social Security and other sources of income in order to make ends meet. The generally accepted approach to reducing portfolio risk is to allocate less to equities and more to fixed income. One school of thought has it that the percentage you have allocated to fixed income should approximate your age, meaning that if you're 60, approximately 60% of your portfolio should be in bonds, CDs, and the like. I don't have a problem with such a policy, except that thanks to the very low interest rate environment we've been in, which I don't see changing any time soon, it has become next to impossible to find high quality fixed income securities that provide a real return in excess of inflation.

Two fixed income products that are popular with people "reaching for yield" are *high-yield bond funds* and *leveraged closed-end bond funds*. I've said what I need to say about high-yield bond funds in the footnote on page 104. As for leveraged closed-end bonds funds, they boost (leverage) the yield on the securities they own by using debt.

[15] It facilitates selling them quickly if they are held at the firm in street name.

Typically, $1 out of every $3 invested by one of these funds comes from extremely short-term borrowings on which the fund pays a lower rate of interest than it earns on the bonds it owns, which are longer term. This works fine so long as the fund is able to roll over its debt when it comes due on favorable terms. But if its cost of borrowing goes up, the fund may run into trouble covering its dividend payments. If your broker suggests you consider putting some small portion of your portfolio in either a high-yield bond fund or a leveraged closed-end bond fund, or a bit in both, that's okay, but be sure to ask lots of questions and make sure before investing anything in a leveraged closed-end fund that there's no actual or foreseeable problem in its covering its dividend.[16]

Don't buy mutual funds through your brokerage firm as asset allocation pie filling. Full-service brokerage firms only sell load funds,[17] and in my opinion, they're not worth it. I say that in spite of owning a number of load funds that have served me well. Don't buy individual stocks either for your equity pieces of the pie. There's no way you can monitor the thirty-plus companies you'd have to own in order to be adequately diversified. My strong recommendation would be to use index ETFs instead. For the domestic equities slice, I would be inclined to use one that tracks the total U.S. stock market, like the Wilshire 5000 or the Dow Jones U.S. Total Market. For foreign developed market stocks, I'd use one that tracks the MSCI Europe, Australasia, and Far East (MSCI EAFE), and for emerging markets one that tracks the MSCI Emerging Markets Free.

Frankly, I would recommend that anyone looking to fill or add to any asset class—including bonds, REITs, and precious metals—do so using ETFs. Certainly for REITs and precious metals, and maybe for Treasuries. I have no problem with buying individual bonds, provided you buy investment-grade bonds, diversify across issuers, and ladder the maturities.

Many full service brokerages offer online trading, which can save you a lot on any stocks you buy, including ETFs (which trade like stocks). My brokerage firm will charge me $29.95 a trade, no matter how large, if I do my buying or selling online. If I

---

[16] Funds, whether open-end or closed-end, have shareholders, so they pay dividends, not interest.
[17] Except in special kinds of accounts.

place my trade through my broker, she'll charge me many times that. Not surprisingly, she has not made a lot of noise about the availability of the online facility.

If you already have an investment portfolio containing numerous individual stocks and mutual funds, what I've just written is no reason for you to jettison them. As I say, I own a number of load funds that I acquired when I was a broker and they have performed well. I'm just saying that going forward, if I need to add to what I have in some asset class, I'll use ETFs because they're a whole lot cheaper and will serve my purposes just as well.

Once you're squared away on what your asset allocation should be, at least for a while, and have all slices of the pie filled with something suitable, leave well enough alone. There's always the impulse to replace stuff that's not doing well for stuff that is. Yielding to this impulse is nearly always a mistake. Consider the results of a Dalbar[18] study several years back. It's instructive. Over the 30 years since 1994 that it had been tracking such data, Dalbar found that the average annualized return on the S&P 500 stock index was 11.1%, while for the average equity mutual fund investor it was only 3.7%.[19] The reason for the disparity was that people chased performance. They sold funds that had underperformed just before they started to outperform and bought funds that had outperformed just before they started to underperform. Don't make the same mistake. Buy index funds (or keep the funds you've got) and leave market timing and "The 10 Best Mutual Funds for the Coming Decade" to the gullible.

At least once a year, you need to visit with your broker to see if your portfolio needs rebalancing. The asset classes that have done well will need to be pared to bring their percentages back in line with what your asset allocation model says they should be, and the cash thus freed up invested in the asset classes whose relative underperformance has resulted in their percentages being below what they should be. This takes discipline.

If you're retired and need to pull money out of your portfolio to make ends meet, discuss your situation with your broker, but try to limit your withdrawals to 4% or less per year, with all or nearly all of that taken in the form of interest and dividends[20]. That's

---

[18] Dalbar is a well-known, highly respected Boston-based financial research firm.
[19] Zweig, Jason. "Just How Dumb Are Investors?" *US News, Breaking News and Headlines*, http://blogs.wsj.com/moneybeat, (May 9, 2014).
[20] The 4% rule is more fully discussed in Chapter 3 on Budgeting.

a rule of thumb aimed at ensuring that you don't outlive your money. In a low interest rate environment such as we're in now, take less than 4% if you can.

There will be stock market corrections; you can depend on it. Keep your head while all around you others are losing theirs. As I well know, this is very hard to do. Remember that that forty-five year average return of 10.28% on the S&P 500 includes nine years of negative returns. The market always recovers and then moves up. As long as we have a capitalist economy, that won't change.

SEVEN

Income Taxes

One of the things I seriously considered doing after retiring from Chiquita Brands was buying a Jackson Hewitt tax service franchise. To gauge whether this was going to be congenial work, I signed up for an H&R Block tax course that fall, hoping to go to work for them during the upcoming tax season. All went according to plan. I took the course, which was excellent, and starting early the following January, went to work for Block at their Ingram, Texas, location. It was all a great learning experience. Among other things, I learned that I did not want to do taxes for a living. I'd have a permanent case of indigestion.

In a rational world, we'd have something like a flat tax. The government's tax receipts would go up, and the estimated 6.1 billion man-hours that Americans spend collectively every year attempting to comply with the tax code could be put to more productive use.[1] But it's never going to happen. Think of all the CPAs and tax lawyers who'd have to find other work, all the people who'd lose their mortgage interest

[1] This number comes from National Taxpayer Advocate Nina Olson's annual report to Congress, as reported in *Forbes*, 1/5/2011.

deduction, all the people who'd have to pay something who presently don't pay anything. There'd be a revolution.

The good news is that even if the Commissioner of the Internal Revenue Service must hire someone to prepare his return, you probably can do yours yourself. Most returns are fairly simple. And even if yours is not simple but you have a personal computer, a modicum of patience, and some general understanding of the task at hand, a software package like *TurboTax*, *TaxACT* or *H&R Block* can take you through the process, step by step, with only a minimum amount of work and head-scratching on your part.

****

Form 1040 and Supporting Schedules

You do your taxes on *Form 1040~U.S. Individual Income Tax Return* or one of its two abbreviated forms—*Form 1040EZ* and *Form 1040A*. I am not going to go into the 1040EZ and 1040A, except to say that if you qualify to use one or the other, you should because they're a whole lot easier to understand and fill out than a regular 1040. The problem is qualifying. To use either form, your taxable income must be under $100,000, and you must take the *standard deduction* as opposed to *itemizing*. Restrictions also apply to the kinds of income being reported. To file a 1040EZ, which is the simpler of the two, your sources of income are pretty much limited to *salaries, wages and tips*, plus *taxable interest* not to exceed a certain amount (presently $1,500), and *unemployment compensation*. To file a 1040A, your income cannot include *tax refunds, alimony, business income, capital gains* from the sale of securities or property, *rents and royalties,* and *gambling winnings*. Also, only single taxpayers and married couples filing jointly who are under 65, not blind, and not claiming any dependents can use the EZ.

The unabbreviated Form 1040 is what I'm going to cover here. This is an uncomplicated looking two-page form with a slew of supporting schedules and forms, whose use or non-use depends on what kinds of income you have and what deductions and tax credits and other benefits you claim. A copy of Form 1040 for the 2015 tax year is included for ready reference at the end of this chapter. The other supporting schedules and forms that will be discussed in this chapter, together with their instructions, can be obtained by doing an internet search using the particular schedule or form as your search term.

To understand the process of doing your taxes, we're going to go through Form 1040, section by section, starting at the top of Page 1. You'll see when we're done that, on a macro level at least, the process is quite straightforward. The devil is in the details.

Label

The first section of Form 1040 is captioned *Label.* It calls for the taxpayer's name, address, and Social Security number. You need to be very careful with your Social Security number that you get it right.

Filing Status

Immediately matters get a bit more complicated: you have to select a *filing status.* Your choices here are the following:

- ***Single,*** meaning unmarried or legally separated at the end of the tax year.
- ***Head of household,*** meaning single and providing more than half the cost of maintaining a household that is the principal residence of an unmarried child or grandchild or any relative who can be claimed as a dependent.
- ***Married filing jointly*** (with your spouse).
- ***Married filing separately*** (from your spouse).
- ***Qualifying Widow(er),*** meaning someone whose spouse died sometime during the two preceding tax years, who hasn't remarried as of the close of the current tax year, and who has at least one child who can be claimed as a dependent. (The taxpayer whose spouse died during the current tax year may file a joint return—i.e., claim *married filing jointly* status.)

Filing status is a big deal because there is a standard deduction associated with each filing status that, subject to certain limitations, goes toward reducing your taxable income. More about this when we get to Page 2 and the section on *Tax and Credits*.

Exemptions

After selecting your filing status, you indicate how many *exemptions* you're claiming. A taxpayer can claim one (1) exemption for himself, one (1) for his spouse if filing a joint return, and one (1) each for every *dependent*. Thus, a married couple filing a joint return and having two dependent children can claim four (4) exemptions.

What an exemption does is exempt a certain amount of income from taxation. Presently (2015), that amount is $4,000. With four (4) exemptions, our couple above could reduce their taxable income by $16,000 ($4,000 × 4). They'd do this on Page 2 in the section on Tax and Credits, right after taking their standard deduction.[2]

Most people claimed as dependents are young children who are still living at home with mom and dad or, if they're not living at home, are away at college but still being supported by mom and dad. Occasionally there can be another relative, not a child, who can be claimed as well. Here are the rules:

To be claimed as your dependent, a *child* must meet four criteria:

- Be your natural born child, step child, adopted child, foster child, brother or sister, or a descendant of one of these.
- Live with you for more than half the year.
- Not have provided more than half of his or her own support during the year.
- Be under the age of 19 (or age 24, if a full-time student for more than five (5) months out of the year) or totally and permanently disabled.

For any other *relative*[3] to be claimed as your dependent, he or she must meet the following criteria:

- Not be a qualifying child of some other taxpayer.
- Have earned less than the personal exemption, which as noted above, is presently $4,000.
- Have received more than half of his or her support during the year from you.

---

[2] Or in lieu of taking the standard deduction, itemizing. More on this in a bit.

[3] To be a *qualifying relative* the individual doesn't actually have to be related to you, but if he or she is not, then in addition to meeting all the criteria above, he or she has to have lived with you all year. In contrast, your mother, who is related to you, would not; she could be in a nursing home.

- If married, not filing a joint return with his or her spouse.
- Be a U.S. citizen or resident alien.

In situations where mom and dad have divorced, disputes can arise over who can claim the children as dependents. If you find yourself with this problem and it's not addressed in your divorce decree, you will need to make inquiries.

Income

All of your income during the year from whatever source derived must be reported here in the *Income* section. Note, however, that as a general rule—there are exceptions—gifts, inheritances, life insurance death benefits, and personal injury awards are not considered income. Almost everything else is—salaries, wages and tips, interest, dividends, alimony (received), business income (or loss), gains (and losses) on the sale of securities and property, IRA distributions, pensions and annuities, rents and royalties, unemployment compensation, Social Security benefits, you name it.

The numbers you report for most of these items will come to you on tax statements sent by the payer of the income. If you had a job, the number you report for your salary or wages will come from a *W-2 ~ Wage and Tax Statement*. If you had interest income, you'll get a *1099-INT* or *1099-OID;*[4] dividends, a *1099-DIV*; a refund of taxes, a *1099-G*; gains or losses on the sale of securities, a *1099-B;*[5] pension and annuity payments and IRA distributions, a *1099-R*; a distribution from a partnership or S corporation, a *K-1*; royalties, a *1099-MISC*; Social Security benefits, an *SSA-1099*. Also, if you performed services for a business as a non-employee and were paid $600 or more, you'll get a *1099-MISC.*[6]

These tax statements are required to be mailed out by January 31, meaning that you should have them by early to mid-February in plenty of time to do your return. As

---

[4] OID stands for *original issue discount*. This refers to a bond originally issued at a price below the face value at which it will be redeemed at maturity – for example, a 10-year zero-coupon bond with a face value of $10,000 issued at $9,500. Instead of being allowed to recognize the $500 gain at maturity, the owner of the bond must "accrete" the gain in $50 annual increments, which is imputed to him as interest, as indeed it is.

[5] This will show your *proceeds* from the sale of securities, but not necessarily your *gain or loss* on their sale. More on this later, as well.

[6] The sole proprietor who receives less than $600 for products or services will not get a 1099-MISC at the end of the year but will still need to report this income.

they come in, you need to put them in a file, or basket, or box dedicated to accumulating such information. If for some reason you misplace something, you can always request that the payer send you a replacement. They may mutter about it, but they cannot refuse. For your part, you need to reconcile yourself to the fact that, for a myriad of reasons and often through no fault of their own, payers sometimes have to send out corrected tax statements. If you have a brokerage account, I'd suggest you hold off as long as safely possible to finalize your return and file it because you're more than likely going to receive a corrected 1099 of some sort along about late March. I invariably do.

A word here about supporting schedules: *Schedule B ~ Interest and Ordinary Dividends*, which is used to detail interest and dividend income exceeding a certain amount (presently $1,500), is a breeze. *Schedule C ~ Profit or Loss from Business* applies to people in business for themselves as sole proprietors, independent contractors, or members of a partnership, and is quite easy to complete provided a) you have a decent understanding of business terminology and b) have kept good records. *Schedule D ~ Capital Gains and Losses* is easy or not depending on the nature of the capital gain(s) and/or loss(es). Those relating to sales of securities, like stocks, bonds, mutual funds, and the like, are quite easy, assuming you can document when you acquired the securities and what you paid for them. Those relating to the sale or involuntary conversion (through casualty loss, theft, or condemnation) of investment property, like an office building or rent house, are likely to be quite complicated, requiring the services of a tax professional to do correctly. *Schedule E ~ Supplemental Income and Loss* relates to "rental real estate, royalties, partnerships, S corporations, estates, trusts, REMICs (real estate mortgage investment conduits), etc." There's basically a section on the schedule devoted to each of these activities, and provided the activities were profitable, none is a problem to complete. But problems can arise with so-called "passive loss disallowance rules" when an activity—a rental operation, for example—was not profitable. Also, if you're dealing with rental property, you will have to depreciate it using IRS tables and keep track of the accumulated depreciation. *Schedule F~ Profit or Loss from Farming* isn't anything I've dealt with since my H&R Block days but does not look intimidating.

Before leaving the Income section, I want to say two important things: One is that the types of income (and deductions) you have tend to be the same year after year, such that your prior years' returns, if done properly, should serve as a reliable guide to how you should do this year's return. Widows and widowers should find this helpful. If, for example, you're unsure how to complete the section on Schedule E dealing with rental property, look at how it was done last year. That may help. The second thing is that a good tax preparation software package can save you a lot of work and uncertainty. It can pretty much reduce your role in doing your taxes to answering questions.

Adjusted Gross Income

In this section, the taxpayer is offered an assortment of mostly unrelated deductions that, to the extent he qualifies to take them, will reduce his income subject to tax. I'm not going to go into these, except to suggest who might find something here that he or she could take advantage of. This would include the teacher who bought teaching supplies out of her own pocket; anyone in a high-deductible health plan (HDHP) who contributed to a qualified health savings account (HSA); the worker who incurred job-related moving expenses; the self-employed guy or gal who shouldered both halves of the Social Security and Medicare payroll taxes and/or who funded his or her own retirement plan and health insurance; anyone who was charged a penalty for withdrawing money from a savings account; anyone who paid alimony to a former spouse; anyone who contributed to a traditional IRA; anyone who paid interest on a student loan; anyone who had kids in college or attended college himself; and those who were engaged in *domestic production activities*, which basically means farming and manufacturing. As you can see from Form 1040, about half of these deductions require working through some paperwork that, like the schedules mentioned in the Income section, must be sent in with your return. Except for *Form 8903* supporting the *domestic production activities deduction*, which I confess to never having dealt with but will admit looks complicated, none is beyond a patient non-tax professional's ability to complete.

When you're done here, you subtract the total of these adjustments from your total income on line 22 to get your *adjusted gross income (AGI)***.** This number goes on the last line on Page 1 (line 37) and is then carried forward to the first line of Page 2 (line 38). It's a number that you likely will need to refer to again and again.

Tax and Credits

Broadly speaking, you do three things in this section: First, you deduct from AGI the larger of a) your *standard deduction* or b) the sum of your *itemized deductions*, and then from the resulting sub-total, you deduct the value of your personal exemptions to arrive at your *taxable income*. Second, you figure your *tax* using the tax tables or tax computation worksheet. Third, you reduce your tax by any *tax credits* that you're entitled to.

Now to elaborate a bit: You have a choice of taking the *standard deduction* that goes with the filing status that you selected earlier or *itemizing*. The standard deduction for each filing status is shown in the margin on Page 2. Itemizing your deductions involves filling out *Schedule A* where you enter what you spent during the tax year on *medical and dental expenses,*[7] *taxes* (state and local income taxes or general sales taxes, property taxes, personal property taxes, etc.), *interest* (mortgage interest[8] and investment interest), *gifts to charity*, *casualty and theft losses*, and *job and certain miscellaneous* items. About half of these deductions are offset by some percentage of adjusted gross income. Medical expenses are reduced by 10% of AGI (unless you're 65 or over, in which case the percentage is 7.5%), casualty and theft losses by 10%,[9] most so-called miscellaneous expenses by 2%. Gifts to charity are also limited by AGI. And, finally, if your AGI exceeds a certain amount, which varies depending on your filing status,[10] your itemized deductions may be further limited. You can probably gauge in your mind whether it will be worth your while to itemize. If it is, you're going to have to be able to document your expenditures in the event you should later be audited.

As previously noted, the deduction you can take for your *personal exemptions* is the product obtained by multiplying the number you claimed on Page 1, line 6d, by whatever dollar amount is allowed, which presently is $4,000. Thus, as I explained

---

[7] Out-of-pocket. You can't claim any expenses for which you were reimbursed by insurance.

[8] If you paid mortgage interest, you'll get a Form 1098 or some other document from your bank or mortgage company showing the amount. If they are also paying your property taxes and insurance out of an escrow account, they'll likely report those amounts as well. The property taxes are also deductible.

[9] After first deducting a $100 "floor." I have no idea why.

[10] If filing *single,* your *itemized deductions* may be limited if your AGI is more than $258,250; if filing *married filing jointly* or *qualifying widow(er)*, if it's over $309,900; if *head of household*, $284,050; if *married filing separately*, $156,000. The maximum reduction is 80%.

earlier, if you're a married couple filing a joint return and can claim two children as dependents, your exemptions will come to $16,000.[11]

After subtracting your allowable deductions from AGI to arrive at your *taxable income,* line 43, you're ready to compute your *tax,* which goes on line 44. If your taxable income is less than $100,000, you do this by going to the *Tax Tables* and looking up the tax corresponding to your taxable income and filing status. If your income is $100,000 or more, you figure your tax using a *Tax Computation* worksheet. Both the tables and worksheet are provided in the instructions and are user-friendly.

There are circumstances where you must plow through another worksheet or two before going to the tax tables or computation worksheet. One situation that gets me every year has to do with *qualified dividends* and *long-term capital gains*, which are presently taxed at rates lower than *ordinary income,*[12] necessitating that these items be dealt with separately. TurboTax does the worksheet for me, but I wouldn't have a problem doing it myself.

The next line in this section (line 45) is the *Alternative Minimum Tax*, the justly infamous *AMT*. This is an additional tax levied on high-income taxpayers who the government thinks wouldn't otherwise be paying their fair share owing to tax breaks they've been able to use to reduce their taxable income for regular tax purposes. Those tax breaks are the key. The mere fact that the number you're reporting on line 43 puts you in a high tax bracket doesn't by itself mean you're going to get hit with AMT.

So what are those tax breaks? Well, they range from simple things that you can understand, like the deduction you may have claimed on Schedule A for state and local income taxes and property taxes paid, to very esoteric things that for the most part only tax wonks do, like accelerated depreciation, intangible drilling costs, net operating loss deductions, and Section 1202 exclusions. The good news is that most people don't utilize any of the esoteric stuff.

---

[11] Subject to limitation if your AGI crosses a certain threshold. For *single* filers, the threshold is $258,250 and for *married joint filers,* it's $309,900. At $380,750 and $432,400, respectively, the deduction is phased out completely.

[12] Ordinary income is pretty much all income except qualified dividends, long-term capital gains and tax-exempt interest.

In your 1040 instructions, there is a listing of seventeen *adjustment* and *preference* items, anyone of which if claimed or received require you to complete *Form 6251*. That's the form used to figure the AMT. Assuming that you understand what each of these items is and none applies, you have cleared one hurdle and can go to the second. That's a little worksheet in the instructions called *Worksheet to See if You Should Fill in Form 6251*. It's easy to complete. If you clear that hurdle too, you don't have to worry about AMT. If you don't, then you do, meaning you must complete Form 6251.

In Part I of Form 6251, you make adjustments to your regular taxable income to purge it of any benefits you received from the twenty-five or so tax breaks listed there. The result is your Alternative Minimum Taxable Income (AMTI).

In Part II, you calculate your AMT. The first step here is to deduct an altogether different and much larger exemption than you were allowed for regular tax purpose from your AMTI. For a single filer or head of household, that number is $53,600; for married couples filing jointly and qualifying widow(er), it's $83,400; and for marrieds filing separately, it's $41,700.[13] If the number you get after deducting your exemption is below a certain threshold ($185,400 for everyone except marrieds filing separately, $92,700 for them), you multiply it by 26%, and if it's over, you multiply it by 28% and subtract a certain amount (equal to 2% of the threshold amount). That's your *tentative minimum tax*. Your AMT, which goes on line 45 of your 1040, is the amount by which your tentative minimum tax exceeds your regular tax (line 44).

The reality of completing Form 6251 can be far more headache-inducing than my quick and dirty explanation here may suggest. Even so, I don't think you should assume that it's beyond your ability. It shouldn't be if the only adjustments you have to make to your regular taxable income to arrive at your Alternative Minimum Taxable is to back out a few deductions you took on Schedule A. If it involves more than that and you're unable to make sense of the 6251 instructions, which are likely gibberish to most folks, you may be wise to get help from a tax professional. That would be less costly in the long run than having the IRS get all over you and having to do an amended return.

---

[13] All subject to phase-out where the taxpayer's AMTI exceeds a certain threshold.

Line 46, which comes next, is new. It relates to the *Premium Tax Credit (PTC),* which is the subsidy that the government gives lower-income taxpayers who bought a *qualified health plan* through a *health insurance exchange.* In most cases, this subsidy is received in advance to the extent that the government pays some, if not all, of the insured's monthly premium based on an estimate of his PTC made at the time of plan enrollment. Come tax time, he must settle up by completing Form 8962 where he calculates his actual PTC. If his estimated PTC was wrong, resulting in his having been advanced more than he should have been, he has to pay back the difference, which he does here. If he's still owed something, he gets a tax credit on line 69 in the *Payments* section, which we'll get to later.

The rest of the Tax and Credits section has to do with tax credits. Credits are different from deductions. *Deductions reduce your taxable income; credits reduce your tax.* If you have a $1,000 deduction and are in a 25% marginal tax bracket, that deduction will end up reducing your tax by $250; if you have a $1,000 tax credit, it will reduce your taxes by the same $1,000. Credits are said to reduce your taxes "dollar-for-dollar."

Lots of people find credits here that they can use. You may too if any of the following apply: you got a 1099-DIV or 1099-INT that reported something on line 6 for *foreign tax paid*; you paid childcare (or daycare for a parent or other relative claimed as a dependent); you paid post-secondary educational expenses for yourself, your spouse, or a dependent; you contributed to an IRA or to an employer-sponsored retirement plan, like a 401(k); you have children under 17; you invested in energy-saving improvements to your home, like solar panels, wind generators, and fuel cells. Assuming that one or more things here apply, there may be two problems claiming the credit. The first is the paperwork you've got to contend with, which ranges from confusing (*Form 1116 ~ Foreign Tax Credit*) to tedious (all the other forms and/or worksheets). The other is your adjusted gross income. Some of these credits are phased out at very modest AGI thresholds.

On line 55, you enter the sum of all your credits from lines 48 through 54. You then subtract line 55 from line 47 and enter the difference on line 56. That is, unless the difference is a negative number, in which case you enter zero.

Other Taxes

In this section, the taxpayer is required to add to his income tax sub-total on line 56 a number of taxes that aren't income taxes per se, but nevertheless get figured in with them.

The first of these (line 57) is *self-employment tax*. People who work for someone else only pay their half of Social Security and Medicare payroll taxes, and their employer pays the other half. Self-employed folks aren't so lucky. Because they fill the roles of employer *and* employee, they are required to pay both halves. They calculate what they owe on *Schedule SE* and then report the tax here. As noted earlier, one-half of the self-employment tax can be taken as a deduction in the Adjustments to Income section on line 27.

Another common item that must be reported here (on line 59) is the penalty, or "tax," as the IRS prefers to call it, on early distributions from qualified retirement plans, like IRAs and 401(k)s, as well as on excess contributions to such plans and to educational and medical/health savings accounts. *Early distributions* refers to pulling money out of a qualified retirement plan account before the owner has attained age 59 ½ The penalty on such early withdrawals is 10%, unless the plan is a SIMPLE IRA, in which case it could be 25%. *Excess contributions* has to do with putting more money into a plan during the year than the law allows. The penalty here is usually 6% of the excess contribution.

There is also a line (58) for reporting the payroll tax (Social Security and Medicare) due on any tips that the taxpayer earned but did not report to his employer, and another (line 60a) for reporting the payroll taxes due on wages exceeding $1,800 annually paid to anyone working in the taxpayer's home.

Right below *household employment taxes*, on line 60b, is a line aptly described as *first-time home-buyer credit repayment*, where anyone who received the $7,500 first-time homebuyer credit in 2008 (agreeing to repay it over 15 years in $500 annual installments starting in 2010) makes his payment.

Like 46, line 61, *health care: individual responsibility*, is also new and stems from the Affordable Care Act, which requires that everyone have "minimum essential (healthcare) coverage," defined as "coverage provided by your employer, coverage you buy through the Health Insurance Marketplace, government-sponsored coverage including Medicare, Medicaid etc., and certain types of coverage you buy directly from an insurance company." Failure to obtain full-year coverage for yourself and your dependents, if you've not been exempted, subjects you to a "shared responsibility payment,"[14] which you make here and figure using a worksheet included in the instructions to Form 8965.

The taxes on line 62, the *additional Medicare tax (Form 8959)* and the *net investment income tax (Form 8960)*, also stem from the Affordable Care Act but only affect high-income taxpayers. For those filing single, head of household or qualifying widow(er), "high income" means $200,000; for those filing married filing jointly, it means $250,000; and for those filing married filing separately, it means $125,000. The first is an additional Medicare tax of .9% on wages and self-employment income exceeding these thresholds. The second is an additional tax of 3.8% on investment income, like dividends, interest, and capital gains, levied on taxpayers whose AGI exceeds these thresholds.

The last line in this section (line 63) is total tax, which is the sum of your net income tax from line 56 and all these *other taxes*.

Payments

We are now, mercifully, near the end. In this section, you report everything you've paid toward satisfying your tax liability. The main things here are the taxes withheld from your pay, which you'll find reported on your W-2, *and* any estimated tax payments you might have sent to the IRS with a quarterly tax voucher (*1040-ES*). You might also have overpayments of last year's income tax or of this year's Social Security and Medicare taxes that you have opted to apply.

In addition to what you have paid in, there are some tax credits that you may qualify for that will go towards satisfying your tax liability. One of these is the *Earned Income Credit* (line 66a). This is a tax credit aimed at redressing the alleged inequities of the Social Security tax and incentivizing unemployed people to find work. Like everything else, it requires doing some paperwork, but unlike all the credits discussed

[14] This has a strangely Orwellian ring to it.

previously, this one (as well as any other in this section) is *refundable*, meaning that to the extent it exceeds your tax liability you get money back.

Two other credits that lots of people can take are the *additional child tax credit* and the *American opportunity credit.* Both are consolation prizes, so to speak, to taxpayers whose utilization of the *child tax credit* and *educational credits* was limited thanks to not having a big enough tax liability.

You need to study this section of the form to see if there's anything else that seems like it might apply to you.

Refund/Amount You Owe

These are actually two separate sections, as you can see, and both are self-explanatory. If your payments (and credits) above exceed your tax liability, you're due a refund, and if the opposite is true, you will owe something still. You could owe interest or a penalty as well.

Third Party Designee/Sign Here/Paid Preparer's Use Only

These are also separate sections, and except for maybe the first, self-explanatory as well. About the Third Party Designee, I would just say that if someone else prepared your return and the whole affair remains a great mystery to you, you might want to designate that person to deal with any queries from the IRS.

****

Here are some things that you probably should be aware of. I'm only going to tell you as much as I know more or less off the top of my head. If anything affects you, you will need to investigate further.

Education Expenses

If you paid higher education expenses, you may be uncertain whether it's best to take them as an adjustment to income on line 34, *tuition and fees*, or to claim them as a tax credit on line 50, *education credits*. To answer that question, you may need to fool around a bit with the numbers. But remember this: if you take the expenses as an adjustment to income, the tax benefit you'll receive is equal to the amount of your deduction, which is capped at $4,000, no matter how much you spent, multiplied by your marginal tax rate, whereas any *credit* you can take on line 50 will reduce your taxes dollar-for-dollar. I say "can" here because your credit may be limited by your tax liability. The other thing to consider is that your ability to take the deduction as an adjustment to income isn't affected by your AGI, but if your AGI is high, it can limit what you take as a credit. As a general rule, I'd offer this: if you have a child in college and your tax liability is not "too low" and your AGI not "too high," you're going to be better off taking a credit.

Sale of a Personal Residence

If you sell your personal residence and you've lived in it for at least two (2) years during the past five (5), any gain that you realize on it, up to $250,000 if you're single or up to $500,000 if you're married filing jointly, is exempt from Federal income tax. You will still need to report the sale, however, if you get a *1099-S ~ Proceeds from Real Estate Transaction* from the title company or whoever handled the closing.

Qualified Dividends and Long-Term Capital Gains

Qualified dividends are simply *ordinary dividends* that qualify for *long-term capital gains* tax treatment, while a long-term capital gain is just a gain on investment property—whether tangible, like a rent house, or intangible, like a stock, bond, or mutual fund—that has been held for more than one (1) year. The special tax treatment that qualified dividends and long-term capital gains receive has to do with the fact that both are taxed at a rate below what the taxpayer is subject to on his next dollar of ordinary income. If you're in a 10% or 15% tax bracket, you pay zero (0%) on qualified dividends and long-term capital gains; if you're in a 25%, 28%, or 33% bracket, you pay 15%; and if you're in the top bracket, which is 39.6%, you pay 20%.

Capital Losses

If you make a lot of money in the stock market, the IRS will tax it all, either as short-term capital gains or long-term capital gains, but if you lose a lot, it will limit what you can deduct to $3,000. It will, however, allow you to carry the balance of your loss over to the following year, and every year after that until used up, to offset capital gains and/or reduce up to another $3,000 of ordinary income. To illustrate, if you had a $25,000 capital loss in 2013 and used $3,000 to reduce your ordinary income, your *loss carryover* into 2014 would be $22,000. Then supposing that in 2014 you had $15,000 in capital gains and $50,000 in ordinary income, you could use your $22,000 carryover to wipe out the capital gains completely and reduce your ordinary income to $47,000. That would still leave you with $4,000 ($22,000 – ($15,000 + $3,000) = $4,000) as a carryover into 2015. If you had capital gains that year of, say, $10,000, and ordinary income of, say, $51,000, the carryover would be used in its entirety to reduce the capital gains, leaving nothing to go against ordinary income.

Rental Real Estate Activities

Although I think most individuals, provided they're patient and methodical, can do their taxes themselves, at least with the help of tax preparation software, there are definitely situations where you may come to grief if you don't engage the services of a CPA or other tax professional. One such situation is where you're involved in rental real estate activities. The tax treatment of rental real estate operations can be complicated. To begin with, rental property, if it's improved—meaning that it's got a building on it, like a house or an office—must be depreciated. But only the improvements, not the land. Among other problems this presents, if you don't have much to go by, is determining how much of your cost basis is attributable to the improvements and how much to the land. Land is not depreciable.

A second problem has to do with the fact that, as the IRS puts it, "rentals generally are passive activities…subject to passive loss disallowance rules." What those rules boil down to is that unless you're a real estate professional[15] as defined by the IRS, *or* your modified adjusted gross income is below $100,000 *and* you actively participate in the management of your rental property,[16] *or* you have disposed of the property, you

---

[15] To be considered a *real estate professional* by the IRS requires that you spend more than half your time in "real estate activities" and more than 750 hours. Real estate professionals are not subject to passive activity loss limitation rules.

[16] If your MAGI is under $100,000 and you're actively involved in managing your rental properties (and not just ratifying the decisions of some property manager), you can deduct up to $25,000 in rental losses from ordinary income. For every $1 that your MAGI exceeds $100,000 what you can deduct is reduced by $0.50, such that at a MAGI of $150,000 you're not allowed to deduct anything.

cannot deduct a rental loss from ordinary income. You can only deduct *passive losses* from *passive income*—a loss on an office building, say, from a gain on a rent house. Absent sufficient passive income from which to fully deduct your passive losses, all you can do is carry your unused losses forward into future years when you may be able to use them.

The third complication has to do with *depreciation recapture*. As explained above, if you own rental property, you must depreciate it. This depreciation charge reduces your net income from the property, which will be taxed as ordinary income. It also reduces your *adjusted basis* in the property, which is to say its cost for purposes of calculating your gain or loss should you later sell. The more years you own the property, the greater will be its *accumulated depreciation*, the lower its adjusted basis, and the higher your gain (or the lower your loss) if you sell. But assuming a gain, which is the more likely outcome, the gain would qualify as a *long-term capital gain*, qualifying for the special tax treatment explained above, except for the fact that the IRS wants to tax it at ordinary rates to the extent that it resulted from depreciation. Thus, if you bought a little rent house for $100,000, depreciated it down to $25,000, and then sold it for $115,000, you'd have a capital gain of $90,000 ($115,000 minus $25,000), of which $75,000, representing *depreciation recapture,* would be taxed at ordinary rates (maximum 25%) and $15,000 as a long-term capital gain at a rate of 0%, 15%, or 20%, depending on your tax bracket.

Who Has to File?

Because over 40% of so-called taxpayers do not actually pay any income taxes, many people wonder if they even have to file. You may wonder, too. For most people, the short answer is you do if your *gross income,* as the IRS defines it for this purpose, exceeds the sum of your standard deduction for your filing status and age and your personal exemption(s). However, for married taxpayers filing separate returns, the threshold ignores the standard deduction, taking only the personal exemption into account. Table 7.1 on the next page explains.

Table 7.1

Thresholds for Filing a Tax Return (2015)					
Taxpayer(s) < 65	Single	Head of Household	Married Filing Jointly	Married Filing Separately	Qualifying Widow(er)
Personal Exemption(s)	$4,000	$4,000	$8,000	$4,000	$4,000
Standard Deduction*	$6,300	$9,250	$12,600	See below	$12,600
Filing Threshold	**$10,300**	**$13,250**	**$20,600**	**$4,000**	**$16,600**
Taxpayer > 65					
Add	$1,550	$1,550	$1,250		$1,250
Filing Threshold	**$11,850**	**$14,800**	**$21,850**	**$4,000**	**$17,850**
Other spouse also > 65					
Add			$1,250		
Filing Threshold			**$23,100**		

* The married taxpayer who files separately cannot claim the standard deduction if his/her spouse itemizes deductions.

You also have to file, even if your gross income is below the filing threshold, if you…

- had $400 or more of income from self-employment;
- had $1,000 or more of *unearned income* (like interest or dividends), or $6,300 or more of *earned income* (like wages), while being claimed as someone else's dependent;
- took taxable and/or early withdrawals from an IRA or other qualified retirement or medical savings account;
- received advance earned income credit (EIC) payments;
- had unpaid Social Security and Medicare taxes on tips.

If any of these other filing requirements sounds like it might apply to you but you're unsure, you will need to make further inquiries.

Reasons to File Even if You Don't Have To

Even if you don't have to file, it might still make sense to. That would be the case certainly if your income was below the filing threshold but you had earned income from which your employer had withheld taxes. The amount withheld would appear in Box 2 of your W-2. By filing a return, you'd get back whatever had been withheld. You might also be entitled to the Earned Income Credit (EIC*)* or some other refundable tax credit.

Filing Deadline

The deadline for filing your tax return for any given year is April 15th of the following year, unless April 15 falls on a Saturday, Sunday, or legal holiday, in which case the date is moved to the next day that's not a Saturday, Sunday, or legal holiday. Three years ago (in 2012) April 15th fell on a Sunday and the 16th was a holiday (Emancipation Day in the District of Columbia), so the deadline became April 17th.

If for some reason you see that you'll be unable to comply with the normal deadline, you can file for an automatic extension until October 15th by filing a *Form 4868 ~ Application for Automatic Extension of Time to File U.S. Individual Income Tax Return.* This is an easy one to complete. Understand, though, that getting an extension does not relieve you of responsibility for paying your taxes on time.

Paying Your Taxes on Time

If you're an employee, your employer will require you to complete a *W-4 ~ Employee's Withholding Allowance Certificate* in order to be able, based on the number of *withholding allowances* you claim, to calculate what to withhold from your paycheck each pay period for remitting to the IRS.

To the extent that you have income not subject to withholding—from, say, self-employment, or investments, or rents, or alimony—Uncle Sam wants you to pay the estimated tax on it in quarterly installments. So that the IRS knows whom to credit with these payments, you're required to enclose with each installment a *Form 1040 ES ~ Payment Voucher*. For the 2015 tax year, your first installment is (was) due on April 15 (2015), the second on June 15, the third on September 15, and the fourth on January 15 of 2016. You'll note that April 15, 2015, was also the deadline for filing your 2014 return and paying any balance due.

Needless to say, when you've got income that's not subject to withholding, it can be problematic figuring out by April 15, which is just three months into the new tax year, what your taxes for the entire year will come to. Understanding this, the IRS offers you an easy way out—just take your total tax from last year's return, divide it by 4 and send them a check for that amount. But that is only if your AGI was $150,000 or less. If it's more, you'll have to use 110% of last year's "total tax" as your basis. If that doesn't seem right to you—because, let's say, you're pretty sure that you won't owe nearly as much this year as last—you'll need to consult *IRS Publication 505*.

If after you've filed the IRS determines that you didn't pay as much in some quarter as you should have, they will charge you interest on the arrearage until such time as it is settled. Typically that will be on April 15. If it's not settled then, they'll hit you with a penalty as well.

Tax Records

Whether you do your taxes yourself (with or without the aid of software) or you pay someone to do them for you, there are all kinds of information you'll need to be able to pull together when the time comes to go to work. Have a file where you accumulate all of the tax statements that will begin to dribble in starting early February—W-2s, 1098s and 1099s—and keep track throughout the year of any expenses that may be claimed as itemized deductions, like medical expenses, charitable contributions, and so on. Almost the worst thing about doing your taxes is not being able to locate some piece of information that you've misplaced.

Record Retention

This refers to how long you need to hang onto to your old returns (short answer: forever) and supporting tax records (short answer: seven (7) years after filing). For discussion, see Chapter Two.

Tax Preparation Software

I said earlier that most people's tax returns tend to include the same old stuff year after year. The numbers change, of course, but the kinds of income people have and the deductions and credits they can claim tend not to. Thus, unless this is the first year you've ever filed, chances are that you can use last year's return, assuming it was done right, as a reliable guide to how this year's return should be done. If a CPA or professional tax preparer or your late husband or wife did your return last year and it was pretty simple, you may wish to save yourself some money this year by doing it yourself. Or by getting a child or another relative or a trustworthy friend to do it. After returning to the U.S. to live and discovering that my mother had been paying a CPA to do her taxes for the past several years, I took over that chore. I should note that this was before my H&R Block work experience. She had some income from a family partnership and one or two other items that I'd never encountered on my own return that probably would have flummoxed me had I not had her prior years' returns to guide me, but as I did, the job was easy. The hour or so that it took me every year always saved her several hundred dollars. And had I felt the need, I could have had someone at our public library check my work for free.

I'm not sure that I have the patience to do my own return unaided, so I do it on a PC using a tax preparation software package. The particular package I use is TurboTax. I don't know that it's any better than the other packages out there—I've just never used any other. You can download TurboTax online or buy a CD at a store like OfficeMax. Once installed, TurboTax takes over. Your role is to answer questions. It will decide which is more advantageous for you—to take the standard deduction or to itemize. If there's a deduction or tax credit that you qualify for, it will complete whatever forms are required for you to take it. If you have a brokerage account, which you can look at online, TurboTax can go into that account, using your PIN and password, and import from there all the information it needs to do Schedule B (interest and dividends) and Schedule D (capital gains and losses), saving you hours of tedium. Whatever you input this year—your name, Social Security number, your spouse's, your address, filing status, number of exemptions, who you receive payments from, their tax ID's, who you make payments to (e.g., what charities), and so on—it will remember next year, again saving you the time and trouble of re-entering all this data. Finally, if you're subject to state income tax, it will do that return as well.

AARP Tax-Aide Program

I have only now, just as I'm ready to go to print, become aware that *AARP* offers free tax preparation services to the public through what they call their *Tax-Aide* program. In our town they work out of a back room at the public library starting about the first week of February. If this program is offered in your community and you need help with your taxes, I suggest you check it out. It sounds like a wonderful resource, and it's my understanding that you don't have to be a member of AARP to avail yourself of it.

Form **1040** Department of the Treasury—Internal Revenue Service (99)
U.S. Individual Income Tax Return 2015

OMB No. 1545-0074 | IRS Use Only—Do not write or staple in this space.

For the year Jan. 1–Dec. 31, 2015, or other tax year beginning , 2015, ending , 20 | See separate instructions.

Your first name and initial	Last name		Your social security number
If a joint return, spouse's first name and initial	Last name		Spouse's social security number
Home address (number and street). If you have a P.O. box, see instructions.		Apt. no.	▲ Make sure the SSN(s) above and on line 6c are correct.
City, town or post office, state, and ZIP code. If you have a foreign address, also complete spaces below (see instructions).			**Presidential Election Campaign** Check here if you, or your spouse if filing jointly, want $3 to go to this fund. Checking a box below will not change your tax or refund. ☐ You ☐ Spouse
Foreign country name	Foreign province/state/county	Foreign postal code	

Filing Status

Check only one box.

1 ☐ Single
2 ☐ Married filing jointly (even if only one had income)
3 ☐ Married filing separately. Enter spouse's SSN above and full name here. ▶
4 ☐ Head of household (with qualifying person). (See instructions.) If the qualifying person is a child but not your dependent, enter this child's name here. ▶
5 ☐ Qualifying widow(er) with dependent child

Exemptions

6a ☐ **Yourself.** If someone can claim you as a dependent, **do not** check box 6a . . . . .
b ☐ **Spouse** . . . . .
} **Boxes checked on 6a and 6b**

c **Dependents:**

(1) First name Last name	(2) Dependent's social security number	(3) Dependent's relationship to you	(4) ✓ if child under age 17 qualifying for child tax credit (see instructions)
			☐
			☐
			☐
			☐

No. of children on 6c who:
- **lived with you**
- **did not live with you due to divorce or separation (see instructions)**

Dependents on 6c not entered above

If more than four dependents, see instructions and check here ▶☐

d Total number of exemptions claimed . . . . . **Add numbers on lines above ▶**

Income

Attach Form(s) W-2 here. Also attach Forms W-2G and 1099-R if tax was withheld.

If you did not get a W-2, see instructions.

Line	Description		Line	Amount
7	Wages, salaries, tips, etc. Attach Form(s) W-2		7	
8a	**Taxable** interest. Attach Schedule B if required		8a	
b	**Tax-exempt** interest. **Do not** include on line 8a . . .	8b		
9a	Ordinary dividends. Attach Schedule B if required		9a	
b	Qualified dividends	9b		
10	Taxable refunds, credits, or offsets of state and local income taxes		10	
11	Alimony received		11	
12	Business income or (loss). Attach Schedule C or C-EZ		12	
13	Capital gain or (loss). Attach Schedule D if required. If not required, check here ▶ ☐		13	
14	Other gains or (losses). Attach Form 4797		14	
15a	IRA distributions . 15a	b Taxable amount . . .	15b	
16a	Pensions and annuities 16a	b Taxable amount . . .	16b	
17	Rental real estate, royalties, partnerships, S corporations, trusts, etc. Attach Schedule E		17	
18	Farm income or (loss). Attach Schedule F		18	
19	Unemployment compensation		19	
20a	Social security benefits 20a	b Taxable amount . . .	20b	
21	Other income. List type and amount		21	
22	Combine the amounts in the far right column for lines 7 through 21. This is your **total income** ▶		22	

Adjusted Gross Income

Line	Description		Line	Amount
23	Educator expenses	23		
24	Certain business expenses of reservists, performing artists, and fee-basis government officials. Attach Form 2106 or 2106-EZ	24		
25	Health savings account deduction. Attach Form 8889 .	25		
26	Moving expenses. Attach Form 3903	26		
27	Deductible part of self-employment tax. Attach Schedule SE .	27		
28	Self-employed SEP, SIMPLE, and qualified plans . .	28		
29	Self-employed health insurance deduction	29		
30	Penalty on early withdrawal of savings	30		
31a	Alimony paid **b** Recipient's SSN ▶	31a		
32	IRA deduction	32		
33	Student loan interest deduction	33		
34	Tuition and fees. Attach Form 8917	34		
35	Domestic production activities deduction. Attach Form 8903	35		
36	Add lines 23 through 35		36	
37	Subtract line 36 from line 22. This is your **adjusted gross income** . . . . . ▶		37	

For Disclosure, Privacy Act, and Paperwork Reduction Act Notice, see separate instructions. Cat. No. 11320B Form **1040** (2015)

Section	Line	Description		
Tax and Credits	38	Amount from line 37 (adjusted gross income)		38
	39a	Check if: ☐ **You** were born before January 2, 1951, ☐ Blind. ☐ **Spouse** was born before January 2, 1951, ☐ Blind. } **Total boxes checked** ▶ 39a		
	b	If your spouse itemizes on a separate return or you were a dual-status alien, check here ▶ 39b☐		
Standard Deduction for— • People who check any box on line 39a or 39b **or** who can be claimed as a dependent, see instructions. • All others: Single or Married filing separately, $6,300 Married filing jointly or Qualifying widow(er), $12,600 Head of household, $9,250	40	**Itemized deductions** (from Schedule A) **or** your **standard deduction** (see left margin)		40
	41	Subtract line 40 from line 38		41
	42	**Exemptions.** If line 38 is $154,950 or less, multiply $4,000 by the number on line 6d. Otherwise, see instructions		42
	43	**Taxable income.** Subtract line 42 from line 41. If line 42 is more than line 41, enter -0-		43
	44	**Tax** (see instructions). Check if any from: **a** ☐ Form(s) 8814 **b** ☐ Form 4972 **c** ☐ ______		44
	45	**Alternative minimum tax** (see instructions). Attach Form 6251		45
	46	Excess advance premium tax credit repayment. Attach Form 8962		46
	47	Add lines 44, 45, and 46 ▶		47
	48	Foreign tax credit. Attach Form 1116 if required	48	
	49	Credit for child and dependent care expenses. Attach Form 2441	49	
	50	Education credits from Form 8863, line 19	50	
	51	Retirement savings contributions credit. Attach Form 8880	51	
	52	Child tax credit. Attach Schedule 8812, if required	52	
	53	Residential energy credits. Attach Form 5695	53	
	54	Other credits from Form: **a** ☐ 3800 **b** ☐ 8801 **c** ☐ ______	54	
	55	Add lines 48 through 54. These are your **total credits**		55
	56	Subtract line 55 from line 47. If line 55 is more than line 47, enter -0- ▶		56
Other Taxes	57	Self-employment tax. Attach Schedule SE		57
	58	Unreported social security and Medicare tax from Form: **a** ☐ 4137 **b** ☐ 8919		58
	59	Additional tax on IRAs, other qualified retirement plans, etc. Attach Form 5329 if required		59
	60a	Household employment taxes from Schedule H		60a
	b	First-time homebuyer credit repayment. Attach Form 5405 if required		60b
	61	Health care: individual responsibility (see instructions) Full-year coverage ☐		61
	62	Taxes from: **a** ☐ Form 8959 **b** ☐ Form 8960 **c** ☐ Instructions; enter code(s) ______		62
	63	Add lines 56 through 62. This is your **total tax** ▶		63
Payments	64	Federal income tax withheld from Forms W-2 and 1099	64	
	65	2015 estimated tax payments and amount applied from 2014 return	65	
If you have a qualifying child, attach Schedule EIC.	66a	**Earned income credit (EIC)**	66a	
	b	Nontaxable combat pay election **66b**		
	67	Additional child tax credit. Attach Schedule 8812	67	
	68	American opportunity credit from Form 8863, line 8	68	
	69	Net premium tax credit. Attach Form 8962	69	
	70	Amount paid with request for extension to file	70	
	71	Excess social security and tier 1 RRTA tax withheld	71	
	72	Credit for federal tax on fuels. Attach Form 4136	72	
	73	Credits from Form: **a** ☐ 2439 **b** ☐ Reserved **c** ☐ 8885 **d** ☐ ______	73	
	74	Add lines 64, 65, 66a, and 67 through 73. These are your **total payments** ▶		74
Refund	75	If line 74 is more than line 63, subtract line 63 from line 74. This is the amount you **overpaid**		75
	76a	Amount of line 75 you want **refunded to you.** If Form 8888 is attached, check here ▶☐		76a
Direct deposit? See instructions.	▶ b	Routing number ▶ c Type: ☐ Checking ☐ Savings		
	▶ d	Account number		
	77	Amount of line 75 you want **applied to your 2016 estimated tax** ▶	77	
Amount You Owe	78	**Amount you owe.** Subtract line 74 from line 63. For details on how to pay, see instructions ▶		78
	79	Estimated tax penalty (see instructions)	79	

Third Party Designee

Do you want to allow another person to discuss this return with the IRS (see instructions)? ☐ **Yes.** Complete below. ☐ **No**

Designee's name ▶ Phone no. ▶ Personal identification number (PIN) ▶

Sign Here

Joint return? See instructions. Keep a copy for your records.

Under penalties of perjury, I declare that I have examined this return and accompanying schedules and statements, and to the best of my knowledge and belief, they are true, correct, and complete. Declaration of preparer (other than taxpayer) is based on all information of which preparer has any knowledge.

Your signature	Date	Your occupation	Daytime phone number
Spouse's signature. If a joint return, **both** must sign.	Date	Spouse's occupation	If the IRS sent you an Identity Protection PIN, enter it here (see inst.)

Paid Preparer Use Only

Print/Type preparer's name	Preparer's signature	Date	Check ☐ if self-employed	PTIN
Firm's name ▶			Firm's EIN ▶	
Firm's address ▶			Phone no.	

www.irs.gov/form1040 Form **1040** (2015)

EIGHT

Auto Insurance

The most perilous thing most of us do on an everyday basis is go somewhere in a car. Car accidents are commonplace. Most are just fender-benders, thankfully, but sometimes they're a whole lot more serious, resulting in serious injury and even death.

You don't have to be irresponsible to cause a car accident. It's enough that at a critical moment you are distracted by something going on around you or inside your head. You fail to stop at a stop light and T-bone another car crossing in front of you; you change lanes without thoroughly looking, side-swiping a car coming up beside you; you don't notice that the traffic in front of you is slowing or stopping and you rear-end the car ahead of you. Even though the 17 year-old single male who's been ticketed a half-dozen times is far more likely to cause an accident than the nice middle-aged lady who's never been cited for anything, we all make mistakes. If you own a car, you'd better have car insurance.

Because it's in the public interest that motorists be able to make restitution to those they injure by their negligence, in the vast majority of states you cannot register a car or renew its registration without proof of insurance. I am going to assume that if you own a car, you've got car insurance (or to call it by its proper name, a *personal auto policy)*. When I use the word "you," I am speaking to you as the *named insured* on your policy's *declarations* page. That's the front page of your policy, which shows the name(s) of the insured(s);[1] the make, model, and serial number of each vehicle insured; and the coverages you have.

****

Policy Overview

If you look at your policy, you will see that it has six parts, the first four of them (Parts A, B, C and D) dealing with coverage against different types of loss, namely:

- ***Liability*** ~ *legal responsibility* for *bodily injury* and/or *property damage* caused to a third party.[2]
- ***Medical Payments*** ~ expenses incurred in dealing with injuries sustained in a car accident by an *insured* or a passenger, or passengers, riding with him or her.
- ***Uninsured Motorists*** ~ bodily injury and property damage suffered by an insured and his or her passengers at the hands of another motorist who doesn't have insurance or who is never apprehended (in other words, a hit-and-run driver).
- ***Damage to Your Auto*** ~ the cost of repairing your car when it is damaged or destroyed in a *collision* or from other perils (causes).

Each of these *coverages* has its own insuring agreement, definitions, exclusions, and other provisions, making the policy in its entirety difficult to get your mind around. I'm sorry about that. I will tell you no more here than I know myself, which is certainly not everything, but I trust enough for a good general understanding.

---

[1] If you're married and the car is in both your names, you'll both be named as *insureds* on the policy.

[2] A third party is anyone who is not a party to your insurance contract.

Liability Coverages (Part A)

Coverages

In plain English, what liability coverage does is provide protection against someone successfully suing you for an injury or property damage that you or a member of your household or someone you let use your car caused. And, of course, in an accident where more than one person got hurt, there could be multiple plaintiffs, all getting their day in court and ultimately receiving personal injury awards. Your coverage here will have three numbers or *limits*— two for *bodily injury* and one for *property damage*. The first of the two bodily injury limits is the maximum the policy will pay to *any one person*, and the second is what it will pay in the aggregate in respect of *any one accident* where more than one person is injured. Our own policy has bodily injury limits of $250,000 for *each person* and $500,000 for *each accident*, and a property damage limit of $100,000. Thus, if one person got a judgment against one of us (my wife or me) for, say, $300,000, our policy would pay up to its "each person" limit of $250,000, but if four people were injured and each were awarded the same $300,000, making the aggregate judgment $1,200,000, our policy would pay up to its "each accident" limit of just $500,000. (This would certainly be an instance where I'd be glad that we also have an *umbrella* policy that affords us excess coverage. I'll discuss umbrellas in just a bit.)

Who's Insured

The policy protects the following people as *insureds*:

- You (the *named insured*), your spouse,[3] and any other family member living with you for "the ownership, maintenance, or use of any auto or trailer."
- Anyone using *your* car (*your covered auto)* with your express or implied permission.
- Any person or organization in whose service you or another insured might be driving *your car* who might be named as a co-defendant if one of you caused an accident resulting in bodily injury or property damage to a third party.

---

[3] Your spouse needs to be living with you to be covered, as does any family member, except a child who is away at college.

- Any person or organization in whose service you or a family member might be driving a car, *other than your car*, who might be named as a co-defendant if one of you caused an accident resulting in bodily injury or property damage to a third party.

The practical meaning of the above, taking the bullet points one by one, is that you and any family member living with you under the same roof has liability coverage whether you're driving a vehicle that you own, or one that someone loaned you, or one that you rented. It means that if you let someone who is not a member of your household use your car, he or she is covered as well. And it means that the policy affords liability protection to any person or organization which might be held legally responsible because you or a family member or another insured *driving your car* was doing something on his or its behalf when one of you caused an accident. Note, however, that *if the car is not your car*—let's say that it's your in-laws', which they've said you can use while they're vacationing in Europe—liability coverage would be extended only to persons or organizations in whose service you or a family member might be acting at the time one of you caused an accident.

Meaning of "Covered Auto"

Another key term here is ***your covered auto.*** Your covered auto, which I shall refer to as "your car," includes the following:

- Any vehicle shown in the Declarations. (Remember that that's the first page of your policy, which shows the Named Insured, etc.)
- A newly acquired auto, meaning acquired subsequent to the issue of the policy.
- Any trailer you own (which doesn't have to be identified in the Declarations).
- Any auto or trailer you're using as a substitute for one of the above while it is unavailable to you because it's broken down, in the shop, stolen, or totaled.

A word about a "newly acquired auto." This could be a replacement vehicle (say, a new Ford that you've traded in your old Suzuki for), or it could be an addition (maybe a nice second-hand car you've bought Junior who is going off to college). As indicated, both replacement and additional vehicles are automatically covered by your policy when acquired, but in the case of an *additional* auto only for a limited time—often just fourteen (14) days.[4] After that, unless you notify your insurer of your new purchase and request that it be covered, all coverages on that additional vehicle—liability, medical payments, uninsured motorist and physical damage—lapse. And after the same number of days, unless you take action, you lose the *physical damage* coverage on any *replacement* auto. (The other three coverages—liability, medical payments and uninsured motorist—remain in force through the end of the policy period.) To be safe, notify your agent right away when you buy or otherwise acquire a new car or used car, regardless of whether it's a replacement or an addition.

Exclusions

Exclusions are all those things you might do that would be grounds for your insurance company to deny coverage if you made a claim. They're things that are either against public policy or haven't been factored into the policy's pricing. At their best, exclusions make for tedious reading; at their worst, they're such an impenetrable tangle of words that it's almost impossible to get at their meaning. That's not to frustrate you, I'm sure, but rather the plaintiff's attorney who would try to take advantage of any little opening or ambiguity to argue to a sympathetic jury that a particular exclusion didn't apply in his client's case. If you want a thorough understanding of your policy's exclusions, which I would certainly encourage, read them and then discuss any questions you have with your agent. Here's my take on the ones applying to liability coverage:

- There's no coverage for either bodily injury or property damage if you or any other insured intentionally causes an accident.
- There's no coverage for property damage to property owned or being transported by any insured, or in his or her "care, custody, or control." The rationale here is that you can't be legally liable to yourself. If you back over your son's mountain bike, which he left parked behind your car, don't look to your auto policy to cover the cost of buying him a new bike.

[4] The time limit on our policy is longer; it's 30 days.

- There's no coverage for bodily injury to an employee—yours or any insured's—during the course of his or her employment, unless the employee is a *domestic employee* not covered by your state's workers' compensation laws. (To be clear, if the employee *is* a domestic employee—a housekeeper, let's say—who is not covered by workers compensation, you would have liability coverage for any bodily injury you caused her by your negligent driving.)
- There's no liability coverage, period, under your personal auto policy if you or any insured is held liable for causing an accident while operating any vehicle for compensation as a taxi or limousine or as a conveyance for picking up or delivering things like newspapers and magazines, or food (e.g., pizza), or other products and materials. Car-pooling is okay.
- There's no coverage for any insured while he's engaged in "selling, repairing, servicing, storing or parking" cars. If the mechanic you let drive your car to see what's causing that worrisome noise doesn't also pay attention to the traffic and as a consequence causes an accident resulting in bodily injury, neither your policy nor his is going to cover his liability. (Presumably the shop he works for has liability insurance that will.)
- There's no coverage for an insured who uses someone else's car without permission…unless the insured happens to be a family member living with you who goes off in your car without your permission. The practical meaning here can best be explained with an example. Suppose that in an emergency you went off in your neighbor's car (the keys to which were always left in the ignition), and on the way to wherever you were going, you caused an accident resulting in bodily injury to a third party. Would your policy pay up? Not if you didn't have your neighbor's okay to use his car.
- There's no coverage for punitive damages (i.e., damages awarded on top of everything else to make an example of you for your egregiously irresponsible behavior.)
- There's no coverage in respect of any non-owned vehicle furnished to you or a family member living with you for your or their use (like a company car).
- There's no coverage for racing or anything having to do with racing.

There are a few other exclusions here having to do with people insured under a nuclear energy liability policy, people whose cars are damaged in drug seizures, and cars that aren't really cars, none of which merits any discussion here. If you would like more information, talk to your agent.

Umbrella Policies

An *umbrella* policy provides liability coverage over and above the limits afforded by your auto and homeowners policies. If you've got substantial assets to protect, or make a handsome salary, or have good prospects, this is something you should look into. A $1 million umbrella is cheaper than you might suppose. The only thing is that it will require that you carry on the order of $300,000 to $500,000 on both your car and home. In the example I gave earlier in which I injured four people in one accident and got stuck with an aggregate judgment of $1,200,000, if I had a $1 million umbrella policy, it would kick in where my auto policy left off. My auto policy would pay $500,000 and my umbrella would then pay $500,000. Note that the umbrella is *excess coverage* up to $1 million, not additional coverage of $1 million. It takes over where your primary coverage—in this case, your auto policy—leaves off.

Medical Payments Coverage (Part B)

Coverage

This covers medical expenses and funeral expenses resulting from bodily injury to an insured that was caused by an accident involving a car. The bare-bones minimum coverage is $1,000, with no maximum per accident. If there were five people including you in the car when you had an accident and all of you were seriously injured, each of you would have up to $1,000 of your medical expenses reimbursed by your policy. For not much extra in premium, you can raise this limit to, say, $5,000 or even $10,000.

Who's Insured

The people covered under the insuring agreement for medical payments are the following:

- The named insured and any family members injured in an accident involving *a* car.

- Anyone injured while in *your* car.

If, for example, you accidentally slam a car door on your fingers, breaking one or two, and go to the hospital to have them attended to, your policy will pay up to its limit toward whatever your bill comes to. The same is true if you get hit while crossing the street on foot.[5] Or if you get hit riding a bicycle. While you or a family member doesn't actually have to be in your car when you're injured to be covered, anybody else does. That is to say that if a friend gets hurt in an accident while riding in your car, he is covered by your policy. But if you're driving a rental, he's not. (In all likelihood, however, he's covered under his own personal auto policy.)

An important point to note here: to be claimable, the expenses must be incurred within three (3) years of the accident. If you think that rear-ender you suffered may have resulted in a case of whiplash, don't put off seeing about it if you want your policy to pay for treatment.

Exclusions

All of the exclusions that apply to Medical Payments coverage are contained within the list that applies to Liability coverage, which is a bit longer. In short, if you're okay with the exclusions on liability coverage, you're okay with those on medical payments.

Why buy this coverage

Only Liability insurance is mandatory. Medical Payments and the other two kinds of coverage are not. You may therefore wonder, if you've got major medical insurance or Medicare to deal with any injuries, whether it makes sense to buy this coverage. From what I understand, it does, because if someone riding with you is hurt in an accident you caused and your insurance deals with his or her injuries, that person is much less likely to sue you than if your insurance hadn't helped.

---

[5] Unless the driver who hits you is never apprehended, your medical expense will almost certainly be reimbursed by his auto liability coverage, assuming he's got insurance.

Uninsured/Underinsured Motorists (Part C)

The last time I checked, all but one state requires motorists to carry car insurance providing liability coverage. The one that doesn't instead requires that drivers show proof of having the financial wherewithal to deal with the legal consequences of being found at fault in an accident causing bodily injury or property damage. Notwithstanding these requirements, there are lots of uninsured people on the road. Think of the millions of illegal aliens driving around. Obviously if you get hit by one of these people and he totals your new Lexus and puts you in the hospital and thence into rehab, you could have a hard time collecting from him.

And even if the man who hit you does have insurance, it may not be enough. The state requirements are all pretty low, with the highest being 50/100/25, meaning, of course, bodily injury limits of $50,000 per person and $100,000 total per accident and property damage of $25,000. Most requirements are on the order of 25/50/25, which might not indemnify you for the loss of your Lexus or pay to fix you up. Suing the guy probably won't help either. If he had much in the way of assets to protect, he doubtless would have had more coverage.

Coverage

Uninsured Motorist coverage is intended to cover your losses in the event you or another insured is injured or suffers a property loss at the hands of either an uninsured motorist or a hit-and-run driver or an insured motorist whose insurance company has become insolvent. In any of these events, your policy pays you what you otherwise could have collected from the driver at fault, up to the limits of your coverage, of course. Generally, the limits here will be the same as your liability limits in Part A.

Whether an insured is entitled to recovery under this coverage, as well as the amount to which he or she is entitled, is a matter to be agreed between the insured and his or her insurance company. If they can't agree, the dispute must be settled through arbitration.

If you want to cover the risk of being hit by an *underinsured* motorist (i.e., someone whose insurance, while meeting state minimum requirements, isn't adequate to deal with a significant loss), you must buy an endorsement to your policy. Underinsured Motorist is not part of the basic coverage.

Who's Insured

For the purposes of this coverage, the following people are insured:

- You (the named insured) and members of your family living with you.
- Anyone "occupying" your car ("your covered auto"), with "occupying" encompassing getting in, being in, riding in, and getting out of your car.
- Anyone entitled to recover damages because of bodily injury sustained by a person described above (i.e., the named insured, a member of his or her family, or anyone occupying your car).

This means that you and any family members would be covered whether you're in your car or not when you were injured. If you were hit walking across the street by a hit-and-run driver, you'd be covered. If you were hit riding your bicycle, you'd be covered. For anybody else to be covered by your policy, however, he or she would have to be "occupying your covered auto," or suffer financial loss as a consequence of one of you being injured or killed. If, for example, a breadwinner is killed, his or her spouse might be able to use this coverage to recover lost wages, up to the policy limit.

Exclusions

Again, the exclusions that apply to Liability coverage cover most of those that apply to Uninsured Motorist, but not all. Here are several exclusions that are unique to Uninsured Motorist:

- There's no coverage if you settle with the negligent party without your insurance company's consent. Your insurance company wants the right to sue the other party to recover what they paid you.
- There's no coverage if you don't have Uninsured Motorist coverage. As noted before, the only mandatory coverage in a personal auto policy is liability.

Physical Damage Coverage (Part D)

Coverage

Here we're dealing with the cost to repair your car if it's damaged, or to pay you its actual cash value if it has been totaled or stolen. Actually, it doesn't have to be your car—it could be a loaner or a rental car. It's enough that the car was in your (or another insured's) possession when something happened to it.

The policy makes a distinction here between two causes of damage or loss. One cause is *Collision*, which you might take to mean running into something—e.g., a tree, utility pole, another vehicle, whatever—*or* being run into by something, which in most cases would be another car. But it also means "upset," or overturning. All other causes fall under the heading of *Other Than By Collision.* The latter is *open-perils* coverage, meaning all causes except those specifically excluded. Other Than By Collision was formerly (and still is) referred to as *Comprehensive*. That's the term I'm going to use.

You can elect to buy coverage for physical damage or not. You can buy Collision, but not Comprehensive, and vice-versa. If you own two cars, you can buy both coverages for one car and one or neither for the other. Some people who own a clunker will waive buying any kind of physical damage coverage, figuring that it isn't worth the premium dollars. Needless to say, if you waive physical damage coverage and you have a loss which is your fault, you're going to bear the loss in its entirety.

One of the advantages of collision coverage is that if your car is damaged by another motorist you don't have to collect from him first to pay to get your car fixed. Your insurance company will pay to repair your car. It may then attempt to recover what it's out from the other guy, who may have no insurance and no money. (We'll discuss *subrogation* near the end of the chapter.)

Non-Owned Auto

As indicated, Physical Damage coverage applies not only to your covered autos, but to non-owned autos as well, excluding those non-owned autos furnished or available for your use, or a family member's use, like a company car. As usual, "auto" here encompasses cars, pick-ups, vans, and trailers. If these vehicles are being used by you or a family member or are in your possession or theirs, they're covered. This could be a car your in-laws left with you while they went on a cruise, or one you're using while yours is in the shop for repairs, or it could be a rental.

There's a bit more to say about rental cars, however. If you've ever rented a car, you know that the agent helping you will always ask if you wish to buy the insurance. The insurance in this case consists of four coverage options—a loss-damage waiver, liability coverage, personal accident coverage and personal effects coverage. The one that's germane to your policy's physical damage coverage is the loss-damage waiver, whereby the rental car agency waives its right to recovery if the vehicle is damaged or stolen while in your possession. Savvy travelers are supposed to know to decline the waiver. Why? Because anything not covered by their auto policy's collision and comprehensive coverages, such as *loss of use* (while the vehicle is being repaired), supposedly will be covered by the credit card they presumably used to pay for the rental. Even the policy deductible.

Based on what the insurance lady who vetted this chapter tells me, that's not necessarily the case. Many credit cards don't pay for losses like "diminished value." What's "diminished value?" I was told that this occurs when the rental car company decides to sell a damaged car at auction, rather than have it repaired, and receives less than book value for it. I have no idea how common this is. Maybe very common. I just know that most auto policies don't cover it and neither do most credit cards.

So what should you do? Well, first, read your auto policy's Physical Damage section and your credit card's Guide to Benefits where it deals with "rental car insurance" to understand what they cover and what they don't.[6] It's conceivable, though not likely, that you're covered against "diminished value." If not, you may wish to consider adopting my insurance lady's practice. She says she buys the waiver, as expensive as it is, if she's going to be driving in a strange, big city where the traffic could be hairy and to decline it if conditions should be okay.

Claims Settlement

It is the insurance company's call as to how it's going to compensate you on any physical damage claim. It can pay to repair your car; it can replace it; or it can give you a

[6] If you have questions, don't wait until you're at the Avis desk to call your credit card company to ask them. You'll go crazy just trying to talk to a human being.

check. If it opts to do the last, it will give you *actual cash value*, which is essentially replacement cost minus a deduction for age and wear and tear.

Car Rental

Most policies will pay you up to so much a day (likely $30 to $50), for up to thirty days to rent a car while yours is being repaired or replaced. Of course, to receive this coverage you have to have the underlying Collision or Comprehensive coverage, whichever applies to the kind of loss you're dealing with.

Deductibles

You will always have some sort of deductible that applies to your two physical damage coverages. A deductible is that portion of any loss that the insured agrees to pay before his insurance pays anything. The deductibles I have on both Collision and Comprehensive is about $500, meaning that if my car is damaged or destroyed I will absorb the first $500 to repair or replace it. The higher your deductible, the lower your premium.

Exclusions

Most of the exclusions that apply to Liability coverage apply here as well, but there are some additional ones, to wit:

- There is no coverage for wear and tear, mechanical and electrical failures, or road damage to tires. If a rock flies up and cracks your windshield, however, that is covered.[7]
- There's no coverage for sound systems, CB radios, fuzz-busters, and other electronics unless they are permanently installed.
- There's no coverage for custom furnishings to pick-ups and vans, although you can add it.
- There's no coverage for camper bodies or trailers not listed in the declarations.

---

[7] This has happened to us multiple times in the past five years. In each instance, the cost to replace the windshield was less than our deductible, so our insurance paid nothing.

Duties after an Accident or Loss (Part E)

This is all just commonsense stuff. As you would expect, when you have an accident—whether you're at fault or the other party is—you need to report it to your insurance company promptly, letting it know how, when, and where it happened, and if you can, the names, telephone numbers, and addresses of any witnesses. Be factual: you'll be on a recorded line.[8] Then, however the matter evolves—into an investigation, lawsuit, out-of-court settlement, whatever—you need to cooperate with your insurance company in every way. You need to provide it with copies of any legal documents or other related correspondence you receive. If it needs you to undergo any kind of medical examination, you'll have to comply. If it needs access to medical records, you must give it. If it asks for proof of loss, you must give that too.

If you or a family member was involved in any mishap involving a hit-and-run driver, you are required to report that to the police right away.

Other Provisions (Part F)

I'm not going to wade through all these provisions as, again, most are just common sense—things you would assume anyway. But there are two worth noting.

The first is that your policy is only good in the U.S., Canada, and Puerto Rico. If you're travelling to Mexico, you need to buy a policy that covers you there.

The second is that if your insurance company pays you on a Medical Payments claim, Uninsured/Underinsured Motorist claim, or Physical Damage claim, where a third party caused your loss, it (i.e., the insurance company) is *subrogated* to your right to seek recovery from the person or persons responsible. You are enjoined (prevented) from doing anything that would prejudice its chances of collecting. If you do, as noted earlier, it could be grounds for the insurance company to deny your claim.

Additional Coverages

I'm not going to go into these either except to note that these additional coverages include such things as towing.

---

[8] Some people object to this, as if they don't want to be held later to what they first reported. Too bad -- there's no way around it.

No-Fault Insurance

Precisely because car accidents are so commonplace and no one, no matter how cautious, is immune to causing one; and because the process of fixing legal responsibility can be agonizingly slow, not to mention wasteful, often benefiting the parties' attorneys more than the parties themselves; and because so many accidents are caused by uninsured/underinsured drivers and people with no means at all of making restitution, there has been a movement afoot for many years to replace the personal auto policy just described with something called no-fault insurance. With no-fault insurance, instead of you trying to collect from me if I run into you, injuring you and messing up your car, and me for my part trying to fend you off, we each say, in effect, "Too bad—stuff happens," and look to our individual policies to pay to fix us up. In this case, if I've got more insurance than you (i.e., higher limits), even though I'm at fault, I may come out better in my settlement than you.

While the no-fault insurance idea has been around a long time, I'm not aware that any state has adopted it in its pure form. I do know that a number of states—twelve, I read somewhere recently—have policies that are a variation on this theme. I'm not going to worry with those here. Ask your agent if yours is a no-fault state, and if so, how it works there.

****

The principle coverage you have with an auto policy is liability protection up to whatever limits you have opted for. You can buy property coverage on your car as well (collision and comprehensive), but that's up to you (*and* if you owe on your car, your lender of course). Public policy doesn't require it, as it does liability coverage.

How much liability coverage you carry on your car, over and above the minimum limits set by your state—and for that matter, how much liability you carry on your homeowners policy—should depend on how much in the way of assets you have to protect, as well as your future earnings potential. The more you have to lose, the more protection you need. Above some figure you may need to consider buying an umbrella policy. If so, the size of the umbrella will dictate the limits of liability you must carry on your auto and homeowners policies.

Your premiums will be lower if you buy your auto and homeowners policies (and your umbrella, too, if you need one) from the same insurance company. So, when shopping for auto insurance, shop your homeowners policy (and umbrella) at the same time. I'd seek quotes from two or three agents or agencies representing companies which rank high in customer satisfaction. You can find these companies by doing an internet search.

You will also reduce the premiums on both your auto and homeowners policies by opting for higher deductibles. Your agent can help you here by explaining the trade-offs.

The most significant thing you can do to minimize the premium on your auto policy is to maintain a spotless driving record. You do that of course by driving carefully, obeying the law, and keeping your mind on what you're doing.

NINE

Homeowners Insurance

If you own a home, you have two major loss exposures: One is the risk of your home and everything in it being damaged or destroyed by a fire or some other such occurrence, and the other is of being sued by someone who was injured on your property. To protect against such eventualities, you buy a *homeowners* policy. You cannot afford *not* to have one.

****

In most states[1] homeowners (HO) policies are written on six standardized *forms*. Four (*HO-2, HO-3, HO-5* and *HO-8*) apply to *owner-occupants*—i.e., people who own and live in their own homes; one (*HO-6*) to condominium unit owners; and one (*HO-4*) to renters.[2]

The discussion here is going to be about the policies for owner-occupants.

[1] Texas, where I live, is not among them.

[2] There's an HO-1 policy which applies to owner-occupants as well, but because it only provides protection against ten named perils, it's apparently not very popular and can't be sold in many states.

Whatever the policy—whether it's for an owner-occupant, a condo owner, or a renter—they all provide property and liability coverages.

Section I – Property Coverages

Coverages

HO policies for owner-occupants distinguish between three types of property. The *dwelling* is the house where you actually live; *other structures* means other fixed improvements to the residence premises, such as a detached garage, storage shed, or greenhouse, as well as some improvements you might not think of as "structures" per se, like fences, driveways, and walkways; and the third is *personal property*, meaning in a practical sense the contents of your house, whether belonging to you or someone else, including furniture, artwork, bric-a-brac, rugs, appliances, computer equipment, music systems, clothing, cookware, foodstuff, jewelry, money, and fire-arms. Other structures are typically insured for 10% of the amount that the dwelling is insured for and personal property for 50% of the dwelling amount. This means that if your house is insured for, say, $250,000, you've likely got $25,000 on other structures and $125,000 on personal property.

There is also coverage for *loss of use*. This reimburses you for the additional expenses you incur and/or rental income you forego if your home is made uninhabitable by some occurrence. The amount of coverage here is either 10% or 20% of the dwelling coverage, depending on the form, so in the example above it would be either $25,000 or $50,000.

Perils

The term used by the insurance industry for the kinds of events that could cause a property loss is *perils*. Property coverage is either on a *named-perils* or *open-perils* basis. The standard HO-2 policy names sixteen (16) perils that it insures against:

- Fire or lightening
- Windstorm (think of hurricanes and tornados) or hail
- Explosion
- Riot or civil commotion

- Damage caused by aircraft (including spacecraft)
- Damage caused by vehicles (like a drunk driver taking out your front fence)
- Smoke damage
- Vandalism or malicious mischief
- Theft
- Volcanic eruption
- Falling objects (like a tree or a big tree limb falling on your house)
- Weight of ice, snow, or sleet (which might cave your roof in)
- Accidental discharge or overflow of water or steam (like the time when as a child I let the upstairs tub overflow, ruining the ceiling below)
- Sudden and accidental tearing apart, cracking, burning or bulging of steam or hot water heating system, air-conditioning, or automatic fire-protection sprinkler system, or an appliance
- Freezing of pipes
- Sudden and accidental damage from artificially generated electric current

If you have an HO-2 policy and suffer damage or loss to your home or its contents that wasn't as a result of one of these sixteen named perils, your policy isn't going to indemnify you in any way.

The HO-3 policy is different from the HO-2 policy in that the HO-3 offers *open-perils* coverage on the dwelling and other structures. (Personal property is still only covered against named perils.) Open-perils means coverage against all perils not specifically excluded. The perils specifically excluded are generally the following:

- Enforcement of building ordinances or law
- Earthquake or other earth movement (like settling, which could damage your slab if you're on that kind of foundation.)
- Flooding and water damage from groundwater seepage, swimming pool leaks, sump pump overflow, etc.
- Power failures

- Neglect in protecting property at the time of loss
- War or nuclear hazard
- Intentional acts
- Government action

In addition to these, which apply to all property—dwelling, other structures and personal property—there may be other exclusions that apply only to the dwelling and other structures, such as:

- Collapse resulting from earthquake, flooding and certain other causes
- Freezing of pipes and the like when the house has been left vacant without heat
- Vandalism and malicious mischief after the house has been left vacant for a certain number of days
- Mold, fungus, or wet rot
- Loss caused by the deliberate or intentional acts of the insured (such as setting your house on fire to collect the insurance)
- Wear and tear, marring, and deterioration
- Mechanical breakdown, latent defect, inherent vice
- Smog, rust, or other corrosion
- Smoke from agricultural smudging or industrial operations
- Discharge, dispersal, release, or escape of contaminants and pollutants
- Settling, shrinking, bulging or expansion of pavements, patios, foundations, sidewalks, etc.
- Birds, vermin, rodents, and insects (like wood ants and termites)
- Animals owned or kept by an insured

If you have an HO-3 policy, you should investigate to see what exclusions other than these may apply to your dwelling and other structures coverage and, if there are any you're not sure you understand, have your insurance agent explain.

The HO-5 policy is like the HO-3 policy except that the HO-5 extends open-perils coverage to personal property (contents) as well. As noted earlier, personal property under an HO-3 policy is covered only against named perils.

Endorsements, Riders & Floaters

If you live on a river or creek or in an earthquake zone, you need to insure against the attendant risk by other means. If you live in a flood zone, you need to buy flood insurance. Flood insurance is sold by insurance companies that participate in the National Flood Insurance Program (NFIP), which is overseen by the Federal Emergency Management Agency (FEMA). The Standard Flood Insurance Policy offers coverage of up to $250,000 on the building property and $100,000 on contents. Premiums are based on the property's susceptibility to flooding according to topographical maps that FEMA maintains.

If you live in an earthquake zone and want to be protected against earthquake damage, you will need to have your HO policy endorsed so that it does. An *endorsement*, aka *rider*, is a document attached to a policy that amends the coverage in some way. Except for "deliberate or intentional acts," nearly any exclusion can be "endorsed" away. For a price, of course.

You also need to know that standard HO policies set very low limits on the amounts that are recoverable on losses by theft of certain types of personal property. Our policy, for example, will not pay more than $500 in the aggregate on rare coins and stamps; not more than $500 on any one article of jewelry or furs, nor more than $1,000 in the aggregate for these; ditto for rugs and carpets; and not more than $500 in the aggregate for silverware, silver-plate, and the like. If you own valuable antiques and artwork, rare coins or stamps, oriental rugs, jewelry, silverware, crystal, and the like, you should look at your HO policy to see what kind of coverage you've got on them if they're stolen, and then consider having them separately insured under a scheduled personal property endorsement. We've done this. It's not cheap, but we sleep a little easier knowing that if any of our valuables are stolen, or for that matter are lost to any other peril, we'll get a check for the insured amount.

Household Inventory

This is probably a good time to talk about an inventory of all your personal property. I've done one, and it's a tedious, time-consuming job, but if you don't have one and you have a fire, or a tornado scatters your things all over North Texas and Oklahoma, you're going to have a difficult time putting together a claim for what you've lost. Besides a good description of each item, your claim would need to indicate when the item was acquired. Photographs or video showing it in your home before the event would be helpful, as would sales slips.

I approached our inventory a room at a time, spending several days each on the kitchen and dining room. As you might imagine, we have tons of stuff whose purchase date we cannot document with sales slips. We've been married over fifty years, and each of us has inherited lots of things that were in turn inherited by our mothers and by them from their mothers. Long story short, I've done the best I could with dates and descriptions, and we've photographed it all. All of this documentation is in the bank safe deposit box where it's safe from any calamity that might result in our needing it.

This is important. If you lose everything, don't assume that the insurance company is just going to hand you a check for the amount of personal property coverage shown on your policy. That's just the limit of their coverage, the maximum amount they will pay. It's up to you to document what you lost. If you don't have a personal property inventory, you need to get to work on one. Your insurance agent may have some worksheets that will make your job easier or be able to suggest where you can find some.

Your agent should also be able to suggest someone qualified to appraise your antiques, artwork, and other high-value possessions for purposes of insuring them separately for their full value.

Replacement Cost vs. *Actual Cash Value*

Property losses are indemnified on the basis of *replacement cost* or *actual cash value (ACV)*. *Replacement cost* is the cost to repair, rebuild, or replace something new. *Actual cash value* is less—it's replacement cost minus *depreciation*, with depreciation meaning how much something is physically used up due to wear and tear. If your refrigerator, which you bought seven years ago, is supposed to last twenty years, its actual cash value in the event of a total loss would be just 65%[3] of replacement cost. Supposing replacement cost to be $1,500, you'd be looking at an ACV recovery of $975.[4]

If your home or one of the other improvements to your premises is damaged or destroyed, your policy will probably pay to repair, rebuild, or replace the property. That is to say, you will receive replacement cost. On the other hand, to the extent that the contents were damaged or destroyed, you're probably only going to be compensated for their actual cash value, unless you've had your standard HO policy endorsed to cover the replacement cost of your possessions. I recommend that you look into this.

Summarizing, coverage on your dwelling and other structures is normally on the basis of replacement cost (up to the policy limit), while for personal property it's on the basis of actual cash value.

The 80% Rule

The complete and total destruction of houses from the perils named above is fairly uncommon, resulting almost exclusively I would think from fires in areas like where I live that are outside the city limits and have no fire hydrants. Most occurrences just do damage. From analyzing and massaging years and years of data, the insurance industry has figured out that if people will insure their homes for at least 80% of replacement cost, the companies can make the numbers work for them and most claims can be settled to the satisfaction of the people who've made them. Accordingly, as long as you meet this 80% threshold, they'll cut you a lot of slack, paying up to the policy limits against a legitimate claim. For example, if the cost to re-build your 3,000 square foot home, with its Italian tile floors in the kitchen and bathrooms, granite countertops, crown molding, plantation shutters, etc., is $500,000, and you have insured it for 80% of that amount, which would be $400,000, and you have hail damage, necessitating the replacement of your roof at a cost of, say, $40,000, the insurance company will reimburse you every cent of that (less your deductible), and you'll doubtless be happy. Of course, if your house is totally destroyed in a fire, all you're going to get is $400,000, leaving you $100,000 short if you rebuild. You'll be very unhappy about that. To obviate that possibility it's wise to insure your house for its full replacement cost.

---

[3] ((20 – 7) ÷ 20 = 65%

[4] 65% × $1,500 = $975

What you must not do is insure your home for less than 80% of its replacement cost. The insurance industry has established that number as a minimum. If you go below that threshold and you have a loss, like the hail damage in the example above, you're not going to be reimbursed for the full cost of replacing your roof. You'll only receive a pro-rata settlement of your claim or the actual cash value of your loss, whichever is the greater amount. Here's how it works: Let's say that, for whatever reason, you bought only $300,000 of coverage, representing just 60% of replacement cost ($300,000 ÷ $500,000 = 60%), when you should have bought at least $400,000, representing 80%. In sum, you only insured your house for three-quarters (75%) of what was minimally required, so three-quarters (75%) of the cost to replace your roof is all you're going to recover from your insurance company. *Unless* of course the actual cash value of your loss was greater, in which case you'd get that. If your 20-year composition roof was very new and its remaining expected life was, say, 18 years, your recovery might be 90% (18 ÷ 20 = 90%). But if the roof was instead 6 years old, making its remaining life expectancy just 70%, then you'd be back to 75% as the larger number. And 75% of a $40,000 roof replacement is only $30,000, which would leave you having to come up with the other $10,000 yourself. And, of course, again, if your $500,000 home is completely destroyed, it will cost you $200,000 out of pocket to replace it. The 80% rule notwithstanding, your policy isn't going to indemnify you for losses that exceed your coverage limits.

There are a myriad of reasons why people under-insure. They're trying to get their premiums down, they confuse market value with replacement cost, they fail to account for the increase in construction costs since they built their homes, etc. Do not make any of these mistakes. If you're uncertain what it would cost today to build a house just like yours, ask your insurance agent to suggest how you find out. Also ask him about *Inflation Guard* and *extended dwelling coverage.* Either will help protect you against construction cost creep. The first is an endorsement you buy that will bump up your property coverage every quarter by some percentage (1%, 2%, 3%, etc.) of your original coverage. Extended dwelling coverage goes beyond this. With it, the insured not only has his coverage on his dwelling bumped up for inflation, but by up to another 25% to 50% if his loss exceeds the limits of coverage per the declarations page of his policy. For example, a home insured for $400,000 might have 25% extended dwelling coverage that in the event of a complete loss would pay up to $500,000 ($400,000 × 1.25% = $500,000) toward the cost of rebuilding. Extended dwelling coverage requires that you insure your home—i.e. the dwelling—for full replacement cost, that you notify the insurance company of any improvements or remodeling that you do that increases its replacement cost by $5,000 or more, and that you accept annual adjustments made by the insurance company to your home's replacement cost to account for building cost increases.

HO - 8

The HO-8 policy form is used to insure homes built in a bygone era whose replacement cost today greatly exceeds their current market value. Coverage is against named perils, and when there is a loss, it is adjusted on the basis of what it will cost to repair or replace the property *functionally* using modern construction methods and materials. It won't pay to replicate the longleaf pine flooring, plastered walls and custom molding you had before.

Condominium-unit and Renter's Forms

If you own a condo, your association will insure the building you're in. Your own policy, then, will only cover the improvements you've made to your unit to finish it out, plus your personal property, and your own personal liability.

Likewise, if you're a renter, you're not going to have property coverage on the house, apartment, or condo where you live, but rather only on your possessions and possibly any leasehold improvements you've made. You'll also have liability coverage.

Deductibles

All policies have a *deductible* that applies to property losses. A deductible is the amount of a loss that you agree to pay out of your own pocket before your policy pays anything. If your deductible is $250, which is typical, and you have a $10,000 fire loss, your reimbursement from the insurance company will be $9,750 ($10,000 - $250 = $9,750).

The higher your deductible, the lower your premium. This is well worth discussing with your insurance agent. The savings can be significant.

Section II – Liability Coverage

Coverages

Homeowners policies provide coverage, usually in the amount of $100,000 to $500,000, against *legal liability* for *bodily injury* or *property damage* suffered by a third party on the residence premises in a mishap or accident imputed to an insured's *negligence* or unintentionally at the hands of any insured, whether on the residence premises or away. The policy also provides some coverage, albeit not much—$1,000 is the standard amount—for *medical expenses* incurred by the third party.

A couple of examples—one where the mishap occurs on the residence premises and another where it occurs away—will help to illustrate what I'm talking about here. First on the residence premises: Suppose that I leave something inherently dangerous lying about in plain sight that the little boy next door is enticed to investigate and in so doing is seriously injured. If my neighbors sue, which is likely, it is all but certain that I will be found guilty of negligence. Another example, away from the residence premises: Out for some early morning exercise with my big, bumptious Airedale, I lose control of him when we come upon an elderly lady who's walked out to the curb with a cat in her arms to pick up the paper and who in the ensuing confusion loses her balance and falls to the ground, breaking her hip, which requires surgery, months of rehab, and is ever after a source of pain and suffering. Again, it's entirely possible that I will be sued, and if so that I will lose. In both cases, it's also probable that my insurance company, knowing that a jury will find me negligent, will attempt to reach an out-of-court settlement with the injured party.[5] Failing at that, it will bear my legal expenses and indemnify me against whatever judgment is rendered against me, up to the policy limits.

The policy is only going to provide coverage for losses resulting in *bodily harm* or *property damage*, and then only if was caused *unintentionally*. If I libel someone and he sues and gets a judgment against me, I'm out of luck. There was no bodily harm or property damage. If I renege on some contract, same thing. If I sic my notoriously bad-

[5] Many, if not most, claims are settled out of court. If your insurance company takes this route in a matter where you think you would be judged not to be negligent, there's nothing you can do about it. How the insurance company wants to deal with a claim is its prerogative.

tempered Rottweiler on the guy who's come to repossess my sofa, I'm on my own if he sues. What I did was intentional.

Insureds

Besides the *named insured* whose name appears on the policy, the following people are also treated as *insureds*: the named insured's spouse, assuming the two live together; any of their relatives living on the premises; and anyone under 21 who is in the charge of one of these people. A friend or neighbor taking care of a pet while an insured is away is also covered as an insured if the pet bites someone while in his or her custody. Employees are covered while on duty. Anyone operating an unregistered vehicle belonging to an insured, like an ATV, golf cart, or tractor mower, is insured too, provided he or she is doing so with the insured's consent.

Exclusions

A host of exclusions apply to these policies, meaning that if the injury or damage stems from, or is related to, any of the following there is no coverage:

- Intentional acts
- Business or professional activities ~ If you own a shop and someone trips on the threshold and is injured, that wouldn't be covered by your homeowners policy.
- Rental property ~ If you have a boarder or two in your home, that's one thing—that's okay—but if you're leasing the whole caboodle while you're away on a two-year assignment to Timbuktu, you need another kind of policy designed for rental property.
- Professional liability ~ Doctors and dentists should look to *malpractice* insurance to protect themselves against lawsuits, while accountants, insurance professionals, lawyers, stockbrokers, real estate agents, and the like whose carelessness can harm their clients financially should buy *errors and omissions* insurance.

- Uninsured premises ~ If the insured has an undeclared home—say, a vacation cabin on a lake somewhere—there is no coverage for anything that might happen there.
- Vehicles, boats, and aircraft ~ There are exceptions to these exclusions, but for all intents and purposes anything bad that happens involving a vehicle, a trailer that is being hauled by a vehicle, a motorized watercraft, or an airplane is not covered. You buy an auto policy, a boat owner's policy, and an aircraft policy to cover those exposures.
- War
- Communicable diseases, sexual molestation or abuse, and controlled substances ~ If an insured is sued for infecting someone with HIV, or for molesting a child, or for an injury sustained in a meth lab explosion—just to throw out three hypotheticals—the insurance company is going to refuse to consider the claim.
- Workers compensation ~ HO policies will not pay for injuries sustained on the job by an employee who is covered by worker's compensation insurance. If there is no workers comp coverage, then it will… notwithstanding the fact that when in the act of operating a vehicle the employee is himself, or herself, an insured.
- Injury to an insured ~ An HO policy will not pay for a judgment that one insured gets against another. If it's your mother-in-law who lives with you who trips on the hose lying across the front walk, whatever ensues from that is of no concern to your insurance company.
- Damage to property owned by, rented to, or in the care, custody, or control of an insured ~ Since you can't be liable to yourself, it's not surprising that there's no coverage for any damage you might do to your own property. Damage to property belonging to someone else that's in your care may be covered under Section I, or if not, up to $500 under "Additional Liability Coverages," which we'll get to in a moment.

Medical Payments to Others

This isn't liability coverage per se. That is to say there doesn't have to be any negligence or carelessness on the part of an insured for the policy to pay. It is enough that the injury took place on the residence premises or at the hand of an insured. If, for example, a guest walks into your patio door, knocking himself flat on his back, and then goes to the emergency room to be examined, his expenses, up to probably $1,000, will be reimbursed to him by your homeowners policy, provided his claim is made and documented within three years of the mishap. All of the exclusions above apply.

Additional Liability Coverages

There are four additional liability coverages:

- Claim expenses ~ In addition to paying up to the policy limit to settle the insured's liability for causing bodily injury or property damage, the insurance company will pay his or her defense costs.
- First aid expenses ~ It will also pick up the tab for first aid given to a person or persons injured in a mishap covered by the policy. This, too, is in addition to any settlement of legal liability.
- Damage to property of others ~ The policy will pay up to $500 for damage caused by an insured to property belonging to someone else, even where there is no legal liability, simply a moral responsibility. This would be the case where your small child accidentally breaks the neighbor's window.
- Loss assessment coverage ~ The policy will pay up to $1,000 if you're assessed by your homeowners, landowners, or condominium association for your share of uninsured liability losses resulting from some occurrence that would be covered by your own policy. For example, let's say that your landowners association owns the roads serving your subdivision and an unsafe condition results in an accident involving a third party who's out there looking at a home for sale. If he or she sues and gets a judgment that surpasses the limits of the association's policy, you might be assessed your share of the deficiency, in which case your HO policy would pay up to $1,000.

Umbrella Liability Insurance

We live in a highly litigious society where it's not unlikely that you'll be sued someday for something—particularly if you are a person of means, or appear to have the potential of earning a lot some day. Judgments against the well-to-do can be huge, far exceeding the liability coverage on their homeowners or automobile policies. To deal with this possibility if you're vulnerable, you should consider buying an *umbrella* policy. An umbrella policy provides you with coverage of $1 million or more against legal liability for bodily injury and property damage, as well as against judgments for libel, slander, defamation of character, mental anguish, false arrest, wrongful entry or eviction, and malicious prosecution. For bodily injury and property damage claims, it picks up where your HO policy or auto policy stops; for the other perils not covered by your HO policy and auto policy, it pays right from the start.

If you want an umbrella, you'll probably have to carry at least $300,000 of liability on both your HO policy and your auto policy, but you'll be surprised at how reasonable the premiums are, particularly if you're rated low risk.

Matters Affecting Costs

All other things being equal, your home will cost significantly less to insure if it is new rather than old; brick or rock rather than wood frame; has a composition shingle roof, not shakes; and in town, where there is a fire hydrant and fire station close by, rather than out in the country. That is just to know. Short of moving, there's not much you can do about these things.

Things that you can do to lower your premium, besides raising your deductible, include installing smoke detectors and a burglar alarm system, putting deadbolt locks on your exterior doors, and placing a fire extinguisher in the kitchen, utility room, and anywhere else in the house you think smart. Your insurance agent can tell you what you'll save doing these things if you haven't already.

What To Do If You Have A Claim

If you have a claim or think you might, you need to call your insurance agent as soon as possible and let him or her guide you as to what you should do next. Whatever they ask you to do, I would do. But besides that I would keep scrupulous notes of these conversations, noting the date and times you talked and who said what. I'd keep receipts for everything I spent that might be recoverable. And I would document any damage with photographs.

****

I will conclude here by emphasizing the importance of reading your policy and clarifying with your agent anything you do not understand.[6] Here are some questions you might ask:

- Does my policy provide property coverage against named perils, or against all perils except those specifically excluded? If named perils, what would it cost me to change to open-perils?
- Would losses to my house and other structures be compensated for on the basis of replacement cost? The answer here is almost certainly "yes," but I would make absolutely sure.
- How can I be sure that my home is insured for at least 80% of its replacement cost?
- How would I be paid on losses to any personal property? Would I receive replacement cost or actual cash value? If the latter, what would it cost me to change it to replacement cost?
- If I have jewelry, silverware, crystal, fine art, oriental rugs, expensive antiques, etc., what would it cost to have these things covered by a scheduled personal property endorsement where I'd recover appraised value if anything were stolen or destroyed?
- If I live in an area subject to flooding, what would flood insurance cost?
- Do I have adequate liability coverage? Should I have an umbrella? What would more coverage cost?

[6] I cannot over-emphasize the importance of reading your policy. If, for example, you live in Texas, as we do, your policy may be on a slightly different form than the HO-2 and HO-3 policies discussed here. Ours is a "named perils" policy that lists sixteen perils, but only fourteen are exactly the same as the sixteen listed on pages 164 and 165. There are many other little differences, as well.

- What can I do to lower my premiums and what are the trade-offs in terms of higher deductibles and/or investments in burglar alarm systems, smoke detectors, and all the rest?

Lastly, if you don't already have one, get to work on that household inventory, and when you're done, show it to your agent to see if he or she thinks that in the event of a fire or burglary it would suffice to document your losses. And as you acquire more stuff, which is the American way, update the inventory.

TEN

Health Insurance

The *Patient Protection and Affordable Care Act (*the *ACA*), more commonly called *ObamaCare*, was passed along strictly party lines in early 2010 when the Democrats controlled both houses of Congress and, for better or for worse, changed the American health care system in major ways. It had a very rocky roll-out in 2014 and two years later remains deeply unpopular with a large segment of the electorate. Thanks in no small measure to the law's unpopularity, the Republicans re-gained the House in 2010 and the Senate in 2014. Just yesterday (January 8, 2016), after numerous failed attempts, they finally put a bill on President Obama's desk that would repeal it. He will veto the bill, and that will be the end of that, for the time being anyway, because the Republicans don't have the two-thirds majorities in both chambers required to override a veto.

Nobody today knows who will succeed Mr. Obama in 2016, but even if it's a Republican and the Republicans manage to retain control of the House and the Senate and are finally in a position to make good on their pledge to repeal the ACA, many observers don't think they actually will, at least not in its entirety. That's because the

ACA does some things that people really like. It says you can't be denied coverage for any reason. It does away with lifetime maximum benefits. It allows young people who can't find work to remain on their parents' policy till age 26. It provides subsidies to people who need help paying their premiums. Repealing the law would mean going back to the status quo ante, and people don't want that. They just want Congress to fix what they see as the law's problems.

****

One of the chief aims of the Affordable Care Act was to reduce the percentage of uninsured in this country, and in that it has succeeded. It has done so through the expansion of Medicaid, by providing help to low-income families with paying their premiums and by fining taxpayers who, ignoring the law, which requires everyone to have healthcare coverage, don't get it. More about these carrots and sticks later.

The latest statistics that I can find on U.S. health care coverage are for 2014 and come from the Kaiser Family Foundation. According to this study, about half (49%) of the U.S. population is covered by employer-sponsored group medical plans, another 6% by non-group plans, 19% by Medicaid, 13% by Medicare, and 2% by the military and Veterans Administration. Only about 10% of the population remains uninsured. This figure used to be around 15%, as I recall.

If you and your family are covered by an employer-sponsored, ACA-compliant *group plan*, lucky for you. While these plans come in different flavors, with some underwritten by regular for-profit insurance companies, some by not-for profits, like Blue Cross/Blue Shield, and some by the employers themselves using third-parties as plan administrators, in nearly all cases the premiums are mostly paid by the employer and offered to the employee as a non-taxable employee benefit. Probably few employees appreciate what a significant benefit it is. According to another (or possibly the same) 2014 Kaiser Family Foundation survey, employers offering health insurance to their employees spent on average $4,598 for single worker coverage and $12,137 for family coverage. Starting in 2015, all companies with more than fifty (50) full-time employees[1] have been required to offer health coverage.

People not serving in the Armed Forces who aren't covered by an employer-sponsored health care plan and aren't eligible for Medicaid, Medicare, or VA benefits must buy insurance in the individual market. For a few of the people in this *non-group* category, nothing much changed with the ACA. They can keep their old policy because— lucky them—it conforms to the new law in terms of providing the *ten essential coverages*. Everybody else in the category is faced with buying a new policy, either through an insurance agent or through one of the healthcare exchanges created by the ACA.

Medicaid is a public health care program for qualifying low-income individuals, including women who are expecting, children up to the age of 18 and their parents, people with disabilities, and old people in long-term care facilities. It is managed by the individual states, whose programs, while slightly different in their particulars, all comply with certain minimum requirements laid down by the federal government, which underwrites at least half of the cost. The ACA allows for expanding Medicaid eligibility, with the federal government picking up the associated cost during the first three years, but states can opt out if they choose. Texas, where I live, is one that has.

Medicare covers nearly everybody over 65. Chapter 14 is all about Medicare.

The *Veterans Administration* takes care of veterans' health care needs at VA hospitals across the country. To qualify for veterans' medical benefits, the individual must have served on active duty and, if no longer in the service, received an "other than dishonorable discharge." There can be other requirements as well relating to when the veteran entered active service.

****

I can't think of another industry, except maybe the oil business, that is talked about as badly as the health insurance industry. Everybody, but especially politicians it seems, talk as though insurance industry greed is the primary cause of the escalating cost

[1] Employees who work more than 30 hours a week are considered "full-time."

of American health care. I doubt this very much. Leaving aside administrative costs and their comparatively modest profits, all these companies do in the final analysis is re-shuffle their policyholders' total annual healthcare costs in such a way as to leave everyone paying their risk-adjusted share. No one disputes that for some years now health care costs have been growing much faster than the overall rate of inflation, but I think the blame must lie elsewhere than with the insurance companies. They just make an easy target.

It's the things that insurance companies do—or did—to contain costs that incline people not to like them. Before the ACA, if you had a pre-existing condition that could portend major future expense, it's likely they would deny you coverage. As you got older and more susceptible to problems, they'd charge you more for coverage. A lot more. If you were on your parent's policy, on reaching a certain age, they'd throw you off. If you hit your lifetime maximum, that was it: you'd have no more coverage. It's doubtful that anyone affected by any of these practices ever thought it was anything but unjust.

Other cost containment measures remain. Your plan may require you to have a *primary care physician (PCP)* who, besides being your regular doctor, keeps a rein on your health care expenses by controlling your access to specialists and deciding what tests or treatments you really need. Your plan may limit you to using specialists, hospitals, labs, etc. that are within its *network* of service providers, and if you go outside the network, bypassing your PCP, you likely will end up paying all or most of the tab yourself. Unless you have a PCP, your plan will almost certainly require you to be *pre-authorized* by the company before having surgery or being admitted to a hospital for other than emergency care, and if you circumvent this requirement, it likely will not cover the charges. There are health care services that you or a family member may want in the worst way that your plan does not cover, like eyeglasses, a hearing aid, or a facelift. People who do not read their plan's *summary of benefits* set themselves up to make some very costly mistakes.

Then, of course, there is the matter of *cost-sharing*. To keep people from abusing their insurance by going to the doctor about every little ache or pain, nearly all plans call for the insured to bear some of his health care costs in the form of a deductible, copayments, and coinsurance. The *deductible* is the first so many dollars of covered healthcare expenses that you must pay every year before your insurance pays anything. It could be any amount between a couple of hundred dollars to over $6,000. Copayments and coinsurance usually, if not always, kick in after you've satisfied your deductible. That is to say they don't count toward it. A *copayment* is a dollar amount, like $25, whereas *coinsurance* is a percentage, like 20%. Your plan could stipulate, among other things, a $25 copayment every time you go to the doctor, $250 every time you go to the emergency room, and $10 for every non-preferred generic drug prescription you have filled, and/or for other types of services and medications, it may call for you to pick up 15% or 20% of the amount charged. Or more. All other things being equal, the higher the share of his health care costs that the insured assumes through his deductible, copays, and coinsurance, the lower his premium, and vice-versa.

****

Most employer-sponsored group plans, as well as plans that an individual would buy for himself and, if he has one, his family, are described as HMO plans, PPO plans, EPO plans, or POS plans.

- *HMO* is an acronym that stands for *Health Maintenance Organization*. HMOs provide *managed care* to their enrollees using doctors and staff who are either employees of, or under contract to, the HMO. Like any successful business model, HMOs have their good points and their not-so-good points. Their main good points are their low premiums and co-pays and their focus on preventive care and staying healthy. Their not-so-good—or, we might say, not so appreciated—points are, first, they require the enrollee to have a primary care physician who under a very businesslike set of guidelines controls the patient's access to specialists and other healthcare services, and, second, they won't pay for any healthcare services, other than emergency room services, that are provided out of network. By law, they have to cover emergency room services.

- *PPO* stands for *Preferred Provider Organization.* This is a network of healthcare service providers, comprised of physicians, hospitals, labs, therapists, etc., with whom the plan has negotiated discounts. You don't have a primary care physician who decides if you need to see a specialist or have some test done, but this doesn't mean you have complete freedom of action or that the freedom you have doesn't come without cost. There are a couple of things you need to be aware of. The first is that if you have anything done that's out of the ordinary and pricey, like surgery or a CT scan, it probably needs to be pre-authorized by your plan provider or plan administrator. If in doubt, it's best to check. If you do need pre-authorization and you proceed without it, the plan may not cover your charges and likely won't. The other thing is that your deductible, copayments, and coinsurance only apply to services provided within the plan's network. Consult a specialist outside your network and you can expect, instead of a modest copayment (assuming you've met your deductible), either to be hit with the bill in its entirety, thanks to the higher deductible applying, or with a hefty amount of coinsurance. To have your insurance pay anything, though, you'd probably first have to pay the service provider's bill in full yourself and then file a claim. Needless to say, this can impose a hardship, which will be all the harder to bear if your insurance company doesn't settle with you promptly.
- *EPO* stands for *Exclusive Provider Organization.* An EPO is like a PPO but for the fact that it won't pay anything toward services provided out-of-network, except emergency room services. In that respect it's like an HMO.
- *POS* stands for *Point of Service Organization.* As with an HMO, a POS plan requires you to have a primary care physician who manages your care, deciding if you need to see a specialist or have some test done or undergo some kind of therapy. But if your PCP thinks you don't and you think you do, you can go around him and the plan will still pay something, which is not the case with an HMO. You can even see a specialist outside the plan's network, if there's one you're particularly keen on. Just be prepared if you decide to do

things your way as opposed to the plan's way, to foot a big share of the cost. You might also have to pay it all before claiming on your insurance.

****

The ACA requires that everyone have health insurance. This requirement is referred to as the *individual mandate*. If you don't have health insurance, you're subject to a fine, which gets figured in with your income taxes. The fine is calculated by subtracting your income tax *filing threshold*[2] from your income and multiplying the result by a small percentage,[3] and then comparing this number to a minimum fine and choosing the greater. It's enough that you will feel it. Someone whose income is below the filing threshold and therefore doesn't have to file is exempt.

For most people, lack of money won't work as an excuse. If you're at or below the poverty level, there's now a good chance you qualify for Medicaid under the ACA, even if you didn't before. In that case your insurance will probably cost you nothing.[4] If you're doing rather better but your income is still pretty modest—between 100% and 400% of the *federal poverty level (FPL)*—where buying insurance might impose a hardship on you, the government will help you by picking up a portion of your premiums. For individuals, couples, and families whose income is between 100% and just 250% of the FPL, there is even more help in the form of reduced deductibles, copayments, and coinsurance. The only hitch is that to qualify for this help, including expanded Medicaid coverage, you've got to apply for it through your state's online insurance exchange.

Your state's online exchange, more properly referred to as its *health insurance marketplace*, is where you'd probably want to shop for a plan anyway because it makes comparing plans easier. To find your state's exchange, go to www.healthcare.gov or just do a search for "my state's health insurance marketplace." Even if *open enrollment* for

---

[2] Your filing threshold is the sum of your *standard deduction* and *personal exemptions*. It's different depending on your *filing status* (*single, married filing jointly* etc.) and the number of *dependents* you have. Income taxes are discussed in Chapter 7.

[3] The percentage was 1% in 2014 and 2% in 2015 and will be 2.5% in 2016. After that, it will be adjusted annually for inflation.

[4] Medicaid may work a little differently from one state to another, but my understanding is that in most states people on Medicaid aren't charged anything for their coverage, nor are they subject to a deductible, copayments, or coinsurance.

the current/upcoming year is closed,[5] you can go to your state's exchange at any time to browse the plans that are being offered.

All of those plans will cover, at a minimum, ten (10) *essential health benefits*, which are:

- Ambulatory patient services (like visits to your doctor)
- Emergency services
- Hospitalization
- Maternity care and newborn care
- Mental health services and substance use disorder services, including behavioral health treatment
- Prescription drugs
- Rehabilitative and habilitative services and devices
- Laboratory services
- Preventive and wellness services and chronic disease management
- Pediatric services, including oral and vision care

The ACA does not require plans to cover cosmetic surgery, chiropractic services, acupuncture, vision and dental care, and some other things. Some do, however, at least to some extent. Before choosing a plan, you should make sure you understand what's covered and what's not.

Plans are ranked according to their *actuarial value*—which is to say the percentage of covered expenses the companies' actuaries expect the plans to pick up. *Bronze plans* are expected to pick up 60% of the individual's covered health care expenses, *silver* plans 70%, *gold* plans 80% and *platinum* plans 90%. In each case, what the plan doesn't pay the insured does by way of his deductible, copayments, and coinsurance. Thus if you enroll in, say, a silver plan, you can expect that your cost-

[5] Open enrollment is the window you have for enrolling in a plan for the upcoming year. Open enrollment for 2016 began on November 1, 2015 and ends on January 31, 2016. If you don't enroll during the open enrollment period, you can't enroll later in the year, unless you qualify for special enrollment by virtue of some major life event, like having a child or losing the healthcare coverage you had because you lost your job.

sharing will work out to around 30%. It makes no difference what kind of plan it is—HMO, PPO, EPO, or POS.

By law all these plans cap the insured's annual out-of-pocket *covered* costs. Remember, though, that covered costs do not include services that are excluded, like, say, cosmetic surgery, or in the case of an HMO that are provided out-of-network, or where pre-authorization is required that are rendered without it. Premiums aren't included either. For 2016, the *out-of-pocket limit* for an individual is $6,850 and for a family $13,700.

With some plans you could hit the out-of-pocket limit just satisfying the deductible. A Blue Cross/Blue Shield of Texas silver PPO plan that I looked at in 2014 had the very same in-network deductibles and out-of-pocket limits of $6,000 per individual and $12,700 for a family.[6]

If your plan qualifies as a *high-deductible health plan (HDHP),* which the company underwriting it can tell you, you might want to consider opening a tax-advantaged *health saving account (HSA)* that you can tap as the need arises to deal with your deductible, copayments, and coinsurance. What you contribute every year, which this year (2016) can be up to $3,300 for an individual and $6,550 for a family, can be taken as an adjustment to income on your tax return (*Form 1040, line 25*), which will reduce your taxable income and the taxes you pay. And these contributions can be invested to grow tax-deferred. Furthermore, withdrawals, provided they are used for qualifying medical expenses, are not subject to tax either. Almost any bank will be happy to help you with opening an account. Once that's accomplished, you'll be issued a debit card with which to pay bills.

HSAs pre-date the ACA, but from what I can see, they continue to make a lot of sense. Lots of employer-sponsored plans are HDHPs with HSAs attached[7].

---

[6] Higher out-of-pocket limits applied to out-of-network services. The numbers were double the in-network numbers, which is to say they were $12,000 and $25,400, respectively. According to something I read just yesterday (on healthinsurance.org), BC/BS of Texas will not offer PPO plans in Texas in 2016 because their claims last year exceeded premiums by hundreds of millions of dollars.

[7] Many employer-sponsored plans come with *flexible spending accounts (FSAs)* attached. An FSA is much like an HSA in that it's to be used for medical expenses not picked up by your plan, and company contributions to it go in pre-tax, but, unlike an HSA, what you don't use doesn't carry over to future years. Anything left in the FSA at the end of the year reverts back to the company.

****

I feel quite certain that how health insurance works today isn't going to be how it works just a few years from now. My guess is that healthcare will soon become an entitlement program, very much like Medicare and Medicaid. That's because I don't think you can fix the things people don't like about the ACA, while keeping all the things they do, and expect that it's not going to result in jacking up the cost of health insurance, which is already sky-high, to the point of being unaffordable. Who, then, will bother with trying to sell it? Nobody in the private sector.

Is government healthcare a bad thing? Maybe not. It's what most economically advanced countries have, and judging by their life expectancies vis-à-vis ours, it works pretty well. Will the government being in charge lead to price controls, less medical research, fewer people going to medical school and rationing? My guess is that it will.

Stay tuned.

ELEVEN

Long-Term Care Insurance

My mother took out a long-term care insurance policy when she was in her late seventies or early eighties. Her policy paid just $60 a day and was not inexpensive owing to her rather advanced age at time of enrollment. Even so, it turned out to be far and away the best investment she ever made, returning every dollar of premium many times over. That's because at around the age of 85 she began a startlingly precipitous descent into Alzheimer's or some other form of dementia that within two years required that we put her in a nursing home. She just got to be more than my sister and brother-in-law, with whom she had been living, could handle.

Every time I think how fortunate we were that Mother had long-term care insurance, I also recall with a smile how very upset she got a number of times that she could not just hit up Bankers Life to pay for a sitter or cleaning lady when she perceived that my sister needed a helping hand. "Why am I paying these people $280 a month for long-term care, if when we need help, they won't provide it," she would say. "I'm going to cancel that damned policy!" And we would always talk her out of it by explaining that long-term care insurance wasn't something that you could just tap, whenever, for random needs, but if and when she ever got to a point where she couldn't take of herself—feed herself, go to the bathroom by herself, bathe herself, dress herself, and so on—we'd be darn glad she had it because the nursing care she'd need wouldn't otherwise be affordable.

Indeed, had it not been for Mother's long-term care insurance, I'm not sure how we would have managed. Just the nursing home alone cost over $3,000 a month. On top of that, she had other outlays for prescription drugs, personal items, hair dresser, etc. It was only by virtue of the $1,800 a month from her long-term care insurance that she was able to bridge the chasm between her expenses and her Social Security and other income. Without it, it would have been my sister and me footing the bill, or Medicaid.

****

What is Long-Term Care Insurance?

Long-term care (LTC) insurance provides financial protection against the eventuality that you may someday be unable to take care of yourself due to either physical or cognitive impairment. It does this by paying you some stipulated amount per day or per month—or what is more likely, up to some stipulated amount per day or per month—until you get well, or die, or the benefit runs out. With most policies, benefits are triggered when a physician certifies that you are unable to perform at least two (2) of the six (6) so-called *activities of daily living (ADLs)* or are suffering from some sort of *cognitive impairment*, such as Alzheimer's. The six ADLs are: *eating, toileting, bathing, dressing, transferring,* and *continence*. Transferring, in case you're wondering, means getting up and moving on your own steam from Point A to Point B, like from your bed to a chair.

Although some policies, once they're triggered, will pay a stipulated amount per day or month irrespective of what the insured's expenses run, most do not. Most, instead, reimburse you for documented expenses that qualify for coverage. This could be room and board and care at a nursing home, assisted living facility, or Alzheimer's facility, or it could be care provided to you in your own home by some licensed care giver. The last is what most people would much prefer. Not all policies, however, will pay for home care, and others will only pay for it on a reduced benefit basis. More about that later.

I said that the daily or monthly benefit goes on "until you die, get well, or the benefit runs out." By the benefit running out, I'm referring to the fact that there is some benefit period, stated or implied, in all long-term care policies. This can be anywhere from one (1) to six (6) years, or indefinitely. You can buy policies that will go on paying until, as I say, you get well or die. As you would suppose, the longer the benefit period, the more expensive the policy.

Like many types of insurance, long-term care insurance has a deductible, only in the parlance of this particular industry it's called an *elimination period.* The metric here is not dollars but days. So, whereas with your auto policy's collision coverage, you pay the first so-many dollars of any repair expenses, with a long-term care policy, you pay the first so-many days of care. This could range, in ten-day increments, from 10 to 120 days. The longer the elimination period, the lower the premium.

Policies that reimburse expenses up to a stipulated monthly amount are sometimes referred to as *pool of money* policies. The particular policies my wife and I have refer to the "pool" as the *lifetime maximum benefit.* The pool or lifetime maximum is calculated by multiplying the maximum monthly benefit by the benefit period. In our case the lifetime maximum comes to $108,000 ($3,000/month × 36 months).

The significance of this lifetime maximum is that it allows you, by spending less than your daily/monthly allowance, to extend your benefit period. Thus, in my case, if I sought reimbursement for only $2,500 of my monthly nursing home expenses, I could keep receiving benefits for more than half a year beyond my otherwise maximum benefit period of 36 months.[1]

Probability of Your Needing LTC

Thanks to better nutrition and far better health care, people today live much longer than they did, say, at the beginning of the last century when life expectancy was 58 years. Today the average is around 78. Better yet, as you steadily advance toward 78,

[1] $108,000 divided by $2,500/month equals 43.2 months.

your life expectancy gets pushed out. According to Social Security actuarial tables, at 73 I can expect to keep going until I'm 85, my wife (72) till she's 87.

This good news about living longer is somewhat muted by the fact that old age is more often than not attended by a number of disagreeable maladies, like worn-out joints, incontinence, and dementia. As my mother was fond of saying, "Old age ain't for sissies."

A statistic I ran across on the Department of Health and Human Services' website[2] states that "about 70% of individuals over 65 will require at least some type of long-term care services during their lifetime." The piece goes on to say that in 2000 about 37% of the 10 million people then receiving long-term care were under 65. Bottom line: anyone, regardless of age, can find him or herself needing long-term care, but if you're over sixty-five (65), you can pretty much count on needing it someday. Ponder that.

What about Medicare and Medicaid

Everybody wonders about this: Won't Medicare or Medicaid pick up the tab for long-term care? Answer: Yes and no. Although Medicare will pay for *skilled nursing* care for up to 100 days following a three-day hospital stay,[3] it does so fully for only 20 days, after which the patient has a big co-payment. This works fine—at least for 20 days—if you've just had something like a hip replacement and require a lengthy convalescence, but it's of no use to the typical long-term care patient. He or she just needs help with the ADLs, not skilled nursing.

Medicaid is an altogether different story. Medicaid will pay for custodial care in a nursing home, but only if you're nearly destitute. Transferring assets to your children is not an acceptable strategy for qualifying for Medicaid. If you do that and the government finds you out, it will claw back every dime it's spent on your behalf and then some.

A more acceptable way of becoming Medicaid-eligible is to go into a nursing home without long-term care insurance and have it reduce you to penury. It can do it in a hurry.

---

[2] "The Basics – Long-term Care Information." U.S. Department of Health and Human Services, http://long-termcare.gov/the- basics/ (June 30, 2016).

[3] The skilled nursing care must be for the same condition as the hospital stay.

The fact that you've got to be at the poverty level to qualify for Medicaid can put older couples in a terrible dilemma if one spouse needs long-term care and the other does not. It used to be that in order to qualify the one needing it—the husband, say—the couple would have to spend down all of their savings on his care, effectively leaving nothing for the wife to get by on. Medicaid rules have since been made more liberal in this regard, but the problem has certainly not gone away altogether.

When to Buy LTC Insurance

As with life insurance and health insurance, the earlier you buy an LTC policy, the more affordable it's going to be. If you wait till you're up in years, as my mother did, coverage will cost you dearly. I'm not suggesting that young people in their twenties and thirties, who may already be struggling to make ends meet, need to make room somehow for LTC—I am not—but I definitely think that by the age of sixty (60) they do.

A friend who sells long-term care insurance shared the numbers shown in Table 11.1 below. The premiums, which are annual, are representative of what you might pay presently (2016) in Texas, depending on your age at the time you applied and assuming you were given a standard rating, for a policy with a 90-day elimination period that pays $150 a day for three (3) years with benefits compounding at 5% per annum. I'll discuss *compounding* later.

Table 11.1 ~ Annual LTC Insurance Premiums

	Age 55	*Age 60*	*Age 65*	*Age 70*
Male	$5,580	$5,730	$6,210	$7,410
Female	$8,310	$8,760	$9,840	$11,535

Married Partner Discount

If you're married and you and your spouse each buy the same LTC coverage from the same company at the same time, you likely will qualify for a "married partner discount" that will reduce your premiums by quite a lot vis-à-vis what you would pay if you bought coverage separately. I was told that the reduction would be around 30%.

Picking an LTC Insurance Provider

There has been major shakeout in the long-term care insurance industry in recent years. There may now be only a half-dozen or so highly rated companies that write this business. Most of the companies that used to write it, including the company we have our policies with, have stopped, having had all their underlying pricing assumptions proven dead wrong.[4] As a result, if you're shopping for LTC insurance, your choice of companies is going to be limited.

From among your limited choices, I think I'd be chiefly interested in how the companies are rated by *A.M. Bests*[5] and whether they have ever hiked the premiums on policies in force and, if so, how many times and how recently. I wouldn't scratch from consideration any company that has *ever* hiked premiums, as there probably is none that hasn't, but I'd still look into the matter. The last thing you want as a retiree living on a mostly fixed income is to buy a policy, sacrifice for years to pay your premiums and then, when it appears relatively certain that you're going to need long-term care in a few years, get hit with a premium hike that you can't afford.[6]

The other thing I'd do as I shopped around is to ask any agent I talked to for references from people he has sold policies to who are now receiving benefits. I can tell you from personal experience that insurance companies do not make the process of qualifying for LTC benefits easy. It was only through the good offices of my mother's

---

[4] There are several reasons for this. One is the low interest rate environment we've been in since 2008. Another is faulty assumptions concerning how many people would actually use the insurance and for how long, as well as how many people, after paying premiums for some number of years, would drop their coverage.

Insurance companies put the premiums they collect to work in very safe investments, like Treasury bonds, and for the past seven years, thanks to Federal Reserve policy, the return on those has been abysmal, suppressing the growth of the reserves from which the companies pay claims.

The degree to which policyholders stay the course, paying their premiums month after month, year after year, through good times and bad, is referred to as "persistency." If persistency is higher than the insurance company's pricing model assumes, meaning that fewer policyholders drop their policies after so many years, that's a bad thing for the company, which was expecting to pocket a lot more unused premiums. This may not sound like a big deal, but it is. Policyholders are loath to drop this coverage, because there's a growing understanding that they'll likely need it.

[5] *Bests* rates insurance companies on a scale of A+ to D, with A+ denoting "a superior ability to meet ongoing insurance obligations" and D denoting "a poor ability."

[6] We were informed last year by our LTC insurance company, which no longer writes new policies but continues to service its old ones (because they have to), that our premiums would be increased 87.5% over the course of the next three years, starting this year (2015). Fortunately, that's from a pretty low base: when I bought our policies in 2002, my monthly premium was only $66.90 and my wife's $63.60.

agent that we ever negotiated Bankers Life's qualifications obstacle course and got them to break out the checkbook. I'd be surprised if our experience was atypical.

****

If you decide to go shopping for long-term care insurance, here's some advice and some things you ought to know.

Daily/Monthly Benefit

The cost of long-term care varies widely, depending on the type of care (nursing home, assisted living, home care, etc.), the "niceness" of the facility, and the region of the country. I remember when my mother was in the Alzheimer's facility in Texarkana, Texas, feeling fortunate that we were only paying $3,000 a month when I was reading that the national average was half again that much. Since then, I'm sure, care has gone up everywhere. In sum, the cost of long-term care is not something that's easy to generalize about. To get some good idea as to what nursing home care, assisted living care, and all the rest runs in your area, you're going to need to make your own inquiries locally.

I enrolled my wife and myself in long-term care insurance via an employer-sponsored group plan and, I regret to say, acquiesced in the general thinking among my co-workers that $100 a day/$3,000 a month was a good, safe number. I know now that $100 a day was too optimistic even for our area.

Assisted Living and Home Care Coverage

There was a time not so long ago when long-term care policies did not cover home care. Period. That's no longer the case, but many policies, including ours, do not pay the same for it as they pay for nursing home care. Ours, for example, reduces the benefit for assisted living to $1,800 a month and for home care to $1,500. As I would much prefer to be cared for at home to being in a nursing home, I'm not too happy about this, but I had no choice at the time, since that's how our particular group policy was written. If you're shopping around, you may want to hold out for a policy that doesn't reduce the home care benefit. I would certainly try to.

Benefit Period

Most nursing home stays end in less than three (3) years. That's because the patient dies. I don't know whether the same can be said of home care recipients. It would not surprise me if they tended to live longer owing to their happier surroundings. Whatever the stats are, I would be inclined to stipulate that you shouldn't opt for a benefit period of less than three years.

The benefit period on my mother's policy was three (3) years. As I recall, she died about two and a half (2 ½) years into her benefit period. Had she outlived it, we would have been thrown back on our own resources. If you've been maxing out the daily benefit, as we had, when the benefit period ends, the payments stop.

Elimination Period

Our policies have a 90-day elimination period. So did my mother's. I selected 90 days because I believe generally in having as large a deductible as I feel I can afford in order to minimize my premium. Some experts feel that the escalating cost of healthcare argues for a shorter elimination period—like 20 days. If you're not sure that you'd be able to handle the projected cost of nursing home care in whatever year you can envision needing it, you may want to opt for 20 days. It will cost you extra, though.

Tax-Qualified

You want a policy that's *tax-qualified.* A tax-qualified policy has many advantages, the first being that if you itemize your deductions on Schedule A of Form 1040 (as opposed to taking the standard deduction), you can include your premium payments as medical expenses. More importantly, any benefits you receive later do not have to be included as income.

Everything I have written here pertains to tax-qualified policies. I'm not aware that non-qualified plans are even being sold these days, although they may. And if you should happen to have bought a policy some years ago, that may be what yours is. Ask your agent if you don't know. If it is a non-qualified policy, it's not the end of the world. It's my understanding that they make it somewhat easier to qualify for benefits. They may have other advantages as well.

Inflation-Protection

Tax-qualified policies conform to *HIPAA* standards. HIPAA is the *Health Insurance Portability & Accountability Act,* which was a major piece of health insurance legislation enacted in 1996. Among those standards is the requirement that all policies offer some form of *inflation protection.* Inflation protection comes in two flavors: *simple* and *compound.* A simple adjustment will bump up the benefit by, say, 5% of the base benefit every year. Compound does the same but, of course, compounds the adjustment. If you have a policy paying $100 a day and a simple 5% annual inflation adjustment, your benefit will mount each year by $5, so that by the end of year 10, you'll be up to $150 a day. If your 5% is compounded, however, you'll be up to $155 and change.[7] Obviously, compounding is to be preferred, and I would strongly recommend it, even though it adds significantly to the cost.

Non-Forfeiture Provisions

HIPAA also requires that all tax-qualified policies offer a non-forfeiture provision whereby someone who pays premiums for some period of time gets something back in the event he or she feels it necessary to cancel coverage. This is done by buying a rider, which costs extra, and how much you get back and all the rest varies from policy to policy. If you were worried that your insurance company might hike your premiums beyond your willingness to pay, you might consider such a rider.

Guaranteed Renewability

All long-term care insurance policies must be guaranteed renewable. That is to say that the insurance company cannot, on any grounds, other than non-payment of premium or fraud, cancel your policy or refuse to renew it on its anniversary date. And after two years it is even proscribed from cancelling your policy on the basis of fraud.

Not only are LTC policies guaranteed renewable, the company cannot increase your premiums selectively. Any premium increase must be applied across the board for everybody.

---

[7] Our polices, my wife's and mine, which we took out in May, 2002, compound benefits at 5% per annum. As a result, thirteen years later, our monthly benefit has gone from $3,000 ($100 a day × 30 days) to nearly $5,400. This makes me feel somewhat better about that 87.5% premium increase.

Protection Against Unintentional Lapses

It doesn't take a lot of imagination to understand how easy it would be for someone slipping into Alzheimer's to forget to pay a bill, including his/her monthly long-term care insurance premium.[8] Against this eventuality, all policies must give the policyholder the opportunity of designating someone else to also receive any notice of cancellation for non-payment of premium. Indeed, if you choose not to designate someone, you must sign a waiver. Ordinarily, your designee would be a family member or guardian—someone who feels responsible for you. We've designated our sons.

You should also know that insurers are required to reinstate any policy that has lapsed due to non-payment of premium if it can be shown that the lapse was due to the insured's being cognitively or physically impaired.

Restoration of Benefits

This is a rider offered by many companies that provides for a restoration of benefits if the person receiving long-term care payments gets well and ceases to need care for some specified period of time. So, for example, if I had a stroke that rendered me incapable of doing much of anything for a year, but thanks to therapy, I then made a miraculous recovery, thereafter requiring no care, this rider would reset my benefits to what they had been before my stroke, once I had satisfied whatever wellness period was required.

Waiver of Premium

Many, if not most, long-term care insurance policies offer what is called *waiver of premium.* What waiver of premium does is allow the insured to stop making premium payments once he's qualified to receive long-term care benefits. I wouldn't buy a long-term care policy without this feature.

****

[8] Which is why I recommended in Chapter 1 and elsewhere that all insurance premiums be set up for payment by monthly bank draft.

I used to think that long-term care insurance was a lot like whole life insurance where the policy premium never changes and you pay it month after month, year after year, in full confidence that when you die—or in this case, require long-term care—it will pay off. It was unthinkable to me that twelve years down the road my company might raise my premium. Why? Well, because I would have thought, being an insurance company, they had everything figured out. And also because it would be so unfair. I'd have no remedy. I couldn't just switch carriers, as I might with my auto policy or homeowners, because by virtue of my being that many years older, the same coverage would cost me a lot more. Assuming I could even find another policy. By then I might be uninsurable.

Had I known then what I know now, would I still have bought long-term care insurance? The answer is yes, because even after an 87.5% increase, our premiums are still affordable. But if you had told me in 2002, just before I bought our policies, that my premiums would likely go up, possibly to the point of being unaffordable, I'm not so sure. I think I would have said, "What kind of insurance is that? There must be another way to deal with the risk."

Maybe so, but so far I haven't found it. The best alternative I can come up with is to take what you might pay for LTC and invest it. For example, if you're a 55-year old female, you might take the $8,310 per year that the policy paying $150 a day that we looked at earlier would cost you and put that to work in an ETF or mutual fund invested in the S&P 500, where historically the average annual return has been around 10%. If you did that—and were lucky— in twenty-five years your investment might be worth on the order of $600,000.[9] That's more than the pool of money you'd have from the long-term care policy, which I figure in twenty-five years would come to $548,589.50.[10] Plus, if you never needed long-term care, or did but died before your resources were used up, your investment would have residual value, which a long-term care policy would not. There's just one huge problem here. It is, of course, that you can't be sure you when you might require long-term care. You might need it long before you could accumulate

[9] I'm assuming an after-tax return of 7.5%.

[10] Compounded at 5% per annum, your $150 daily benefit would grow to $507.95 a day. Multiplied times 30, that would be $15,238.60 per month. Multiplied times 36 months, as in three years, that comes to $548,589.50.

enough money from investing to match the pool of money you'd have with a long-term care policy.

As much as I can find not to like about long-term care insurance these days, for those who can afford it, I don't presently see a better alternative.

TWELVE

Life Insurance

My father died at thirty-four, leaving his wife with two children—me, eleven at the time, and my sister, who was then nearly two. Fortunately for us, several years before he became ill, my father bought a life insurance policy from a guy in McAllen, Texas, named Sam Weems, who, according to my mother, heckled Dad so much about the need to protect his family that he finally gave in and did something. I think that it must have been a very small policy—it didn't pay off any mortgage, it didn't keep my mother from having to go to work, and it didn't pay to send me and my sister to college—but without it and my angel grandmother who took us in—Mother would have been quite destitute. Her gratitude to Mr. Weems was such that sixty-three years later I still remember the man's name.

****

What is Life Insurance?

When you buy a life insurance policy, you enter into a contract with an insurance company, which, knowing the odds of your dying within any period of time, will bet you a large sum of money (the policy's face value) against a much smaller premium that you won't be among the unlucky few who die prematurely.

The parties to this contract are the *owner* of the policy, who is usually but not always the *insured*—i.e., the person whose death would trigger the *death benefit* payment—and the insurance company. The owner of the policy makes the *premium* payments and designates the *beneficiary* who is to receive the death benefit. I say "beneficiary," but you could have more than one. You can also have contingent, or secondary, and tertiary beneficiaries to provide for the possibility that a primary or secondary beneficiary dies before the insured. The death benefit is not taxable to the beneficiary.[1]

To take out an insurance policy on someone else's life, you must have an *insurable interest* in that person, meaning an interest (financial, emotional, or otherwise) in the person staying alive. This will prevent you from taking out a big policy on the teenager next door who acts and drives crazy and seems destined for an early grave.

Who Needs Life Insurance? What For?

Not everyone needs life insurance. If you're widowed, or divorced, or have never married and have no dependent family and have made other provisions for your earthly remains to be disposed of when you die, there is no reason I can think of why you should need life insurance. On the other hand, regardless of your marital status, if you have loved ones who would be in a real financial bind if something were to happen to you, that's a good reason to think that you do.

Here are some typical uses for life insurance:

- Settling your final expenses, such as medical bills, funeral costs, and legal fees and court costs related to probating your estate.
- Paying any income taxes you may owe.

[1] Provided it is taken as a lump sum. When taken in installments, where the principal is left to earn interest, a portion will be interest and subject to tax.

- Paying estate taxes, assuming your estate is above a certain threshold and you are not married.
- Paying off the mortgage.
- Replacing your income, less any expenses that would end with you, to the extent that the people you leave behind cannot make up the shortfall.
- Putting your children through college.
- Continuing financial support to aged parents who cannot make it on their own.
- Providing for special-needs children.

Identifying and Quantifying Life Insurance Needs

Most people who buy life insurance just buy what sounds like a good number. Our older son may be typical. He called me up one day shortly after the birth of his little girl and said, "Hey, I'm thinking that I maybe should buy $1 million of term life insurance. I hear that at my age it's pretty cheap. Would you get me some quotes?" I did, it was cheap, and he bought a policy.

Other people just buy what they think they can afford, irrespective of what they need, which is often significantly more.

A man (or a woman) may not give much thought to how much insurance he needs to protect his family if he should die because: a) he doesn't want to think about it; b) he doesn't know how to go about it; and c) he doesn't want to consult an insurance agent for fear that once in the agent's embrace he won't be able to wiggle free.

There are a number of ways of coming up with a reasonable number on what you need. All require that you know how much money your dependents would need if you suddenly departed this world. Assuming that your dependents here are a spouse and one or more children, answering that question requires that you know what your yearly household expenses run,[2] how much they would go down (or go up[3]) in your absence, and to what extent they could be met, or at least partially offset, by the surviving spouse's earnings and Social Security survivors' benefits.[4]

---

[2] Chapter 3 explains how to prepare an annual budget and cash f low summary.
[3] I'm thinking here of employer-provided health care and, in the case of the stay-at-home mom, day care.
[4] Social Security Online has a "Quick Calculator" that can help you figure this.

Once you know how much income your dependents would need, one quick-and-dirty approach to determining how much insurance to buy is to divide the need by whatever after-tax return you think is achievable on a conservative investment portfolio. If the annual need is, say, $50,000 and you and your broker think 5% is a good, safe return, you need a $1 million policy.[5] One weakness in this approach is that it does not take inflation into account. As the years go by, it will take more than $50,000 to buy the same basket of goods and services that $50,000 will buy today.

Another approach, which is almost as easy, is to go to the Internet and do a search, entering something like "how much life insurance do I need?" This will take you to a host of websites with online calculators, each of which will ask you a series of questions: What do you estimate your funeral and final expenses would run? What's the balance on your mortgage? What other debt do you have that you would want to be paid off if you died? How much income would your dependents need? How long would they need it? How much do you have in the way of non-retirement investment assets? And so on. It will also want to know what you expect inflation to run and what you would expect as a return on your investments. As soon as you've answered the last question, up pops the answer. I have two problems with these calculators: 1) I am sometimes uncertain how to understand the question, so that I worry about garbage in, garbage out, and 2) I cannot imagine how, with the little bit of data they ask for, they can possibly crank out a good number. But I must admit that the sponsors of these calculators all seem to be serious folks.

The most satisfactory approach is to bite the bullet and consult an insurance person. My understanding, based on a conversation I had with an agent, is that the software programs they use are similar to the online calculators.[6] The advantage of working with an insurance agent, though, is that he or she will understand the meaning of each and every question, so that if you don't understand what's being asked, you can get clarification. In that way you are more likely to get a number in which you can feel confident.

---

[5] $50,000 ÷ 5% = $1,000,000. $1 million invested at 5% will throw off $50,000 a year.

[6] Although I was licensed to sell life insurance when I was at A G Edwards, the only policy I ever sold was to my son, who had made up his mind beforehand how much coverage he wanted.

Types of Insurance

For many years there were only two kinds of insurance policies—*term life* policies and *whole life* policies. Nowadays there are a number of others, of which *universal life* and *variable universal life* are probably the most popular.

Term

Term life is pure insurance. You buy term to cover you for a certain period of time, which can be one year, five years, ten years, fifteen years, and so on, out to thirty. You can also buy a term policy that will cover you from age of issue out to age 65. If you die while the policy is in force, your beneficiary collects. If you don't die, which is many times the more likely scenario, you'll have nothing to show at the end of the term for all the premiums you paid. There is no residual value with term life.

Term is just what the doctor ordered for the young head-of-household whose insurance needs are large and his budget small. He can buy a lot of coverage for not much money. My son's 30-year $1 million *level term* policy, purchased when he was three months shy of 32, costs him just $113.40 per month. That seems really cheap. If he wanted to, he could have also bought a *decreasing term* policy that would closely track the balance on his mortgage, ending in twenty-five years when his house is paid off.[7]

For a few extra bucks of premium, you can buy level term life insurance that is guaranteed *renewable*, meaning you can renew it for another 5, 10, or 20 years without showing proof of insurability. You can also buy term that is *convertible* to whole life insurance, which would be a godsend if some years down the road you developed a disease that promised to take you before your time. I think it's essential that any young person buying term get it with these two options.

The only disadvantage to term life is that the premiums go up as you get older. If you buy a level term policy, the premiums won't change while it remains in force, but if and when you renew or try to buy another policy with the same face value, it will cost you a lot more. This makes sense, inasmuch as the older you get, the less unlikely it is that you will die over the next twelve months, five years, or whatever. If my son chooses to continue his policy, his premium in year 31 will be $3,030.83 per month!

[7] I'm told that many insurance companies no longer offer decreasing term, so perhaps it isn't as available today as it was just a few years ago.

Whole Life

Whole life insurance combines insurance with savings. It is also different from term in that it doesn't end in a certain number of years but rather remains in force for the insured's entire life, which is why it's called "whole life." I had an old textbook that described term as *if* insurance and whole life as *when* insurance. Unless the insured dies prematurely, there'll be no death benefit paid on a term policy; unless the owner cancels or allows his policy to lapse, there definitely will be one paid on a whole life policy. For that and other reasons, whole life is more expensive than term.

I said above that whole life is a combination of insurance and savings, but it would be more accurate to say that it is a combination of term insurance that decreases over time as the cash value increases and that it is so structured that the sum of the two values—insurance plus cash value—always equals the face value of the policy. Premiums are credited to the policy's cash reserve, which earns interest at a fixed rate spelled out in the policy, and out of this reserve, the insurance company deducts the cost of insurance (referred to as the "mortality charge"), as well as its administrative and other expenses.

You have a number of premium payment options with whole life. You can elect to pay the premiums for your entire life, paying so much monthly, quarterly, or annually; you can pay them all in one single payment at the outset of the policy; or you can pay them for some limited number of years, like 20 or 30, or until you turn a certain age, like 65 or 85. There may be other options still.

With whole life you can also borrow against the policy's cash value. As you would expect, if the insured dies before the loan is repaid, any outstanding balance will be deducted from the death benefit.

Universal Life

Universal life (UL) is another form of *permanent* insurance. It works pretty much like whole life. There are, however, some important differences. One is that with a whole life policy you can't see what's going on inside the policy, whereas with universal life you can. There's full disclosure, for whatever that's worth. Also, with universal life you have some flexibility as to when you pay your premiums and in what amount. So long as there's enough cash value to cover the mortality charge and administrative expenses, there's no coverage lapse as there is with whole life. The third big difference is that you can increase the amount of coverage up and down within the same policy, which you cannot do with whole life. Personally, I don't see this as a really big deal, inasmuch as increasing coverage requires showing evidence of insurability, but I suppose having one policy instead of two can save you *some* money.

Variable Universal Life

Variable universal life (VUL) is just like universal life, except that instead of the cash value being invested in the insurance company's general account where it earns interest, the money is invested in so-called *separate accounts*, which for all intents and purposes are mutual funds that own either stocks or bonds or both. The corollary to this is that the death benefit on a VUL policy is variable, depending on the performance of the investments in the separate accounts. Anyone who is not pretty investment-savvy might want to think twice before buying a VUL policy.

There are all sorts of iterations on the four types of policies described above. For example, you can buy Type A and Type B universal life policies. The UL policy I described is a Type A policy, where over time as the cash value increases the term insurance decreases by the same amount, such that the death benefit always stays the same. Under a Type B policy, the amount of insurance stays level, but the death benefit increases in lockstep with the increase in cash value. You can also buy policies covering the lives of two or more people, where the death benefit is paid to the survivor(s) of the first to die and others where the death benefit isn't paid until the last to go dies. First-to-die policies are commonly used by business partners to provide surviving partners with the wherewithal to buy a deceased partner's interest from his or her heirs. Last-to-die policies are commonly used by wealthy couples to provide funds to pay estate taxes on the money trapped in the estate of the second spouse to die.

The Term vs. Whole Life Debate

Some knowledgeable people advise against buying whole life insurance. They point out that, generally speaking, insurance is something you mostly need when your children are young, you've got a big mortgage, and you haven't built up any significant wealth. That's when you need to buy 20- or 30-year level term, they say. It's cheap.

Nobody expects you die. Whole life insurance is not cheap because, provided you continue to pay your premiums, there is the certainty of a death benefit being paid and that has to be priced in. Whole life's critics also point to the high commissions paid to the agents who sell this product, which can be nearly as much as the sum of all of the first year's premiums, and to the low interest rate implied by the slow buildup in cash value. It makes more sense, they say, to buy term, which is much cheaper, and invest the savings in a good mutual fund.

The proponents of whole life counter that, while there's something to these arguments, the fact is that many people who need insurance die without any because when their term life expired, the cost of buying a new policy was seen as prohibitive. They also point out that even if people would be better off buying term and investing the savings in a good mutual fund, they are more likely to just spend the savings. The interest earned on a whole life policy, while low, is better than nothing.

The middle ground here is to use term for covering needs that in time will go away, like paying off the mortgage or sending the kids through college, and whole life for needs that won't go away, like funding an investment to provide a dependent with an income stream.[8]

Death Benefit Settlement Options

The beneficiary on a life insurance policy has a number of settlement options. One, of course, is to receive the death benefit as a lump sum payment. That's far and away the most popular election. A second is to take it in equal installments over some specified period of time. In this case you're saying something like, "I want the death benefit paid to me monthly over the next ten years." A third option, similar to the second, is to take it in the form of a fixed amount paid out on some periodic basis until the principal and interest are exhausted. Here you're saying something like, "I want to receive $500 a month for as long as the money lasts." And the fourth way is to take payment in the form of a life income, or annuity, where the beneficiary receives so much per month for as long as he or she lives. This last option comes with options of its own. The simplest is the single-life annuity, where payments cease when the annuitant dies.

[8] It would appear that, in spite of whole life being more suitable in certain situations, it is losing popularity and as a consequence is becoming less available.

There's another option where payments are guaranteed for a certain number of years, such that if the annuitant dies before the specified period is up, his or her beneficiary will receive whatever payments remain to be made. A third option provides that if the beneficiary dies before the death benefit is paid out, his or her beneficiary, or a contingent beneficiary, will receive the amount remaining. There are others.

Policy Lapses

If you have a term policy and you do not pay the premium within thirty or thirty-one (30 or 31) days of its due date (i.e., during the so-called *grace period*), your policy will lapse, voiding your coverage. For that reason alone, it is advisable that you arrange for your premiums to be paid by monthly bank draft.

If your policy is some form of permanent, or cash value, insurance, like whole life, universal life, or variable universal life, which you purchased within the last year or two, meaning that it has had no time really to build up any cash value, failure to make a scheduled premium will also cause the policy to lapse. However, once there's enough cash value built up to allow tapping it to cover the premium payments, that's what will happen. Indeed, I've already noted that one of the distinguishing features of universal life or variable universal life policies is that you have considerable flexibility as to when you pay your premiums and in what amount. If you have a whole life policy, the company will convert your policy to extended term, dipping into the cash value to pay the premiums. Once the cash value is used up, you have no insurance.

Reinstatements

Most policies, if not all, allow you a certain number of years, like five to seven, to reinstate your insurance if it lapses for non-payment of premiums. This is usually conditional on your showing proof of insurability, making up all missed premium payments (plus interest), and paying off any policy loans.

A policy that is surrendered for its cash value cannot be reinstated.

Non-Forfeiture Options

Cash value policies, like whole life, universal life, and variable universal life, have what are called *non-forfeiture provisions*, which provide the policyholder who wishes to stop making premium payments with three options concerning what to do with the policy's cash value. He can elect to surrender the policy and receive the cash surrender value in a check. He can have the cash surrender value used to buy a paid-up whole life policy for a lesser face value. He can have the cash surrender value used to buy an extended term policy with the same face value. This extended term policy will remain in effect only so long as there is enough cash value remaining to pay the premiums. When there's no more cash value, the policy ends for good.

****

All life insurance policies have some standard clauses in them that are worth noting. If you have a policy, you will find these there:

Misstatements

If the insured dies and the insurance company learns that the insured misstated his or her age or sex on the application, it will adjust the death benefit to the amount of insurance that the premiums paid would have purchased based on the correct information.

Incontestability

The insurance company has two (2) years after it issues a policy to contest any statements made in the application for insurance submitted by the insured. If, for example, the insured did not disclose that he smoked and the doctor who examined him didn't detect that he did and three years later he died from some smoking-related disease, the insurance company could not refuse to pay, alleging that it had been lied to.

You may wonder what happens in a case like this if the insured dies within two years. My best guess is that if the company believed it could prove that the insured's application was fraudulent, it would deny the death benefit claim and simply refund the premiums paid.

Suicide

The suicide clause is similar to the "incontestability" clause to the extent that after two years the policy must pay even if the insured dies at his or her own hand. If the insured commits suicide within two years of the policy issue date, the company is only required to refund the premiums paid up till then.

****

Quotes

Life insurance agents abound. Finding one to come talk to you at your convenience should be real easy. However, some experts (of which I am definitely not one) would advise against going to the Yellow Pages and calling one up. They would also advise against approaching that nice guy or gal who goes to your church and sells insurance. You want people to whom you don't feel beholden competing for your business.

The best place to start, they say, is with one of the quote services, like any of those listed below. You might want to contact them all.

- AccuQuote ~ www.accuquote.com ~ 800-654-2079
- IntelliQuote ~ www.intelliquote.com ~ 800-963-6405
- MatrixDirect ~ www.matrixdirect.com ~ 800-914-8376
- SelectQuote ~ www.selectquote.com ~ 800-977-5173)

You can call these people or go to their websites and complete their questionnaires. Either way you will end up talking to someone. To save time, you should explain to your interlocutor at the outset of your conversation that you're not interested in quotes from companies that are not A-rated or better by one of the insurance company credit ratings services, like A.M. Best, Standard & Poor's, and Moody's. He or she will take it from there.

Reviews

As I've already said, no matter how much effort you and your advisor invest in quantifying your insurance needs, unless you die within a few years, the numbers you develop will not hold up. No one can divine what inflation will average over the coming years, how far tax rates may go up,[9] where interest rates are headed, and so on. Be off just

[9] Given the enormity of our national debt, I cannot conceive of them going down.

a little bit on any of these assumptions and time will magnify the effect. Also, over time your circumstances will change. The balance on your mortgage will go down or go away. Luckily, you didn't die, but unfortunately your mother, whom you had been helping to support, did, and two of your children are through college and have left the nest. Or maybe you suddenly develop needs that you didn't have before: you get married, have a family, and buy a house, which saddles you with a mortgage. Whatever, your needs will not remain static. Every five years or so, and sooner if your circumstances change in any significant way, you need to review matters with your insurance agent to see if you have too much protection or too little.

****

In summing up here, I would say that the most important thing in buying insurance is that you buy your policy from a company that is sound, one that's rated A or better. You cannot risk buying a level term policy or some type of permanent life insurance only to discover years down the road, when insurance will cost you more due to your age, or is unavailable due to your health, that your company has become insolvent. I would lean toward level term, but with the caveat that you contribute faithfully toward college and retirement, so that if you don't die prematurely these needs can be met.

Next, remember what I just said about reviewing your needs every five years or sooner if circumstances warrant.

And finally, if and when you buy a policy, don't risk letting it lapse. Don't rely on your memory to make the premium payments on time; arrange to have the premiums paid by bank draft (ACH debit). And having bought a policy, don't decide you can't afford it. If you bought it, you need it. Economize somewhere else.

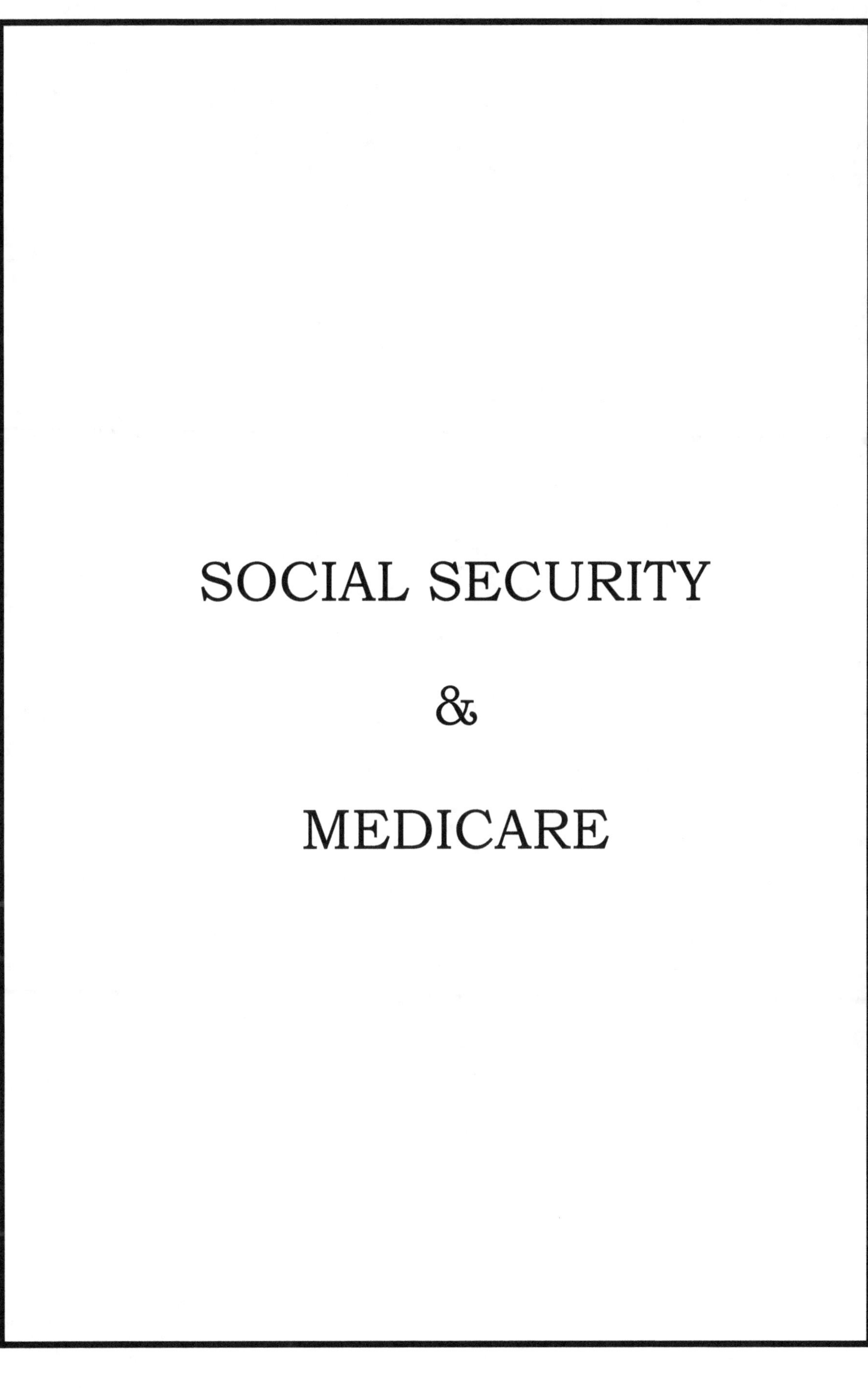

SOCIAL SECURITY

&

MEDICARE

THIRTEEN

Social Security

About 49 million Americans get a check every month from Social Security—from its *Old-Age, Survivors & Disability Insurance (OASDI)* program.[1] For most that check is their financial mainstay. Without it they'd have trouble making ends meet.

The checks that go out from Social Security pay three kinds of benefits—*retirement benefits, survivors benefits* and *disability insurance benefits*. Social Security retirement benefits are what every working person looks forward to someday—a monthly check from Uncle Sam that will enable him to quit the rat race. The people who get these pension checks are mostly enjoying their golden years. Survivors' benefits go to those dependents the worker or retired worker leaves behind after dying. Disability benefits go to people who have been beset by some physical or mental impairment that prevents them from continuing to earn a living. Together with Medicare and Medicaid, these programs make up the great American social safety net.

[1] "Monthly Statistical Snapshot, January 2016." Social Security Administration, www.ssa.gov/policy/docs/quickfacts, (released February, 2016)

The OASDI program is said to be a pay-as-you-go program, meaning that the benefits paid out come from taxes paid in. While that may be so, not everyone who's getting a benefit was once a worker who paid in. Lots of beneficiaries can claim benefits based on someone else's earnings record, like a spouse's, or in the case of a dependent child, a parent's. My wife, who didn't work outside the house long enough to qualify on her own for Social Security retirement benefits, nonetheless qualifies for them based on my earnings record. We both get a check every month. Upon the death of my father at age 34, my mother and my infant sister and I received survivors benefits based on his earnings record. Had disability benefits been available during his year-long illness back then, the three of us might have received those as well.

Workers pay into the OASDI program through the *FICA*[2] tax, which is levied on nearly all earnings from gainful employment in this country.[3] FICA, as you know if you've ever had a paying job, has two components—the Social Security component, which is 12.4% on all earnings up to the *contribution and benefit base* ceiling, which is presently (2016) $118,500; and the Medicare component, which is 2.9% on all earnings, period.[4] If the worker is employed by someone else, he pays half of these taxes and his employer pays half. If he's self-employed, he pays the whole 15.3% himself.

Until just a few years ago (2010), the OASDI program took in far more in taxes every year than it paid out in benefits, and taking into account interest earned on its trust fund assets—special bonds issued by the U.S. Treasury[5]—the program still generates surpluses. However, by 2023 or thereabouts, unless Congress takes some action, it is projected that the program will begin to pay out more than it takes in. It will then have to tap its reserves of Treasury bonds to meet its obligations to retirees and others. That can

---

[2] Federal Insurance Contributions Act

[3] Some workers don't pay the OASDI/Social Security piece of FICA. These include federal employees hired before 1984 who've had no break in service and are still working, railroad employees covered by the Railroad Retirement System, and state and local employees who are exempted by virtue of being members of their government employer's retirement system. They do pay the Medicare piece.

[4] Workers pay an additional 0.09% on earnings exceeding $200,000.

[5] The Social Security Trust Fund and the U.S. Treasury are joined in a marriage of convenience. The Trust Fund has an enormous surplus every year that it must invest, while the Treasury has an enormous fiscal deficit that it must finance. The way the Treasury finances the deficit—i.e., the shortfall resulting from federal government expenditures exceeding tax receipts—is by borrowing. To the extent that the Social Security Trust Fund has surplus funds, Treasury borrows those, and to the extent that those don't make up the shortfall, it borrows from the public. In each case, the lender gets an interest-bearing bill, note or bond from the Treasury. The Treasury bonds that the Social Security Trust Funds get are different from the bonds sold to the public, which is why I call them "special."

go on for another dozen years (until about 2033) before those assets are used up and benefits have to be reduced. One assumes that Congress will act in time to prevent that.

The problem with Social Security comes down to demographic trends. When Congress enacted the first piece of Social Security legislation back in 1935 creating old-age retirement benefits, life expectancy in this country was 61 years, benefits didn't begin until age 65, and the ratio of workers to beneficiaries was better than 40 to 1. Now life expectancy is 78 and trending up, retirement benefits can begin as early as age 62, and the ratio of workers to beneficiaries is just a hair over 3 to 1 and trending down. Something will have to give.

****

The discussion in this chapter will be limited to *retirement benefits*. My first draft dealt with survivors and disability benefits as well, but when I returned to the draft months later to see how it read, I realized that spending time on benefits that were of no interest to most readers served little purpose. I would direct anyone who *is* interested in survivors' benefits or disability benefits to his or her nearest Social Security office or to Social Security's website at www.social security.gov.

****

There are four terms that need to be understood before we get into a discussion of who's eligible to receive Social Security retirement benefits and what they're entitled to. The terms are *insured status, average indexed monthly earnings (AIME)*, *primary insurance amount (PIA)* and *normal retirement age (NRA).*

Insured Status

If you've ever worked as an employee, you know that sometime in January you can expect to receive a *W-2 ~ Wage & Tax Statement* from your employer showing among a number of things how much you earned during the preceding year that was subject to Social Security (*Box 3 ~ Social Security wages*) and how much tax you paid (*Box 4 ~ Social Security tax withheld*). And if you've ever worked for yourself, you know that as part of doing your taxes you've got to do a *Schedule SE ~ Self-employment Tax* where you compute the Social Security and Medicare taxes you owe on your net earnings subject to these two taxes. These two tax documents—the W-2 and the Schedule SE—allow the Social Security Administration to keep track of every worker's earnings history and to determine how many *credits* he's earned. That in turn will determine his *insured status*, on which his and his dependents' eligibility for benefits depends.

If you do further research on Social Security, you may find the term *credits* replaced by the term *quarters of coverage.*[6] But since by definition a quarter of coverage is nothing more than a credit awarded to a worker for having paid Social Security tax on some minimal amount earnings during the year, I prefer "credits." It's also more economical.

Presently (2016) a credit is earned on every multiple of $1,260 in earnings, up to four (4). If Box 3 on your W-2 shows $1,500, you earned one (1) credit (quarter of coverage) last year. (You don't get fractional credits.) If it shows $2,800, you earned two (2). If it shows $118,500, the maximum annual earnings subject to Social Security tax, you earned just four (4) credits, even though $118,500 is more than ninety-four times $1,260. To repeat, four (4) credits are the most you can earn in a year. Note, however, that you can earn them all in just one pay period

To receive retirement benefits a worker must have *fully insured* status, and for that he needs forty (40) credits. For a full-time worker, that's more or less the same thing as saying that he needs to have been paying into the system for ten (10) years.

Average Indexed Monthly Earnings (AIME)

The worker's insured status has no bearing whatsoever on the amount of the benefit to which he and/or his dependents may be entitled. All it does is make them eligible for benefits from the standpoint of his having satisfied the work requirement.

Benefits are based on the worker's *average indexed monthly earnings (AIME)*, from which another number called the *primary insurance amount (PIA)* is derived. PIA is the reference number for every benefit calculation. We'll get to PIA next. But first we need to understand how AIME is figured.

---

[6] The term *quarters of coverage* stems from the way these credits were figured prior to 1978 and the fact that you can't earn more than 4 in a year.

In Table 13.1 on the next page, there's an illustration of how the Social Security Administration figures someone's average indexed monthly earnings. I borrowed this from their website, www.ssa.gov. This is for a worker born in 1950, whom I'm going to call Gerald, who started to work in 1976 at age 26 and is retiring this year (2016) at his normal retirement age of 66. All told, Gerald has worked forty years.

In the column headed "Actual Earnings," you see Gerald's complete earnings history, year by year, which, as explained earlier, Social Security has kept track of. Actually, it is not his complete earnings history as it ignores earnings in excess of the contribution and benefit base. Gerald apparently bumped up against the ceiling every single year, including those at the beginning of his career, which I would think is unusual. (Maybe Gerald went to work for an investment banking firm right out of Wharton.)

The next column headed "National Average Earnings" shows what the average U.S. worker paying into Social Security earned during each of the years that Gerald worked up to the year he turned 60. These national average earnings numbers are used to construct the index in the next column headed "Indexing Factor." This is done by dividing the average wage index in the year Gerald turned 60 (2010) by the average wage index for each of the preceding years. For example, dividing the average for 2010, which was $41,673.83, by the average for 1976, which was $9,226.48, gives you 4.51676. This is a measure of the wage inflation that took place between 1976 and 2010. Just as the price of groceries and gas and other staples tend to go up over time, so do wages.[7]

Multiplying the worker's actual earnings by the indexing factors results in his "Indexed Earnings." Indexed earnings is just another, shorter way of saying "actual earnings adjusted for wage inflation." It is important to note, however, that the indexing stops at age 60, two years before the worker becomes eligible for retirement benefits at age 62. From that point on, the worker's actual earnings and indexed earnings are one and the same.

The next three steps are to 1) select the highest 35 years of indexed earnings, 2) sum them, and 3) divide the total by 420. That gives you the average indexed monthly

[7] Only faster, which explains the general improvement in workers' standard of living.

Table 13.1 ~ Average Indexed Monthly Earnings (AIME)

	Year	Age	Actual Earnings	National Average Earnings	Indexing Factor	Indexed Earnings
1	1976	26	$ 15,300.00	$ 9,226.48	4.51676	*$69,106*
2	1977	27	$ 16,500.00	$ 9,779.44	4.26137	*$70,313*
3	1978	28	$ 17,700.00	$ 10,556.03	3.94787	*$69,877*
4	1979	29	$ 22,900.00	$ 11,479.46	3.63030	*$83,134*
5	1980	30	$ 25,900.00	$ 12,513.46	3.33032	*$86,255*
6	1981	31	$ 29,700.00	$ 13,773.10	3.02574	$89,865
7	1982	32	$ 32,400.00	$ 14,531.34	2.86786	$92,919
8	1983	33	$ 35,700.00	$ 15,239.24	2.73464	$97,627
9	1984	34	$ 37,800.00	$ 16,135.07	2.58281	$97,630
10	1985	35	$ 39,600.00	$ 16,822.51	2.47727	$98,100
11	1986	36	$ 42,000.00	$ 17,321.82	2.40586	$101,046
12	1987	37	$ 43,800.00	$ 18,426.51	2.26162	$99,059
13	1988	38	$ 45,000.00	$ 19,334.04	2.15546	$96,996
14	1989	39	$ 48,000.00	$ 20,099.55	2.07337	$99,522
15	1990	40	$ 51,300.00	$ 21,027.98	1.98183	$101,668
16	1991	41	$ 53,400.00	$ 21,811.60	1.91063	$102,027
17	1992	42	$ 55,500.00	$ 22,935.42	1.81701	$100,844
18	1993	43	$ 57,600.00	$ 23,132.67	1.80151	$103,767
19	1994	44	$ 60,600.00	$ 23,753.53	1.75443	$106,318
20	1995	45	$ 61,200.00	$ 24,705.66	1.68681	$103,233
21	1996	46	$ 62,700.00	$ 25,913.90	1.60817	$100,832
22	1997	47	$ 65,400.00	$ 27,426.00	1.51950	$99,375
23	1998	48	$ 68,400.00	$ 28,861.44	1.44393	$98,765
24	1999	49	$ 72,600.00	$ 30,469.84	1.36771	$99,296
25	2000	50	$ 76,200.00	$ 32,154.82	1.29604	$98,758
26	2001	51	$ 80,400.00	$ 32,921.92	1.26584	$101,773
27	2002	52	$ 84,900.00	$ 33,252.09	1.25327	$106,403
28	2003	53	$ 87,000.00	$ 34,064.95	1.22336	$106,433
29	2004	54	$ 87,900.00	$ 35,648.55	1.16902	$102,757
30	2005	55	$ 90,000.00	$ 36,952.94	1.12775	$101,498
31	2006	56	$ 94,200.00	$ 38,651.41	1.07820	$101,566
32	2007	57	$ 97,500.00	$ 40,405.48	1.03139	$100,561
33	2008	58	$ 102,000.00	$ 41,334.97	1.00820	$102,836
34	2009	59	$ 106,800.00	$ 40,711.61	1.02364	$109,324
35	**2010**	**60**	**$ 106,800.00**	**$ 41,673.83**	**1.00000**	**$106,800**
36	2011	61	$ 106,800.00		1.00000	$106,800
37	2012	62	$ 110,100.00		1.00000	$110,100
38	2013	63	$ 113,700.00		1.00000	$113,700
39	2014	64	$ 117,000.00		1.00000	$117,000
40	2015	65	$ 118,500.00		1.00000	$118,500
	Sum of highest 35 yrs of indexed earnings..............................					$3,593,696
	Avg indexed monthly earnings: ($3,593,696 ÷ (35 yrs X 12 mos.))......					$8,556

earnings, which you round to the next lowest dollar. Four hundred and twenty (420) is, of course, the number of months in 35 years.

The question comes up: What happens when a worker who's retiring doesn't have 35 years of earnings history? The answer is that he'll have zeros in those years he's short. That will result in lowering his average because his total is still going to be divided by 420.[8]

Note also that if Gerald had elected to start receiving retirement benefits when he first became eligible at age 62, his AIME would be less. I figure it would drop to $8,200.[9]

Primary Insurance Amount (PIA)

A worker's PIA is derived from his average indexed monthly earnings. This is a two-step exercise. In Step 1 the worker's AIME is divided up into as many as three pieces at what Social Security calls *bend points*. These bend points change every year, but in 2012, the year Gerald turned 62 and first became eligible for benefits, they were $767 and $4,624. For him, then, the three pieces of his AIME would be $767, $3,857 ($4,624 - $767) and $3,932 ($8,556 - $4,624). In Step 2 each piece of the worker's AIME is assigned some weight and then the weighted pieces are summed. The first piece is multiplied by 90%, the second by 32% and the third by 15%. Unlike the bend points, these percentages stay the same year after year. Applying them to Gerald's numbers, we'd figure his PIA as shown in Table 13.2 below.

Table 13.2 ~ Primary Insurance Amount (PIA)

	First $767	Over $767 thru $4,624	Over $4,624	Total
AIME	$767	$ 3,857.00	$ 3,932.00	$ 8,556.00
Weight	90%	32%	15%	29%
PIA	$ 690.30	$ 1,234.24	$ 589.80	$ 2,514.34
Rounded to next lowest dime..........................				$ 2,514.30

[8] Something to give you pause if you're hoping to retire at 55.

[9] If he began benefits at age 62, his indexed earnings for 2012 through 2015 would need to be replaced by those for 1977 through 1980, which would make the sum of his highest 35 years $3,443,975, which divided by 420 would make his AIME $8,200.

The bend points used to divide up the worker's AIME are always those applicable to the year he first became eligible for benefits, which in the case of retirement benefits is the year he turned 62.

Note that the way PIA is calculated, with the worker getting 90% of that piece of his AIME that is under the first bend point and significantly less of anything over, the so-called "little guy's" benefit will always work out to a higher percentage of his average indexed monthly earnings than the high wage earner's will. That's by design. The guy who earned a lot is assumed to be less dependent in retirement on his Social Security than the guy whose wages were low.

Normal Retirement Age (NRA)

A worker's *normal retirement age (*aka *full retirement age)* is the age at which he can retire with full pension benefits. That used to be 65, but thanks to some reforms in the OASDI program that went into effect in 2000 with people born in 1938, it's been ratcheted up to age 66. And starting with people born in 1955, it begins stair-stepping up again in two month increments until reaching a new plateau of 67 for anyone born in 1960 or later. Table 13.3 shows everyone's normal retirement age and early retirement age by year of birth.

Table 13.3 ~ Normal Retirement Age

Birth Year	Normal Retirement Age (NRA)	Early Retirement Age
1937 and before	65	62
1938	65 & 2 months	62
1939	65 & 4 months	62
1940	65 & 6 months	62
1941	65 & 8 months	62
1942	65 & 10 months	62
1943 thru 1954	66	62
1955	66 & 2 months	62
1956	66 & 4 months	62
1957	66 & 6 months	62
1958	66 & 8 months	62
1959	66 & 10 months	62
1960 and after	67	62

Applying for benefits

To begin receiving a retirement benefit, you have to apply for it. Unbidden, the Social Security Administration won't just start sending you a check every month when you turn 66 and quit your job.

You can apply for benefits by going to the Social Security office in your hometown, assuming there's one there. If there's not, you can apply online at www.socialsecurity.gov. You can also call Social Security at 800-772-1213. People who wish to start drawing Social Security are encouraged to apply three months in advance of when they'd like to receive their first check.

Benefits~ Who's entitled to what

Worker's Benefit

The worker must be at least 62 and fully insured, meaning have earned no less than 40 credits. The normal retirement age (NRA) for someone who turns 62 in 2016 is age 66. At 66 the worker's pension benefit is 100% of PIA. If he opts to retire early, his pension will be reduced by some fraction of 1% for every month that he's under his NRA. The reduction is 5/9th of 1% per month for every month, up to 36 months, that he's under and 5/12th of 1% for every additional month. This means that if the worker elects to start his pension at age 62, it will be reduced by 25% (66 – 62 = 4 yrs or 48 months; 36 mos. × 5/9 of 1% = 20%, plus 12 mos. × 5/12 of 1% = 5%; 20% + 5% = 25%). In Gerald's case that would reduce his benefit from $2,461 a month, which is what I figure his PIA would be if he retired at 62,[10] to about $1,845 ($2,461 × 75%).

The worker can also delay taking his retirement benefit until age 70. Assuming his NRA to be age 66, for every month that he delays, his benefit will be increased by 2/3rd of 1%. That works out to 8% a year and 32% (nearly a third) in 4 years.

Spouse's Benefit

To be eligible for benefits, the worker's spouse must either be a) at least 62 and have been married to the worker for at least 1 year, or b) regardless of her age, taking

[10] If his AIME at age 62 was, as I said, $8,200, his PIA would be figured as follows: ($767 × 90%) + ($3,857 × 32%) + ($3,576 × 15%) = $2,461.

care of the worker's child who is under 16 or disabled. In the first instance the spouse is entitled to 50% of the worker's PIA at her NRA, but like him, she can, if she wishes, take a reduced benefit, starting as early as age 62. In the spouse's case, however, the early retirement penalty is more severe—at least during the first 36 months, when it is 25/36th of 1% per month versus 5/9th. Beyond that it's the same—5/12th of 1% per month. If Gerald's spouse, whom I'm going to call Geraldine, opts to wait till her 66th birthday to start taking retirement benefits (notwithstanding the fact that Gerald started at 62), her monthly check will come to $1,231 ($2,461 × 50%). However, if like him, Geraldine elects to start at 62, her $1,231 a month will be reduced to just $861 (66 - 62 = 4 yrs. or 48 mos.; 36 mos. × 25/36 of 1% = 25%, plus 12 mos. × 5/12th of 1% = 5%; 100% - 30% = 70%; $1,231 × 70% = $861).

In the second instance, where the spouse is taking care of a child who is either under 16 or disabled, she's entitled to 50% of the worker's PIA, period. There's no reduction for being under her NRA. Thus, if Geraldine were taking care of a child under 16 or one who was disabled, it wouldn't make any difference what her age was—she'd get the full 50%. However, if the deal was simply that the child was under 16, upon his turning 16, Geraldine would lose her pension until or unless she could qualify for early retirement benefits on the basis of having attained age 62.

The spouse who waits beyond her NRA to start her benefits, unlike the worker, gains nothing.

Children's Benefit

This includes any child of the worker, whether natural-born, adopted, or stepchild, who is under age 18 (or 19 if still a full-time high school student), or over 18 but unable to work owing to a disability that began before he turned 22. The child is entitled to 50% of the worker's PIA, but his benefit, like the spouse's, may be reduced to fit within the *maximum family benefit,* which I'll get to in a bit. The child who receives retirement benefits simply on the basis of being under 18 (or 19) loses them upon attaining that age.

Former spouse

The former spouse must have been married to the worker for at least 10 years but be unmarried and at least 62 at the time of applying for benefits. Her benefit is figured the same way as a current spouse's but, unlike the current spouse's, is not subject to reduction to fit within the maximum family benefit.

It should be noted that lots of wives now work and are entitled on their own to Social Security retirement benefits. Where that's the case and the earned benefit (100% at NRA) is more than the spousal benefit (50% at NRA), the wife can claim nothing on the husband's record. However, if it's less, she can claim enough of a spousal benefit to make up the difference.

Widow's/Widower's Benefit

Although the widow/widower benefit comes under the heading of survivors' benefits, I'm going to note here that a widow or widower who's reached full retirement age and who was receiving retirement benefits based on his or her spouse's earnings record is entitled to receive 100% of the spouse's benefit. It will be in lieu of the benefit he or she was receiving. To illustrate, if at age 70 Gerald were receiving a monthly pension of $2,700 a month and Geraldine one of $1,350 and he died, Social Security would stop sending him a check but increase hers from $1,350 to $2,700.

Maximum Family Benefit (MFB)

This is the maximum monthly benefit that can be paid out to a worker and/or his dependents, and it's figured in much the same way that his primary insurance amount is figured, except that: a) it's figured on the worker's PIA, rather than his average indexed monthly earnings; b) breaks up the reference number into as many as four pieces, rather than three; and c) weights each piece more generously. In 2012, when Gerald turned 62 and became eligible for retirement benefits, the three bend points were $980, $1,415 and $1,845,[11] and the weightings applied to the four possible pieces (which never change) were 90%, 272%, 134% and 175%. Table 13.4 on the next page shows how we'd apply these numbers to his PIA ($2,514)[12] to come up with his family maximum benefit.

---

[11] There are many workers whose PIA is less than the upper *bend point*, so it follows that the theirs cannot be broken into four pieces.

[12] I'm assuming in this instance that Gerald waited till age 66 to draw Social Security.

Table 13.4 ~ Maximum Family Benefit

	First $980	Over $980 thru $1,415	Over $1,415 thru $1,845	Over $1,803	Total
PIA	$980	$ 435.00	$ 430.00	$ 669.00	$ 2,514.00
Weight	150%	272%	134%	175%	175%
Fam Max	$ 1,470.00	$ 1,183.20	$ 576.20	$ 1,170.75	$ 4,400.15
Rounded to next lowest dime					$ 4,400.10

How is the family maximum applied? That's easy. You subtract the worker's PIA from the maximum family benefit and what's left is what's available to the worker's dependents. Let's say that besides his wife Geraldine, Gerald has four 4 children all under 18. His benefit would be $2,514—that's not affected by the family maximum—but Geraldine's and the children's are. Individually, they might be entitled to $1,257[13] each, but collectively there's only the difference between $4,400 and $2,514 for them to split, so each gets just $377 ($4,400 - $2,514 = $1,886; $1,886 ÷ 5 = $377). The good news, I suppose, is that as each child turns 18 and loses his benefit, the amount available to those still qualifying as dependents will be divided by a smaller number, raising each remaining dependent's share. When the last child turns 18, Geraldine will get her full 50% .

****

You should know that besides running up against the family maximum and starting them early, there are several other things that can cause benefits to be reduced. You should also understand the extent to which benefits are subject to income taxes.

How earnings can reduce benefits

If you retire under Social Security before your normal retirement age and continue to work, your benefit will be reduced by $1 for every $2 you earn above a certain amount, which presently (2016) is $15,720. What exactly does this mean? I'll explain with an example. Let's say that you apply for early retirement benefits to begin in July, the month after you turn 62, that your monthly benefit is $1,500 a month and that you'll continue to work part-time through the end of the year at your old job for $2,750 a month. As you are required to do, you advise Social Security of this. Thanks to your

---

[13] $2,514 × 50% = $1,257

forthcomingness, Social Security will take \$390 out your *first month's* check. They will have arrived at the \$390 as follows: \$2,750 × 6 = \$16,500; \$16,500 - \$15,720 = \$780; \$780 ÷ 2 = \$390. Instead of a check for \$1,500, you'll get one for \$1,110. The following month and every month for the rest of the year, your check will be for \$1,500, unless something changes. Social Security doesn't spread the amount they're going to take away from you over the remaining months in the year. They take it up front.

There is one small exception to the foregoing. In the year that a worker reaches his normal retirement age, the benefit reduction is only \$1 for every \$3 earned above a much higher threshold. Presently, that threshold is \$41,880.

Once someone has attained his normal retirement age, there is no limitation on how much he can earn without having his benefits affected.

It is the Social Security recipient's responsibility to inform the Social Security Administration of what he expects to earn if he's under his normal retirement age. Failure to do this in a timely manner will result in his having to pay a penalty, in addition to giving back what he was over-paid.

Windfall Elimination Provision

This applies to any worker with enough quarters of coverage to be fully insured but whose AIME is low because it does not reflect his real earnings history, which includes substantial earnings from non-covered employment on which he's entitled to a pension. I think here of our public school teachers in Texas who can retire at a relatively young age with a pension from the Texas Teacher Retirement System and then go to work at something else, from which after paying FICA tax for 10 years, they can retire again and draw Social Security. Dividing their indexed earnings for fewer than 35 years by 420 (35 yrs. × 12 mos.) will result in rather modest average indexed monthly earnings it's true, but because a low wage-earner's PIA will ordinarily be a higher percentage of his AIME than a high wage-earner's, owing to the way PIA is calculated, unless some provision is made to eliminate it, these teachers would get a retirement benefit that is disproportionate to what they would have gotten had all their earnings been considered. Suffice it to say that the government construes this as a "windfall" and has taken measures to see that no one gets away with it. If this could affect you and you'd like to know more, go to the Social Security Administration's website at www.socialsecurity.gov and do a search on this subject.

How Social Security Benefits are taxed

Social Security benefits are taxable to the extent that the taxpayer's *combined income* exceeds a certain threshold, which is one thing for *single* filers and another for couples filing a *joint* return. *Combined income* is not a line on *Form 1040*—it's just a calculation. It's the sum of all the income items included in the taxpayer's *adjusted gross income (AGI)* except *Social Security* (Line 20), plus any *tax-exempt interest,* plus one-half of *Social Security* as reported on the taxpayer's *SSA-1099.* If the single filer's combined income is less than $25,000, none of his Social Security benefit is taxable. He can enter zero on *Line 20b* of *Form 1040.* But if it's over $25,000, he will have something to report. For every $1 that his combined income exceeds $25,000 but is less than $34,001, half (50%) of his Social Security benefits will be taxable, and for every $1 that it exceeds $34,000, 85% of his benefits will be. Table 13.5 below, positing six different levels of non-Social Security income, will help to clarify the exercise. In each case, the assumption is that the taxpayer's Social Security benefit, as reported on his SSA-1099, was $20,000 exactly.

Table 13.5 ~ Taxable Social Security Benefits

1 AGI-SS+Tax exempt Int	2 1/2 of Soc Sec	3 Combined Income	4 Amt 'tween $25K & $34K	5 Amount > $34,000	7 50% of Col. 4	8 85% of Col 5	9 Total Taxable SS
$11,200	$10,000	$21,200	$0	$0	$0	$0	$0
$15,000	$10,000	$25,000	$0	$0	$0	$0	$0
$18,267	$10,000	$28,267	$3,267	$0	$1,634	$0	$1,634
$24,000	$10,000	$34,000	$9,000	$0	$4,500	$0	$4,500
$33,757	$10,000	$43,757	$9,000	$9,757	$4,500	$8,293	$12,793
$38,706	$10,000	$48,706	$9,000	$14,706	$4,500	$12,500	$17,000

For married taxpayers filing joint returns, the two breakpoints corresponding to the $25,000 and $34,000 above are $32,000 and $44,000. For married taxpayers filing separately, there are no breakpoints. These filers must include 85% of their benefits on Line 20b.

CHAPTER 13 ~ SOCIAL SECURITY

****

If there is something here that you'd like to understand better, you'll find Social Security's website at www.socialsecurity.gov. to be an outstanding resource. It's where nearly all of this came from.

FOURTEEN

Medicare

By the time you turn 65 there's a good chance that you will have had some kind of health issue that portends future problems, but even if your record is unblemished, you can be pretty sure that it won't stay that way indefinitely. There are many positive things to be said for the golden years, but improving health is not one of them. Nobody understands this better than the insurance companies, whose profitability hinges on being able to measure and price risk. So thank goodness for Medicare. Without it many seniors couldn't afford health insurance, and without it they might be in a real fix. Some might have to forgo having something done that they need; others might have to choose between not having something done and having it done at the cost of using up all their savings.

Medicare isn't free, of course, but if you qualify for premium-free Part A coverage, which most seniors do, the rest of what you need to be fully insured probably won't send you to the poor house. For Medicare Part B, plus our Medicare Supplement policy and Prescription Drug Plan, which together cover most of what Medicare doesn't, my wife and I each paid $3,917 last year (2015). Times two, that comes to a significant sum, but compared to what our premiums would run for private healthcare policies providing comparable coverage, it's a bargain.

Most years our lives are medically uneventful, but 2011 was a lesson in why, even if you've always been quite healthy, health insurance isn't a waste of money. Without it we'd have ended the year $40,245.83 poorer. That at least was what Medicare was billed by the hospitals, doctors, anesthesiologists, and others for services they provided the two of us. Not that they expected to be paid that much. All these service providers accept what is called *assignment*, meaning that what they bill notwithstanding, they'll accept as payment in full whatever Medicare is pleased to approve. In our case, that worked out to almost exactly 33¢ on the dollar, because what Medicare approved was only $13,504.70. Of this amount, Medicare paid $10,526.73 (78%) and our Medicare Supplement paid the rest, consisting of our deductibles and co-payments amounting to $2,977.94 (22%). We paid nothing.

****

Let's begin here by looking at the big picture.

Medicare Parts A, B, C, and D and Medicare Supplements

Medicare has four parts, with some being mutually exclusive. Parts A and B make up what is referred to as *Original Medicare*; Part C is more commonly called *Medicare Advantage*; and Part D is *Prescription Drug Plan* insurance. If you've got Original Medicare, you won't have Medicare Advantage, and vice-versa. Also, if you have a Medicare Advantage plan that provides prescription drug coverage, you can't participate in a Prescription Drug Plan.

Part A of Original Medicare is so-called *hospital insurance*. We'll get into the details a bit later, but suffice it here to say that it covers the services you receive as an *inpatient* at a hospital or *skilled nursing facility*, plus a few other things. The funding for Part A comes partly from the Medicare HI[1] component of FICA taxes, which was discussed in the previous chapter on Social Security, and partly from general tax

---

[1] HI stands for Hospital Insurance, just as you would expect.

revenues. Having paid for this coverage throughout his or her working career, the worker and his or her spouse get the coverage free upon reaching age 65. People who haven't earned the sufficient number of credits, which is forty (40), can buy it provided they're American citizens and have turned 65. It's not cheap if you have to buy it. The premium this year (2016) runs up to $411 a month.

Part B covers other medical services, like those from physicians and outpatient care providers. It is not free. Presently, the cost of Part B for people whose *modified adjusted gross income* (or share of *MAGI* in the case of married people) is under $85,000 is $104.90 a month. Anyone receiving Social Security, Railroad Retirement Benefits, or Civil Service Retirement benefits will have his Part B premiums deducted from his monthly check. You can have premium-free Part A and choose not to buy Part B, but as a general rule you cannot buy Part A and not also buy Part B.

With Original Medicare, you can receive medical services from any health care provider who accepts Medicare. With a Medicare Advantage plan that's not the case. You're mostly limited to receiving services from within your particular Health Maintenance Organization (HMO), Preferred Provider Organization (PPO), or some other such private healthcare network. If you go outside the network for non-emergency care, your Medicare Advantage plan probably isn't going to cover the charges, or at least not in their entirety. Many, if not most, Medicare Advantage plans provide prescription drug coverage.

Medicare prescription drug coverage, aka Part D, is insurance you buy to help reduce the cost of prescription medications. As with Medicare Advantage plans and Medicare Supplement insurance, you buy this coverage from a private health insurance company, not from the government as you do Parts A and B. My wife and I each pay $65.90 a month for our Humana "enhanced" prescription drug plan. She rarely uses hers, but I make up for her by taking half a dozen medications daily that I get from Humana's mail order pharmacy at either no cost or at prices that are a fraction of what I'd pay retail.

A Medicare Supplement policy (aka *Medigap* policy) is insurance you buy from a private insurance company to cover some, most, or all of what Original Medicare doesn't pay. As we'll see, Part A and Part B both shift some of the cost of services onto the Medicare beneficiary via an *annual deductible* and *copayments* and *coinsurance.* Ten standard Medicare supplement plans are offered in most states to plug these gaps. The plan we have is Plan F, which covers virtually everything that we would otherwise have to pay out of pocket. We're 74 and pay $173.91 a month each for this coverage. As we get older our premiums will continue to stairstep up.[2] Other companies offering the exact same plan will have different premiums, some lower, some higher.

Eligibility

You become eligible for Medicare at age 65 if you or your spouse has paid into the program via FICA taxes long enough to have earned forty (40) *credits* (aka *quarters of coverage*). As explained in the previous chapter on Social Security, you earn one (1) credit for each multiple, up to four (4), of some minimal amount of earnings during the year on which you paid FICA. An easier but less precise way of expressing what is required is to say that you need to have paid Medicare taxes for at least ten (10) years.

Enrollment

It's important to understand *when* you should sign up for whatever parts of Medicare you want because it can cost you dearly if you delay.

Parts A & B

If you opted to begin receiving Social Security retirement benefits before turning 65, you'll be automatically enrolled in Medicare Parts A and B when you do get there. You won't have to do anything. Your coverage will be effective the first day of your birth month, unless it so happens that your birthday is on the 1st of the month, in which case, your coverage will begin on the first day of the previous month. In other words, if your birthday is July 5, your coverage will start July 1, but if your birthday is July 1, your coverage will start June 1. If for some reason you don't want Part B, you'll need to waive the coverage following the instructions on the back of your Medicare card, which you will have gotten in the mail some three (3) months before your birthday.

If you're not already receiving Social Security retirement benefits, you will need to take the initiative. This means signing yourself up during the 7-month *initial*

---

[2] Last year, we each paid $54.20 monthly for our prescription drug coverage and $167.28 monthly for our Medicare supplement.

enrollment period, which begins three (3) months before the month you turn 65 and ends three (3) months after. If, let's say, your birthday was on July 5, that period would include the months of April, May and June (the three months *before* your birth month), July (your birth month) and August, September and October (the three months *following* your birth month). To sign up for Parts A and B, call Social Security at 1-800-772-1213 or go online to www.socialsecurity.gov/retirement.

If for some reason you fail to sign up during the initial enrollment period, you can sign up during the *general enrollment period*, which runs from January1 through March 31 of every year. Understand, though, that if you want your coverage to start the month you turn 65, you need to sign up during the first three months of the initial enrollment period, because if you delay your coverage will also be delayed. Anyone who waits until the general enrollment period rolls around won't be covered till July 1. This means that if your 65th birthday fell on July 5, 2016, and through either ignorance or inertia you didn't get yourself enrolled by October 31, you won't have another chance to do so until the following January 1 and the earliest you could have coverage would be July 1, 2017.

People who don't sign up because they're still working and covered by a group healthcare plan have eight (8) months after the termination of either their employment or their healthcare coverage, whichever comes first, to sign up and avoid the late enrollment penalty. This 8-month window is referred to as the *special enrollment period.* Anyone who doesn't sign up for Medicare during the special enrollment period will have to wait till the general enrollment period comes around again in January.

Failure to sign up for Medicare when you first become eligible can result in your having to pay higher premiums if later you do decide to enroll. Let's say that at the ripe old age of 70 you become seriously ill and need an operation and don't have any insurance. If you're not entitled to premium-free Part A, that coverage will now cost you 10% more, and you'll have to pay this higher premium for the next ten years, that being twice the number of years that have elapsed since you were first eligible, which is the way the penalty is figured. And for Part B, it's worse. You'll have to pay 10% extra for each full year that you delayed, which in your case here might be five years, which would make the penalty 50%, and you'd be saddled with this higher premium for as long as you remained on Medicare.

Part C -- Medicare Advantage

Your first opportunity to enroll in a *Medicare Advantage* Plan is during the 7-month initial enrollment period discussed above. Assuming you're not automatically enrolled in Medicare, you'll need to take care of that first since you cannot enroll in an Advantage Plan unless you're already signed up for Parts A and B. Once that's taken care of, you're good to go.

The next opportunity to sign up for a Medicare Advantage Plan is between October 15 and December 7. During this period you can also drop a plan or switch from one plan to another. Whatever you choose to do, it will become effective on the upcoming January 1.

After December 7 there are only two things you can do. One—which you can only do between January 1 and February 14—is to switch from your Medicare Advantage Plan to Original Medicare and, if you do that, to join a Prescription Drug Plan. The second thing you can do—which you can do at pretty much any time during the year[3]—is switch from a plan that isn't 5-star rated to one that is. A 5-star rating is given to plans that Medicare deems excellent based on member satisfaction surveys and other data.

Leaving aside the foregoing two exceptions, once enrolled in a Medicare Advantage plan, you must stay in that plan for the full calendar year that your coverage began unless you move out of the plan's service area.

Part D – Prescription Drug Coverage

Virtually everything I just said about when you can join a Medicare Advantage Plan, drop a plan, or switch from one plan to another also applies to a Prescription Drug Plan. You can join a plan during your 7-month initial enrollment period; you can join a plan, drop a plan, or switch plans during the period October 15 through December 7; and you can switch from a plan that's not 5-star rated to one that is at any time during the year.

[3] The *5-star special enrollment period* this year began on December 8, 2015 and runs through November 30, 2016.

Unless you have what Medicare calls *creditable coverage* under a company or union-sponsored prescription drug plan, failing to enroll in a Medicare drug plan within sixty-three (63) days of the end of your initial enrollment period will result in your paying more for your coverage if and when you do. Presently that penalty is figured by multiplying 1% of the so-called *national base beneficiary premium* of $34.10 (2016) times the number of months without coverage. So, suppose at 70, having gone sixty months without joining a plan or having other creditable coverage, you learn that you've got a rare condition that will require you to take expensive meds for the rest of your life. Just as soon as you can, which will be October 15, you join the plan that you think will work best for you. Fortunately for you, they can't decline to cover you. Unfortunately for you, your premium, which otherwise might run, as mine did when I was 70, $39.90, will cost you $60.36 (1% × $34.10 × 60 = $20.46; $20.46 + $39.90 = $60.36).

Medicare Supplements

The time to buy a Medigap policy is during the 6-month period that begins with the first day of the month you are both a) 65 or older and b) enrolled in Medicare Part B. So, let's say you turned 65 on February 9, 2016, but didn't sign up for Medicare until May 1 after retiring on April 30 with exactly forty years of service from your old job where you were covered by the company's healthcare plan. Your 6-month period would begin May 1 and end October 31. If you act within this window of opportunity, you can buy any Medigap policy you like at standard rates, regardless of any pre-existing conditions. However, if you procrastinate and do nothing and then decide to act, you may find that no company wants to insure you or that your coverage will cost significantly more.

Coverages

Original Medicare ~ Part A

Part A, which is commonly understood to be "hospital insurance," covers five kinds of care:

- *Inpatient care* at a hospital
- Inpatient care in a *skilled nursing facility (SNF)*

- *Home health care services*
- *Hospice care*
- Inpatient care in a *religious nonmedical health care institution*

Here's what you need to know about each:

Inpatient care at a hospital ~ The key thing here is understanding the meaning of *inpatient care*. For you to receive "inpatient care," you've got to be admitted to a hospital on a doctor's orders for at least one overnight stay. If your doctor sends you to the hospital for a chest X-ray, that's not going to be covered by Part A. If you go to the emergency room because you've got chest pains and after being checked out are released that same day, that's not going to be covered by Part A either. For starters, neither visit requires an overnight stay. They'll both be covered by Part B, which deals with *outpatient* services.

But suppose that you go to the hospital's emergency room because you're having chest pains, and after doing an EKG and whatever other tests they do to determine whether someone has had a heart attack, the doctor in charge orders that you be kept under "observation" overnight. What then? Well, to me this sounds like it ought to qualify as inpatient care, but somehow it doesn't quite make the grade. Why not? I'm not sure. All that's clear is that being "held in a hospital under observation" doesn't come to quite the same thing as "being admitted to a hospital on a doctor's order."

Now let's suppose that it is several weeks later and you've been referred to a good cardiologist who, having determined that you've got some badly blocked arteries, has scheduled you for bypass surgery at a regional heart hospital. His office will make the arrangements for the operating room, the anesthesiologists, and all the rest and see to having you admitted to the hospital on the day of your surgery. When that day arrives, pretty much everything that is supplied by the hospital, which is to say the operating room, operating room equipment, blood, surgical supplies, dressings and bandages, etc., as well as the recovery room, your room,[4] your meals, your nursing care, and your meds and supplies, will be covered by Part A. What won't be covered by Part A are the

[4] Provided that your hospital offers semi-private rooms and it's not medically necessary that you be by yourself, a semi-private room is what Medicare pays for. If you insist on a private room, you'll pay the difference. You'll also pay for a telephone and TV unless your room comes equipped with those at no extra charge.

services of your surgeon and the anesthesiologist. Their charges will be covered by Part B.

Why is it important whether something is picked up by Part A or Part B? Two reasons: First, because what Medicare pays and what you pay is different under Parts A and B. More about this in a minute. Second, in the event that you need care in a *skilled nursing facility* after leaving the hospital but before going home—which is often the case with people who've had serious surgery—Medicare isn't going to pick up the tab unless your inpatient hospital stay was at least three (3) days, not counting the day you were released.

Most hospital stays aren't very long, averaging, according to the Centers for Disease Control and Prevention, just four to nine days. In comparison, Medicare Part A covers ninety (90) days of inpatient hospital care per *benefit period*, which as Medicare explains,

> "...begins the day you are admitted to a hospital or skilled nursing facility...and ends when you haven't received any inpatient hospital care (or skilled care in a SNF) for 60 days in a row. If you go into a hospital or skilled nursing facility after one benefit period has ended, a new benefit period begins. You must pay the inpatient hospital deductible for each benefit period. There is no limit to the number of benefit periods."

During the first sixty (60) days of each benefit period, Medicare pays everything except your *deductible*, which (in 2016) is $1,288. For days 61 through 90, Medicare pays everything except your *copayment*, which is $322 a day. Then after day 90, provided that you haven't already used them up, you've got sixty (60) *lifetime reserve days* that you can avail yourself of. For each lifetime reserve day that you tap, Medicare pays all covered costs except your co-pay, which presently is $644 a day (double that for days 61 through 90). After day 150, Medicare pays nothing—you're on your own. I wouldn't worry about it, however. There's not much likelihood of your ever being confined to a hospital for 150 days. Or even ninety. And if you have a Medigap policy, regardless of the plan you've got, it will cover up to an additional 365 days of hospital care after your Medicare benefits are used up. That's in addition to picking up your copayments and possibly part or all of your deductible.

Inpatient care in a skilled nursing facility (SNF) ~ Although the term "skilled nursing facility" may suggest a stand-alone facility somewhere, the reality is that lots of nursing homes qualify as SNFs and lots, if not most, hospitals have a wing or a floor that is designated as a SNF. To be accredited as a SNF by Medicare, the facility must meet certain staffing criteria and be equipped to provide rehabilitation services and to perform a host of medical and nursing procedures.

Now, lest I have muddied the waters by observing that lots of nursing homes are also skilled nursing facilities, let me be clear that we're not talking here about custodial nursing home care. Medicare does not cover that. We're talking here about something altogether different—namely, the skilled nursing care that enables someone to successfully transition from hospital to home. Hospitalization is now so expensive, and room availability at some hospitals so tight, that the minute a patient can be unhooked from his monitors, feeding tubes, IVs, etc., everyone wants him released. If he can go home with no further ado, great. Often, though, in order to fully recover from whatever put him in the hospital in the first place, the patient will need rehab and skilled nursing care that no one at home—if indeed there is someone else at home—is qualified or equipped to give. My mother-in-law, when she was in her late eighties, fell off a small ladder breaking her hip on one side and shattering her leg below the knee on the other and, after undergoing major orthopedic surgery, spent a number of days in the hospital and then many weeks as an inpatient in a skilled nursing facility across the street undergoing rehab. As an elderly widow living by herself, there was no way after being discharged from the hospital that she could have managed at home on her own.

There are 100 days in an inpatient SNF care period. During the first 20 days Medicare presently pays everything—no deductible or copayments apply. For days 21 through 100, Medicare pays everything except the patient's copayment of $161 a day. I feel pretty sure that my mother-in-law's hospital deductible and SNF copayments, to the extent she had any, were covered by her Medicare supplement.

Home Health Services ~ Medicare Part A will also cover "medically-necessary part-time or intermittent skilled nursing care, and/or…therapy" that is delivered by a

Medicare-licensed home health agency to someone who is homebound. The term for this kind of care is "home health services." A Medicare-enrolled doctor must order the care, after certifying that the patient needs it. Medicare foots the bill in its entirety; the patient pays nothing.

I have two friends, both married, who were sent home within a day or two of having a knee replacement. Both had someone from a local Medicare-approved home health agency come to their home five times a week for several weeks to give them physical therapy for an hour, change their dressings, draw blood, and so on.[5] I mention that both friends were married in order to make the point that, had they not been, they might have been transferred from the hospital to a skilled nursing facility, rather than sent home. As it was, they had a spouse at home who could see about their meals and help them with getting dressed and undressed, bathing, going to the bathroom, etc.

Hospice Care ~ Think of hospice care as being palliative care given to someone whose illness or condition is such that nothing more can be done, really, to bring about recovery. The focus is on trying to manage the patient's pain and symptoms and make him as comfortable as possible in the time he has remaining. In addition, hospice offers other kinds of support to the patient and his family, like spiritual counseling, help with planning diets, respite care,[6] and plain old human companionship. Hospice staff is made up of paid professionals and volunteers.

To receive Medicare-paid hospice care, the patient's personal physician must certify that his condition is terminal and his life expectancy is six (6) months or less. If after six months the patient remains alive but his outlook is unchanged, his doctor must re-certify him.

Medicare pays all of the costs of hospice care, except for 1) a small copayment (limited to $5) in respect of the patient's prescription drugs and 2) 5% of the cost of inpatient respite care.

---

[5] For home health services to be covered by Part A, they must follow a hospital stay of at least 3 days. Since my friends were released from the hospital sooner, the home health care they received was probably covered under Part B.

[6] Respite care is inpatient care for the person on hospice at a Medicare-approved facility so that the usual caregiver, usually a spouse or other family member, can get a break. Each respite care stay is limited to 5 days.

Inpatient Care at a Religious Nonmedical Health Care Institution ~ My step-father was a Christian Scientist, as were all of his blood relations, and I remember that one of his elderly aunts who lived in our town spent some time in a Christian Science nursing facility up in the Dallas-Ft. Worth area after suffering a bad fall that resulted in a broken hip. That was back in the late 1960's. Whether Medicare covered her charges back then I do not know, but I feel sure that it would nowadays under this category of covered care. Maybe not all of her charges—certainly not those relating to any practitioner who may have worked with her—but at least her room and board, nursing care, and most supplies. If you're a Christian Scientist and need to know more, I'm sure your church can point you to people who can answer your questions.

Original Medicare ~ Part B

Leaving aside for the moment the few things that Original Medicare doesn't cover, Part B covers just about everything that's medically-necessary that Part A doesn't cover.

It covers:

- The services of doctors and other outpatient healthcare providers
- Hospital outpatient services
- Screenings and tests
- Therapy of all kinds
- Home health services
- Durable medical equipment
- Defibrillators
- Prosthetic and orthotic items
- Chemotherapy
- Diabetes self-manage training and diabetes supplies
- Kidney disease education services and dialysis
- Tobacco cessation counseling
- Shots
- Ambulance service

I won't go into all of these because some are pretty self-explanatory, but a word or two about those that aren't may be helpful.

Doctors and other outpatient health care provider services ~ This takes in visits to your doctor or to a specialist you may be seeing about some particular issues you're dealing with, like allergies, skin problems, COPD, cancer, heart trouble, etc. Also the services of the surgeon who operates on you and the anesthesiologist who keeps you resting peacefully and pain-free while you're being worked on. Also the services of any other professional, including the physician assistant, nurse practitioner, and therapist who works on you.

Hospital outpatient services ~ This encompasses visits to the Emergency Room, overnight stays in the hospital for observation, and tests like X-rays, MRIs, CT scans, and EKGs that require very expensive equipment usually only found at a hospital.

Screenings and tests ~ This includes bone density tests; mammograms; blood tests to measure cholesterol, lipid, and triglyceride levels; Pap tests and pelvic exams; colonoscopies and other colorectal cancer screenings; diabetes screenings; glaucoma tests; HIV screenings; PSA tests and digital exams; and urinalyses. Many of these are free on some periodic basis, like every twelve months or every twenty-four months, to people who have, or are at risk of developing, whatever disease or condition the screenings are intended to monitor or detect. A doctor has to order the tests, and the provider has to accept assignment.

Home health services ~ You will recall that "home health services" are also provided at no cost under Part A.

Therapy and rehab of all kinds ~ Listing these in alphabetical order, we're talking here about cardiac rehab, medical nutrition therapy (for diabetics and people with kidney disease), occupational therapy, physical therapy, and speech therapy.

Durable medical equipment ~ This means things like oxygen tanks and supplies, walkers, wheel chairs, and special beds, some of which can only be rented. The supplier has to be Medicare-approved, and your doctor has to write an order for the item.

Prosthetic and orthotic items ~ This includes back and neck braces and the like; artificial eyes; artificial limbs; prostheses for use after a mastectomy; and prosthetic devices needed to replace an internal body part or function (including ostomy supplies and "parenteral" and "enteral" nutrition therapy) ordered by your doctor or another Medicare-enrolled health care provider.

Shots ~ This includes an annual flu shot during flu season, a Hepatitis B shot for those at high or medium risk, and a once-in-a-lifetime pneumonia shot. There is no charge for these shots.

In addition to the foregoing, you are entitled upon enrolling in Medicare to a *Welcome to Medicare* preventative care visit with your doctor for the purpose of developing a personalized plan to keep you healthy or, if you're not healthy, to improve your health. You can arrange for this visit at any time during the first twelve (12) months that you've got Part B. You pay nothing; the cost is all borne by Medicare.

Twelve months after this initial visit, and every twelve months afterwards, you're entitled to an *annual wellness visit*, also fully paid by Medicare, to evaluate your current health status and update the plan for what you should be doing to stay healthy or address any problems.

Except for your Welcome to Medicare visit and subsequent annual wellness visits, all doctor and other outpatient health care provider services are subject to an annual deductible and 20% coinsurance. That's true, too, of most of the other things covered by Part B, some of the screenings and the three shots being exceptions. The deductible isn't a big deal—this year (2016) it's just $166—but the coinsurance can mount to a significant sum over the course of a year if you become seriously ill or have surgery. Keep this in mind when we get to Medicare supplement insurance.

Original Medicare ~ Things that are not covered

Things that Original Medicare doesn't cover include:

- Custodial nursing home care – you need a long term care insurance policy for this.
- Prescription drugs – You need a prescription drug plan for this.
- Routine dental care and dentures
- Acupuncture
- Cosmetic surgery
- Hearing aids

- Eyeglasses – Except after cataract surgery that implants an intraocular lens. In this case, Medicare will pay for one pair of glasses with standard frames (or one set of contacts). The Part B deductible applies, as does the 20% coinsurance.
- Chiropractic services – Except to help correct a "subluxation" (whatever that is).

Medicare Advantage ~ Part C

Medicare Advantage Plans cover all the same things that Original Medicare does, except hospice care, and many offer important benefits that Original Medicare doesn't, such as prescription drug coverage and wellness programs. Overall, Medicare Advantage Plans are seen by many to be a bargain.

As already noted, however, there is the disadvantage with them that you can't go outside your network, except in an emergency, without compromising your coverage. It's important, too, to note that no two Medicare Advantage Plans are exactly alike. They don't all cost the same, and what you're on the hook for in the way of deductibles and copayments will vary from one plan to the next.

If you do not live in a metropolitan area, a Medicare Advantage plan may not be an option. If it is an option, you may want to attend some of the marketing seminars put on by the various plan providers.

Prescription Drug Plan ~ Part D

Each prescription drug plan has its own *formulary* and differs to some extent from other plans in terms of what it pays and what the plan member pays. However, all plans have to meet certain minimum requirements.

A plan's formulary consists of the drugs the plan covers. If you're shopping Prescription Drugs Plans, you need to find one that has the meds you take (at least any expensive ones) on its formulary. I recall that after enrolling my wife and me in our Humana "Enhanced" Plan, we discovered that something pricey she took wasn't on its formulary.[7] Not only would our plan not cover this med, what we paid would not even count toward satisfying our annual deductible. As it happens, however, our plan doesn't

[7] Fortunately, sometime later her doctor took her off the medication.

have an annual deductible. Most plans do. The annual deductible corresponds to the first of four so-called *payment stages*. By law, the annual deductible cannot be higher than a certain amount. In 2016, that ceiling is $360.

Stage 2 is referred to as the *initial coverage stage*. You remain in this stage until your total drug costs, including anything you paid, as well as anything the plan paid, cross a certain dollar threshold, which presently is $3,310. Through June 30, 2016, which is the date of my last *Explanation of Benefits (EOB)* statement from Humana, my current year's total drug costs have amounted to $258.51, of which I paid $43.30 (±17%) and my plan $215.21 (±83%).

The $258.51 isn't the retail price of the drugs I've taken. According to Humana the retail price is $3,147.45. Also, if the 17% suggests that I pay a certain percentage of the cost of my drugs, I (usually) don't. For *preferred generic drugs*, I pay $3.00 per prescription; for *non-preferred generics*, $7.00; and for *preferred brand drugs*, $42.00. Only for *non-preferred brand drugs* and *specialty drugs*, do I pay a percentage of the cost (44% and 33%, respectively). All of these co-pays assume that I buy my meds through a *preferred* pharmacy; through a *non-preferred* pharmacy the co-pays are somewhat higher. For any generics purchased through Humana's mail order service, my co-pays are zero. That is so long as I remain in Stage 2.

I do not foresee my total drug costs this year reaching $3,310, but if they should, that will move me into Stage 3, which is known as the *coverage gap*, or "donut hole." For all intents and purposes, the plan member pays 100% of the cost of his meds while he remains in the coverage gap. Fifteen hundred and forty dollars ($1,540) later when his total drug costs have reached $4,850, he pops out of the donut hole into Stage 4.

Stage 4 is referred to as *catastrophic coverage*. In Stage 4 the Plan picks up all but maybe 5% of the member's drug costs. Needless to say, you never want to get to this stage, but if you do, you'll at least get some relief for the rest of the year.

People with limited income and resources may qualify for what Medicare calls "Extra Help" with paying for their prescription drug costs. Suffice it to say, this "extra help" is very significant. If it's something you would like to investigate, you should call Social Security at 1-800-772-1213.

Medicare Supplements

I said earlier that there are ten standardized Medicare Supplement Insurance plans, but actually there are fourteen, identified by the letters A through N. The thing is that Plans E, I, H and J are no longer offered. People who have these plans, however, may keep them.

When I say the plans are standardized, I mean that all plans with the same letter, by whatever insurance company offered, provide the same array of benefits.[8] Understand, though, that the fact that the plans are standardized doesn't mean that every company charges the same premium for the same plan to people of the same age; they don't. If you're in the market for a Medigap policy, it would pay to shop around.

Plan benefits basically consist in picking up the deductibles, coinsurance, and co-payments that the Medicare recipient would otherwise be responsible for. As shown in Table 13.1 below, Plan F, which is what we have, provides the most comprehensive coverage. In addition to covering all of our deductibles, coinsurance and copayments, it

Table 13.1 ~ Medicare Supplement Insurance Plans

Benefits	A	B	C	D	F	G	K	L	M	N
Medicare Part A Coinsurance and Hospital Costs (up to an additional 365 days after Medicare benefits are used).	100%	100%	100%	100%	100%	100%	100%	100%	100%	100%
Medicare Part B Coinsurance or Copayment	100%	100%	100%	100%	100%	100%	50%	75%	100%	100%
Blood (first 3 pints)	100%	100%	100%	100%	100%	100%	50%	75%	100%	100%
Part A Hospice Care Coinsurance or Copayment	100%	100%	100%	100%	100%	100%	50%	75%	100%	100%
Skilled Nursing Facility Care Coinsurance or Copayment			100%	100%	100%	100%	50%	75%	100%	100%
Medicare Part A Deductible		100%	100%	100%	100%	100%	50%	75%	50%	100%
Medicare Part B Deductible			100%		100%					
Medicare Part B Excess Charges					100%	100%				
Foreign Travel Emergency (up to plan limits)			80%	80%	80%	80%			80%	80%

Note: Plans K and L have limits on the insured's out-of-pocket expenses, which presently are $4,940 and $2,470, respectively.

[8] Except, I understand, in Massachusetts, Minnesota and Wisconsin, where the plans apparently are standardized somewhat differently.

also picks up Medicare Part B *excess charges* and up to certain limits *foreign travel emergency* medical expenses. Excess charges refers to the extra 15% that Part B health care providers who don't accept assignment are allowed to charge over and above the Medicare-approved amount.

****

My source for all of the factual information presented here is the 2015 edition of a publication put out by the Centers for Medicare and Medicaid Services entitled *Medicare and You,* which I picked up at the local Social Security office. It's very clear and readable. Medicare's website at www.medicare.gov is also an excellent resource.

LOOSE

ENDS

FIFTEEN

Loose Ends

After thinking that I had covered just about everything, several other topics have come to mind that I feel I ought to say something about.

Goals, Objectives & Strategies

Except for the severely depressed, we all have goals. Not many of us, however, have a plan for realizing our goals. One of the reasons for this is that we don't understand how to go about putting a plan together or where to go to get help. That's a shame. Without a plan our chances of attaining our goals are much diminished.

The terms "goal" and "objective" are often used interchangeably, but when you're doing personal financial planning, you need to make a distinction between the two. Think of a *goal* as being a broadly happy state or condition you hope to enjoy someday. Being "healthy" is a goal. So is being "wealthy." An *objective,* on the other hand, is a very specific, measurable thing you want or need by some future date or over some future period. Getting your weight down to 185 lbs. by the end of the year is an objective. Having a $1 million investment portfolio by the time you're age 67 is another.

Achieving a goal is always predicated on meeting at least one objective, and usually more. For example, to feel wealthy you may stipulate that when you're 67 you'll need a $1 million investment portfolio, plus an annuity paying $60 thousand a year to supplement your Social Security, plus have paid off the mortgage on your home, plus have gotten Junior through college. Financial plans are constructed around objectives, not goals.

Strategies are the means by which you achieve your objectives. For example, your strategy for being able to put Junior through four years at Texas A&M may be to open a tax-qualified 529 College Savings Plan account into which you will invest $409 monthly over the next eight years. You could, of course, need more than one strategy to achieve a particular objective. Often you do.

Table 15.1 below illustrates this hierarchy of goals, objectives and strategies:

Table 15.1 ~ Goals, Objectives & Strategies

Goal: Enjoy a financially comfortable retirement
Objective: Finish paying off our mortgage by July, 2023.
Strategies: Continue making scheduled monthly amortization payments.
Objective: Accumulate over $1 million in our two IRAs by the time we're 67.
Strategies: Continue to max out our annual IRA contributions, including 'catch-ups'.
Objective: By age 67, accumulate $780,000 in a deferred annuity that will then pay us $5,000 a month for 25 years.
Strategies: Starting in August 2023 and for the next 21 years, invest the $1,530 per month that we were paying on our mortgage into a deferred annuity returning an estimated 6% per annum.
Objective: Put Junior through 4 years at Texas A&M.
Strategies: Continue over the next 8 years to put $409 a month into his 529 college savings plan.

Quantifying objectives is not something most folks excel at. As discussed earlier, a good financial advisor or financial planner can help with this. These people have software programs to figure about anything you might want to know.

Personal Financial Statements

In Chapter 3, I explained that a *Cash Flow Summary* is for an individual what an *earning statement* is for a business enterprise. Both summarize *financial performance* over a period of time, like a month or year, in terms of *income* and *expenses*. For an individual the difference between income and expenses is called a *surplus* or a *shortfall*, depending on whether it's positive or negative. For a business this difference is referred to as *profit* or *loss*. In Chapter 3, I discussed a cash flow summary in the context of a budget where all the numbers are estimates. Obviously, if we are preparing a cash flow summary for the period ended December 31 of last year, we need to use actual numbers.

A *Net Worth Statement* is the other personal financial you need to be familiar with. It corresponds to a business's *Balance Sheet*. Both summarize *financial condition* at a point in time, like month-end or year-end, in terms of *assets* and *liabilities*. Assets are things you own, like the money in your checking account, the securities in your IRA, 401(k), and brokerage account, the cash value of any life insurance, and the market value of your house, your car, and your other material possessions. Liabilities are things you owe, like the balances on your credit cards, your mortgage, and your car loan. The difference between your assets and liabilities is your *net worth*.[1] Table 15.2 on the next page shows what a Net Worth Statement looks like.

It should be noted that this statement ignores household contents, i.e., furnishings and personal effects. That's because valuing this stuff is all but impossible, and it can't be readily sold without pretty much giving it away. If you doubt this, go to an estate sale.

Preparing a net worth statement is infinitely easier than doing a cash flow summary because there's no need to go through a month's or year's worth of transactions and classify them all by income and expense category. With a Net Worth Statement there's just one number for each kind of asset and liability, and with just two or three exceptions, the numbers are available to you from month-end statements. Depending on what month-end[2] you choose for your Net Worth statement, you might have to call your insurance company to ask for your policy's cash surrender value. And to come up with

[1] Some people object to the use of the term "net worth" on the grounds that an individual's value as a human being has nothing to do with how much money he has.
[2] Net Worth Statements are always dated at the end of a month.

the approximate market value of your car(s) and any real property you own, like your home, you may have to rely on some online resource. For autos and pick-ups, Kelly Blue

Table 15.2 ~ Net Worth Statement

ASSETS		
Cash in Bank		$ 5,758.77
Acct #1	$ 2,219.34	
Acct #2	$ 603.48	
Sinking Fund	$ 2,935.95	
Cash Value of Life Insurance		$ 67,398.00
IRAs		$ 257,670.07
John's Traditional	$ 58,370.17	
John's Roth	$ 134,998.05	
Ana's Traditional	$ 64,301.85	
John's 401(k)		$ 315,876.43
Brokerage Acct @ Chas. Scwhab		$ 1,001,297.03
Residence @ 1219 Warbler - Mkt Value		$ 425,000.00
Cars - Blue Book		$ 15,000.00
Buick	$ 10,000.00	
Honda	$ 5,000.00	
Total Assets		$ 2,088,000.30
LIABILITIES		
Credit Card Debt		$ 2,447.70
Visa	$ 1,590.03	
Mastercard	$ 857.67	
American Express	$ -	
Mortgage		$ -
Car Loan		$ 12,855.25
Total Liabilities		$ 15,302.95
NET WORTH		**$ 2,072,697.35**
Total Liabilities & Net Worth		$ 2,088,000.30

Book (www.kellybluebook.com) is a good resource, and for your home, you might try Zillow (www.zillow.com).[3] I'm sure that answering questions on Zillow doesn't sound like the best way of obtaining the market value of what is likely your most valuable asset, but it's certainly the most economical. To have your home appraised by a licensed appraiser will cost on the order of $300 or $400 and maybe more. Other than that, all I can suggest is that if you have a Realtor® friend, you try imposing on him or her to estimate what your house might sell for based on what properties comparable to yours in

---

[3] Some people mistakenly assume that the *assessed value* of their home, as shown on their annual property tax statement, reflects its *market value*. It maybe should, but likely doesn't. Others confuse *replacement cost*, which is what they have their home insured for, with market value. They're two different things. Replacement cost is what it would cost to re-build a home; market value is what it can be sold for.

the same area have recently sold for. The term for this kind of estimate is *comparative market analysis* or *CMA*.

About the only time you'll be required to prepare a Net Worth Statement is if you apply for a loan, and in that case the bank or lending institution will have its own form they'll want you to use. Also, if you work with a financial planner, he may ask you to do one, again using his form. Often, of course, people do one for no other reason than that they're curious.

Leverage

Leverage is the use of debt to improve the return on an investment. A couple of examples will help to explain how it works.

Suppose you have the opportunity to buy a parcel of unimproved land for $100,000 that you feel certain you can re-sell within a year for at least $125,000. (We'll assume you know something that everyone else doesn't.) Acting on this belief, you pull $100,000 from savings and buy the land. And, sure enough, just as you foresaw, exactly one year later, a developer comes along and takes the property off your hands for $125,000 to build a strip mall. You can be forgiven for feeling pleased with yourself. It's not every day that somebody realizes a return of 25% on an investment.

The thing is, though, you could probably have done much better than 25% had you financed your purchase rather than putting up all the money yourself. Let's say that you could have borrowed 80% of the $100,000 purchase price at 5% over ten years. In that case, all you would have had to invest yourself would be $20,000. It's true that you'd have monthly payments, the interest piece of which would reduce your profit by $3,235.66 over the course of twelve months, but so what. Your return on investment would jump to 96%. Plus the $80,000 you didn't have to pull from savings would remain undisturbed, continuing to earn whatever it was making. The math supporting the 96% ROI is laid out in the footnote below.[4]

Another, more extreme example of the use of leverage would be the better than 30 to 1 ratio of debt to equity that many big banks and investment banks used to pump up

[4] $125,000 sale price minus $100,000 cost equals $25,000 gain; $25,000 gain less $3,235.66 in interest payments equals $21,764.34 net profit; $21,764.34 net profit divided by $20,000 plus $2,624.77 (average amount of monthly payments applied to loan principal) equals 96.2%.

their returns on the mortgage-backed securities (MBS) and such that they invested in during the go-go years leading up to the housing market collapse in 2008 and 2009. These guys used their access to capital markets to borrow huge amounts of cheap money for very short periods of time to buy longer dated, high-yielding securities like MBS. The risk they ran was the ongoing challenge of being able every thirty days or so to roll their debt over on favorable terms. However, as long as they could, they made tons of money. On a $1 million MBS paying 5%, where they invested just $30 thousand of their own money and paid for the remaining $970 thousand using funds borrowed at 3%, their annualized ROI would be around 70%.[5]

Leverage works wonders until it doesn't, as those banks learned when people began to default in droves on their mortgages, making MBS so toxic nobody would touch them. The ensuing write-downs not only wiped out the banks' stakes in such leveraged investments; it nearly wiped them out too, and would have had the Treasury and Federal Reserve not intervened to save them.

Reconciling Bank Accounts

At the risk of being accused of encouraging sloth, I must confess that we long ago stopped keeping a check register (checkbook) and reconciling what it shows as our account balance with what our bank reports on its monthly statement. There are several reasons for this. The first is that virtually all the money that we have coming in every month comes in by direct deposit and most of what goes out is by ACH debit. We write very few checks. Second, by looking at our accounts online, which we do every few days, we can follow all the activity in them in more or less real time. To the extent that a deposit we mailed in remains in transit or any checks we've written haven't cleared, I can add or subtract these missing items from what the bank is showing as our balance to know what the real number is. In the rare instance that something seems amiss—and I cannot remember when that last happened—I call my bank and straighten it out over the phone[6].

[5] Interest earned ($1,000,000 × 5% = $50,000) minus interest paid ($970,000 × 3% = $29,100) equals $20,100; $20,100 ÷ $30,000 invested = 70%.

[6] I am far more likely to see something in our credit card accounts that I'm not expecting.

If you aren't able to monitor your checking account(s) online, or for whatever reason don't want to, you will need to keep a check register and reconcile the balance in it to your monthly bank statement when you get it. If you're new to all of this, Table 15.3 below shows what a check register looks like and how you record transactions. Deposits, including direct deposits (ACH credits), and interest earned add to your balance, while checks, drafts (ACH debits), and fees subtract from it.

Table 15.3 ~ Checking Account Register

Ref	Date	Transaction	Withdrawal	Deposit	Balance
		Opening balance			$ 1,000.00
1001	8/15/16	Tommy Smith	$ 100.00		$ 900.00
1002	8/17/16	Peyton's Jewelers	$ 257.33		$ 642.67
	8/22/15	Social Security		$ 2,023.00	$ 2,665.67
1003	8/22/15	HEB	$ 54.55		$ 2,611.12
1004	8/25/15	Keerville PUB	$ 54.20		$ 2,556.92
	8/26/15	Sheridan		$ 115.97	$ 2,672.89
1005	08/27/15	Jimmy Jones	$ 23.98		$ 2,648.91
1006	08/28/15	Tommy Smith	$ 100.00		$ 2,548.91

If you don't have online access to your account, or you do but don't want to bother with using it, you won't know how much interest you earned or fees you were charged until you get your bank statement. That's also true of ACH credits and debits where the funds being direct deposited into your account or pulled from it to settle something you owe can vary from one month to the next. Of course, if you do have online access to your account and log into it regularly, keeping your check register up to date shouldn't be a problem.

But even if you do go online to keep your register current, your balance there may not agree with what's shown on your bank statement when it comes in the mail. That's because, as I alluded to earlier, it's not unlikely that you will have written a few checks that hadn't cleared the bank by the statement closing date and perhaps mailed in a deposit or two that hadn't gotten there in time to be credited. Those *outstanding checks* have to be subtracted from the statement balance and the deposits added to it in order to reconcile it to the balance per your register.

On the back of your bank statement you will find a bank reconciliation form that will enable you by filling in the blanks to adjust the balances per both your statement and your check register so that the two agree. It will resemble Table 15.4 below, which I have completed to illustrate how it works.

Table 15.4 ~ Bank Reconciliation

BANK BALANCE			CHECKBOOK BALANCE		
Balance per this statement		$ 2,653.28	Balance per your check register....................................		$ 2,548.91
Add Deposits not shown on this statement	+	$ 115.97	Add credits not yet recorded in your check register:		
			ACH Credits	+	$ 109.97
Sub-total	=	$ 2,769.25	Interest..................................	+	$ 0.09
Subtract total of checks outstanding per detail below	-	$ 178.18	Sub-total	=	$ 2,658.97
Adjusted bank blance	=	$ 2,591.07	Subtract bank charges not yet recorded in check register:		
			Bank fees	-	
CHECKS OUTSTANDING			ATMs	-	
#1004		$ 54.20	ACH Debits	-	$ 67.90
#1005		$ 23.98			
#1006		$ 100.00	Adjusted check register		
Total checks outstanding		$ 178.18	balance	=	$ 2,591.07

My illustration assumes that my check register reflects the numbers shown in Table 15.3, where on August 28 I show a balance of $2,548.91, and that on that very same day my bank statement arrives in the mail showing a balance on August 26 (two days before) of $2,653.28. Going right to work, I enter each balance where it goes on the form. I adjust the bank statement balance first. I quickly see that the statement doesn't reflect the deposit of $115.97 I mailed to the bank on August 26, so I add that. That gives me a sub-total of $2,769.25. Next I look to see if any checks I wrote hadn't cleared. It comes as no surprise that the last three hadn't. I list and total these, and then subtract their total, $178.18, from the $2,769.25 above. That gives me an adjusted balance of $2,591.07. Assuming no mistakes on my part or the bank's, that's the number to which I must reconcile my checkbook balance.

First, though, there are some transactions shown in my bank statement that aren't reflected in my check register because I never go online to check things. The first thing I see is a direct deposit of $109.97 from a company that pays me royalties. I also see that I earned $.09 in interest. I enter these numbers on the form where they go and then record the transactions in my checkbook. This gives me a new total of $2,658.97. I'm not done, however, because there's also a $67.90 debit on the statement for my auto insurance premium, which I hadn't remembered to enter in my checkbook even though it comes around every month and the amount doesn't change but once a year. After taking that into account, my adjusted balance becomes $2,591.07. I give a sigh of relief. That was my adjusted statement balance and the number I was looking for.

If the two adjusted balances did not agree, I'd have to investigate to see why. It might be a posting error on the bank's part, or it might be because I recorded a number incorrectly or made an addition or subtraction mistake. If the difference were evenly divisible by 9, it's highly likely that one of us—the bank or I—transposed some numbers.[7]

****

I started to close here by sharing some of my concerns about the future and then decided against it. The truth is that the things I worry about, like slow economic growth, the growth in entitlements, the Fed's low-interest rate policy, and our mushrooming national debt, are not matters that I, as a non-economist, am really qualified to discuss. If no two trained economists can agree on what to say about these things, it's better that I not weigh in.

I'll just say this: I am not as optimistic as some people (including Warren Buffet, who's very smart) that the next generation is going to have it better than mine. I think our children and grandchildren are going to face some very big challenges.

I think people in my generation likely will live out their days with things rocking along about as they are. My advice to them, if I may presume to give some, is to try to

[7] An example of a transposition would be where the right number is 72 and I write 27 instead. The difference is 45. Divide 45 by 9 and you get 5 even.

stay healthy, stay off ladders, be careful about “reaching for yield” in this low-interest rate environment we’re in, and watch your spending that you don’t outlive your money.

Younger people, as I say, will likely face serious challenges. That, at least, is my prediction. My advice to them, some of which is not attuned to the times, is to adopt a healthy lifestyle, marry someone who’s intelligent and emotionally mature, stay married, be a good parent, cultivate a spiritual life, save as much as you can, use credit wisely, and invest in making yourself valuable.

Bibliography

Davis, Elizabeth. "Can You Get a Health Insurance Exemption?" About.com, May 29, 2014. (*www.healthinsurance.about.com*).

Davis, Elizabeth. "HMO, PPO, EPO & POS—What's the Difference & Which Is Best?" About.com, June 17, 2014. (*www.healthinsurance.about.com*).

Davis, Elizabeth. "How Much Is the Health Insurance Penalty for an Individual?" About.com, June 13, 2014. (*www.healthinsurance.about.com*).

Davis, Elizabeth. "How Much Is the Health Insurance Penalty for Families?" About.com, June 10, 2014. (*www.healthinsurance.about.com*).

Davis, Elizabeth. "Uninsured? What You Need to Know About Obamacare." About.com, June 24, 2014. (*www.healthinsurance.about.com*).

Estate Planning, Modules 1–8. Certified Financial Planner™ Professional Education Program. (Centennial, CO: College for Financial Planning, 1981–2003).

Folger, Jean. "How to Choose Between Bronze, Silver, Gold and Platinum Health Insurance Plans." Forbes.com, September 24, 2013. (*www.forbes.com/sites/investopedia*).

Gibson, Roger C. *Asset Allocation: Balancing Financial Risk*, 3rd ed. (New York: McGraw-Hill, 2000).

Hebner, Mark T. *Index Funds: The 12-Step Program for Active Investors*. (Irvine, CA: IFA Publishing, 2007).

Hemphill, Barbara. *Taming the Paper Tiger*. (Washington, DC: Kiplinger Books, 1998).

Income Tax Planning, Modules 1–8. Certified Financial Planner™ Professional Education Program. (Centennial, CO: College for Financial Planning, 1981–2003).

Jones, Sally M. *Principles of Taxation for Business and Investment Planning*. (New York: McGraw-Hill, 2003).

Kaiser Family Foundation. "Health Insurance Coverage of the Total Population." February 23, 2016. (*http://kff.org*).

Malkiel, Burton G. *A Random Walk Down Wall Street*. (New York: W.W. Norton & Company, 2003).

Mayo, Herbert B. *Investments: An Introduction*, 7th ed. (Mason, OH: Thomson South-Western, 2003).

McGee, Malcolm and Ramsey, Ben. *Life & Health Insurance for Texas Agents*. (Arlington, TX: Dearborn Financial Publishing, 2000).

Morgenstern, Julie. *Organizing from the Inside Out*, 2nd ed. (New York: Henry Holt & Co., 2004).

"ObamaCare Facts: An Independent Site For ACA Advice." ObamaCare Facts, June 16, 2016. (*http://obamacarefacts.com*).

Retirement Planning & Employee Benefits, Modules 1–9. Certified Financial Planner™ Professional Education Program. (Centennial, CO: College for Financial Planning, 1985–2003).

Schumacher, Vickie and Jim. *Understanding Living Trusts,* 5th ed. (Los Angeles: Schumacher Publishing, 2000).

Social Security Administration. (*www.ssa.gov*).

Swenson, David F. *Unconventional Success: A Fundamental Approach to Personal Investment.* (New York: Free Press, 2005).

U.S. Department of Health and Human Services. Centers for Medicare & Medicaid Services. *Medicare & You 2015*. (Washington, DC: GPO, 2016).

U.S. Department of the Treasury. Internal Revenue Service. "1040 Instructions." *Forms and Publications*. (Department of the Treasury, January 2016).

Vaughn, Emmett J. and Therese. *Fundamentals of Risk and Insurance,* 8th ed. (New York: John Wiley & Sons, 1999).

www.ingramcontent.com/pod-product-compliance
Lightning Source LLC
Chambersburg PA
CBHW081435170526
45166CB00008B/2208

* 9 7 8 1 5 1 9 7 6 6 7 1 7 *